Cambridge Studies in Social Anthropology

GENERAL EDITOR: JACK GOODY

No. 19

The Fate of Shechem

Cambridge Studies and Papers in Social Anthropology

The Fate of Shechem

or The Politics of Sex

**Essays in the Anthropology of
the Mediterranean**

JULIAN PITT-RIVERS ·

Cambridge University Press

CAMBRIDGE

LONDON   NEW YORK   MELBOURNE

Published by the Syndics of the Cambridge University Press
The Pitt Building, Trumpington Street, Cambridge CB2 1RP
Bentley House, 200 Euston Road, London NW1 2DB
32 East 57th Street, New York, NY 10022, USA
296 Beaconsfield Parade, Middle Park, Melbourne 3206, Australia

First published 1977

Printed in Great Britain at the
University Press, Cambridge

Library of Congress Cataloguing in Publication Data
Pitt-Pivers, Julian Alfred.
The fate of Shechem.
(Cambridge studies in Social anthropology; 19)
Includes Index.
1. Ethnology – Mediterranean region – Addresses,
essays, lectures. 2. Honor – Addresses, essays,
lectures. 3. Sex customs – Mediterranean region –
Addresses, essays, lectures. 4. Ethnology – Spain –
Andalusia – Addresses, essays, lectures. I. Title.
GN588.P57 301.2′1 76–27913
ISBN 0–521–21427–0

Contents

Contents

Preface

This book has honour as its central theme. It is composed of essays written independently of one another over the last ten years or more, but they represent the development of a single point of view and a common preoccupation. They are intended to be read in the order of presentation for the later chapters take as given the conclusions of the earlier ones. Thus chapter six which concerns sexual hospitality and shows how in terms of general theory it must be related to the rules of marriage is the expansion of a point made in 'The law of hospitality' (Chapter five) and 'The fate of Shechem' leans not only upon this but upon the analysis of honour with which the book begins, and upon 'The moral foundations of the family' (Chapter four).

The idea of sexual hospitality would strike the modern peoples of the Mediterranean as most uncouth, the very antithesis of honour in fact, and the contradiction between ancient and modern attitudes to this rather neglected institution appears at first sight total, yet I have sought to demonstrate how it was possible to pass from practising to abhorring it. To explain this reversal one must not only view it in relation to the establishment of monotheism – a connection set forth eloquently and repeatedly in the Old Testament – but above all place it within the context of the kinship system, for permanent alliance through marriage and transient alliance through sexual congress are both forms of the exchange of women. Both derive from the political significance accorded to sex. If the area surrounding the Mediterranean is in historic times so strikingly different in its attitude to marriage alliance from the rest of the world it is because here the politics of marriage conform to different rules from those which govern exogamic systems. But the attempt to explain this anthropological conundrum cannot overlook the previous practice of sexual hospitality. My thesis is that the origins of Mediterranean sexual honour are bound up in this transition.

Unlike many of my British colleagues, I am very much concerned with origins, as is apparent in the importance accorded in this book to Genesis and the Odyssey, but this is not to say that I think anything can be explained by being termed a 'survival'. On the contrary, the concept of survival is almost a confession of defeat before the challenge to find a contemporary sense in anything. Rather, I believe societies can only be understood in the present as a point of transition between a former and a future state; their structure is always a transformation of what went before. Mediterranean honour is a product of such a transformation. It is not of course a single conception common to all the peoples who dwell along the littoral of that sea – how could it be with such a variety of cultures? – but rather a common premise found in all the societies of that area regarding the relations between power, sex and religion; hierarchy, endogamy and the sacred are the three principles which come together in the notion of honour. Thus it is a multi-faceted notion[1] and, as the first chapter explains, it is this which gives it its essential character and function and which also makes it so paradoxical in usage. The various institutions discussed in these essays all therefore concern honour in one way or another, and this is the justification for bringing them together into a book.

It is sub-titled 'essays in Mediterranean anthropology' yet in fact it is largely about Spain, for this is where most of my field-work in the area was done. Such a grandiose expansion of perspective surely warrants a word of explanation, for it could not be assumed simply that what goes for Spain goes for the rest, even if it were possible to generalise for the Iberian Peninsula, which in fact contains contrasts of culture and social structure almost as sharp as the whole area. Moreover its cultural unity is today very much less than it was two thousand years ago when the Roman empire gave at least a semblance of homogeneity. Thus the early anthropologists, who were classical scholars, were on the face of it more clearly entitled to treat it as a whole than are those of us who twenty-odd years ago set out to bring the Mediterranean back into the focus of social anthropology by doing the empirical research that our intellectual forebears, interested only in the ancient past, never envisaged. The disparities we face are greater than were theirs, but if we have come to talk about Mediterranean anthropology it is not out of the obvious and vapid truism that the former Roman empire shares a common cultural heritage but because we have found that our problems are sufficiently similar to merit detailed comparison. The Mediterranean is, in the first place, a concept of heuristic convenience not a 'culture area' in the sense given this phrase by American cultural anthropology. Yet it is worth glancing at the common features and variance to see whether it is anything more than a scholarly device. It is certainly not geographically uniform and distinct,[2] for the land masses divide along the lines of the seaboard into Europe, Asia and Africa. But these land masses again are diversified to at least as great an extent even though there are no clear lines of divison between southern and northern Europe, between Asia

Minor and the rest of Asia and between north Africa and the lands to the south of the Sahara. The French geographers readily speak of the Mediterranean as a stereotype, but perhaps the greatest import of geography with regard to the question is not in the similarities and dissimilarities of the environment but in the fact that it erects barriers to communications inland, much more formidable than those represented by the sea. All Mediterranean societies face the sea and their enemies – and customers – on the far side of it.

Politically, moreover, if the Mediterranean lost its unity with the fall of Rome, the continents that surround it have not managed to establish any subsequently, so that if one were to think in terms of national states the choice is between grouping them in accordance with the linguistic or religious or cultural criteria of the present or of those of some previous period. To Fernand Braudel, the Mediterranean in the sixteenth century appeared to be a world of its own.[3] Most of the littoral has been at one time or another both Christian and Muslim – all has been Christian and all, save from the Gulf of Lyons to the Adriatic (and excluding Sicily), has been Muslim – as far as official religion goes, but if anthropology has anything to bring to the study of the civilised world it is in going behind the façade of official religions and national cultures to the populations and communities that compose the national states but do not necessarily conform to their self-image. The cultural continuities of local communities respond to the political hegemonies imposed upon them, but do not easily cut adrift from their own past, least of all in those aspects of culture that cannot be submitted to official control: the modes of thought and assumptions underlying personal behaviour. It is in this field that the comparison of different areas has proved most fruitful for anthropologists and that, by examining the general problems of kinship, the family and honour, this book aims to make its contribution. If therefore I have used the term 'Mediterranean' rather loosely it is in the aim of relating what I have studied at close quarters to the general tradition of that part of the world. The axes of contrast vary: sometimes what I have to say goes for much more than the Mediterranean, sometimes Mediterranean Europe is contrasted with the lands north of the Massif Central and the Alps (where ritual kinship has long since been lost and where the code of honour is today very different), sometimes the 'People of the Book', the descendants of Abraham, Christians, Muslims and Jews, are contrasted with the rest of the world, but since I am not attempting to define a culture area, but rather to find the general terms of analysis for certain institutions which seem important within it, this does not appear to me to matter.

It might be possible theoretically to relate them to their geographical distribution, noting first of all the general structural characteristics of the Mediterranean communities: their moral cohesiveness and the absence of the contrast between town and country which was so important in England and northern Europe (and from which the concept of *bourgeoisie* emerged), the significance of social class, the forms of agricultural exploitation and commerce, *etcetera*, and then examining the variations, but this seems to me too vast an undertaking if done on any scale and inconclusive if not done on a very grand scale. I have been content to explain only their internal structure and to show at certain points the connections between them and with the notion of honour, which has indeed impressed many of us as the aspect of culture where the Christian and Islamic sides of the Mediterranean have most in common. Nevertheless, if similar, the two are far from identical and this poses a theoretical problem which is worth examining before going further: what is or should be meant by the word 'honour'? As long as we remain within the cultures of the Romance languages we know roughly – how very roughly will soon be clear – what is implied. But can we talk about honour in relation to cultures which possess no such word and not even any that is equivalent in sense? Is it a word to include in the analytical vocabulary of anthropology or only a conception that belongs to our own civilisation and can be exported only at the price of committing an ethnocentrism? If we opt for restricting it to the areas of Romance language we are still left with the problem of how to define analytically the behaviour of those who act under the pressure of their notion of honour and how to analyse similar behaviour in other cultures. However we may express it we must still distinguish between honour as a general principle of conduct relating individuals to their community and honour as a particular conception found in the ethnography. It might be likened to hospitality in the sense that there is, so I have maintained, a general and universal law of hospitality, yet each culture produces its own variant, conforming to the law yet different and sometimes contrary to others in its prescriptions. Thus there is first of all a general law of honour, as there is of hospitality, reminiscent of the concept of natural law except that it rests upon social necessity rather than moral absolutes, and then, providing the basis of action at a specific time and place, the various codes of honour as of hospitality like the legal codes of different nations. Much confusion is caused by failure to distinguish between the analytical and ethnographical levels of discourse and the fact that the same words – such as 'law' – may be used at both makes the confusion only easier, so it might be wise to confine 'honour' to the sphere of the romance languages and use a different word at the analytical level. We might patent the word 'analhon' for this purpose or we might describe honour at the general level as the principle of personal moral supremacy – 'P.P.M.S.' for short. But this would only palliate not resolve our difficulty. It would save us from talking about the *mana* of the Polynesian chiefs as honour and crediting such a notion to the scalp-takers of north America or Borneo, but it would not overcome the problem that differences nonetheless exist in this regard between the peoples of Europe and this, if we are to make any comparisons, forces us to the analytical level. To talk about 'analhon' or 'P.P.M.S.' would arouse the reverse objection of making obscurantist heavy weather of a theoretical point when all we mean is 'honour'. But there is more to this objection. For if we compare southern Europe with northern and with south-eastern Europe and with the further shores of the Mediterranean it becomes evident that, while honour covers a number of very different notions in western Europe and always has done, in those other areas a very similar conception is found expressed in a number of quite different words such as Greek *timé*, Arabic *ḥorma*, *nif*, etc. whose linguistic structure is different but which correspond essentially to the same values. In the first case the same root gives different conceptions, in the second the same conception bears different names. Language relates to culture we would all admit, but it is not identical with it, and to equate the two is merely to shirk the real problem of translation, for language places limitations on what can be said but it does not tell its speakers what to say; the problem of translation is not 'just a matter of words'. There is, alas, no sovereign prophylactic against its dangers, and the invention of a specialised jargon, though it may be necessary when no concept exists in our own language that is even approximately similar – and this explains the proliferation of the vocabulary of anthropology in the field of kinship where this is indeed the case – is hardly the solution when our vocabulary is already rich and our difficulty arises, not from the poverty of ordinary speech but from the complexity of the concept concerned. It would in fact take as much as I have written in this book to make reasonably clear the connotations of the word 'moral' in the 'principle of personal moral supremacy'.

So let us be watchful rather than inventive and trust to the context to make clear the distinguishing features of the different notions of honour. How they conform to its general principles will be apparent only when we view them in their social setting and relate them to the other conceptions of their society. For meanings are never simply given, as in a dictionary, but are part of a way of life and of an intellectual system,[4] yet it is first of all a system lived and only analysed with a view to comparison, an operation that requires general principles, afterwards. Hence the first chapter, devoted to generalities, contains the conclusions that are in fact to be drawn from the essays that form the remainder of the book, even though most of them were published subsequently.

I am grateful to the previous publishers for permission to reprint them. Thus to Messrs George Weidenfeld and Nicolson and the University of Chicago Press for the first two chapters which appeared in *Honour and shame: the values of Mediterranean Society*, edited by John Peristiany, a volume which is all highly relevant to this book for it provides studies of different notions of honour in different parts of the Mediterranean and shows that they have much in common. To the *Bulletin of the New York Academy of Sciences* for a part of the essay here called 'Spiritual Kinship in Andalusia'. To Messrs Mouton and Co. for 'The Law of Hospitality' (in *Contributions to Mediterranean Sociology*) and for 'Women and Sanctuary in the Mediterranean' in *Echanges et Communications*. The article 'The moral foundations of the family' was originally written for the symposium *Seven Studies of the Traditional Family in Southern Europe*, edited by J. K. Campbell and due to be published in Spring 1977. We acknowledge permission from the Clarendon Press, Oxford, to reproduce it here. 'The Fate of Shechem' has not previously appeared in print.

With regard to the content of the book, the list of acknowledgements would indeed be long were I to mention all those in whose debt I stand for help over the past fifteen years in elaborating the theories presented here. All those anthropologists who have worked in the Mediterranean would find a place and in particular John Peristiany who has periodically brought together specialists on different parts of the area to discuss their common interests – and there would be many others besides. But there are some whose help specifically with 'The Fate of Shechem' I would like to mention.

Sir Edmund Leach who generously helped me to understand the basis of our disagreement with regard to the interpretation of Genesis, but who will, I very much fear, remain unconvinced by my thesis. The members of the departments of Anthropology at the London School of Economics, Cambridge, Chicago, Kent, Vassar, Yale and Stockholm where I presented verbally parts of my argument. Professors I. M. Lewis and Jean Pouillon who were kind enough to read critically the essay in manuscript and give me the benefit of their comments. Mr François Heim who gave me the value of his great knowledge and remarkable archive to track down pictorial representations of Dinah and Shechem, including that which graces the cover of this book, and Mr Robert Martin who guided me to some illustrations of the story in illuminated manuscripts. My greatest debt of all, however, goes to Canon Osty's annotated translation of the Bible whose cross-references make it possible for a novice like myself to find his way around the complex text of the Old Testament.

Finally I would like to thank Professor I. Schapera, who has himself contributed notably to our anthopological understanding of Genesis in an essay called 'The Sin of Cain', for reading the proofs and Mrs Hilda Jarrett for coping indefatigably with the revised versions of 'Shechem'.

At the time of going to press I had not yet read D. F. Pocock's interesting article 'North and South in the Book of Genesis'. It adds yet another example to the variety of the ways in which Genesis can be analysed.

1 The anthropology of honour

The theme of honour invites the moralist more often than the social scientist. An honour, a man of honour or the epithet honourable can be applied appropriately in any society, since they are evaluatory terms, but this fact has tended to conceal from the moralists that not only what is honourable but what honour *is* have varied within Europe from one period to another, from one region to another and above all from one class to another. The notion of honour is something more than a means of expressing approval or disapproval. It possesses a general structure which is seen in the institutions and customary evaluations which are particular to a given culture. We might liken it to the concept of magic in the sense that, while its principles can be detected anywhere, they are clothed in conceptions which are not exactly equivalent from one place to another. Like magic also, it validates itself by an appeal to the facts (on which it imposes its own interpretations) and becomes thereby involved in contradictions which reflect the conflicts of the social structure and which this chapter will attempt to unravel. In the first part I shall examine this general structure as it is found in Western Europe without much concern for the local and temporal variations. In the second part I shall examine the semantic range of the notion of honour in modern Andalusian society and attempt to draw conclusions regarding the relation of concepts to society.

The concept of honour

Honour is the value of a person in his own eyes, but also in the eyes of his society. It is his estimation of his own worth, his *claim* to pride, but it is also the acknowledgement of that claim, his excellence recognised by society, his *right* to pride. Students of the minutiae of personal relations have observed that they are much concerned with the ways in which people extort from others the validation of the image which they cherish of themselves[1] and the two aspects of honour may be reconciled in those terms. Honour, therefore, provides a nexus between the ideals of a society and their reproduction in the individual through his aspiration to personify them. As such, it implies not merely an habitual preference for a given mode of conduct, but the entitlement to a certain treatment in return. The right to pride is the right to status (in the popular as well

1

as the anthropological sense of the word), and status is established through the recognition of a certain social identity. When the English girl claims to be 'not that kind of a girl' she is talking about her honour, and in Calderón's plays the heroes invoke their honour with a standard phrase, *Soy quién soy*, I am who I am.

The claimant to honour must get himself accepted at his own evaluation, must be granted reputation, or his claim becomes mere vanity, an object of ridicule or contempt – but granted by whom? The moralist retains the right to arbitrate the claims to honour in accordance with his own values (and many of the treatises on honour are, in fact, tirades against the mores of the day),[2] but the social scientist is concerned with the facts and processes of recognition: how, on what grounds and by whom is the claim to honour recognised?

Every political authority displays the pretension to incarnate the moral values of the society which it governs, to 'command what is right and prohibit what is wrong' in Blackstone's ponderous question-begging words; it therefore claims the right to bestow 'honours' and it follows that those whom it honours are, so it maintains, honourable. When this is accepted by the whole population then the problem of honour presents no quandary. The argument goes like this: the sentiment of honour inspires conduct which is honourable, the conduct receives recognition and establishes reputation, and reputation is finally sanctified by the bestowal of honours. Honour felt becomes honour claimed and honour claimed becomes honour paid. But this argument is not always justified in a complex society where consensus is not uniform. The individual's worth is not the same in the view of one group as in that of another, while the political authorities may view him in a different light again. Moreover, it is not only a question of differing evaluations of the same person. The qualities needed to exert leadership in a rural community are not those which please at court. Honour as a sentiment and mode of conduct becomes separated from honour as a qualification for the Honours List. The two conceptions might be placed at the poles between which common usage fluctuates: at one pole we might put the notion of honour derived from conduct in the sense in which 'All is lost save honour', and at the other, the titles which are piled by the usurper upon the traitors who helped him to power. Adherence to the code of honour is thus opposed to the possession of honours.[3]

If honour establishes status, the converse is also true, and where status is ascribed by birth, honour derives not only from individual reputation but from antecedence. The dual origin is reflected by the former meanings of the English word *valour* which was the leading qualification of honour; it referred both to social status and to personal excellence. But the two conceptions can conflict. The theme of the story of the Cid is the triumph of honour derived from excellence over honour derived from birth, a theme which remains as popular today as ever. The well-born are supposed to possess by inheritance the appropriate character and sentiments which will be seen in their conduct, but when it is asserted they do not, as in the case of the Cid's antagonists, the heirs of Carrión, the concept of honour faces an ambiguity which can only be resolved by an appeal to some tribunal, the 'fount of honour': public opinion, the monarch, or the ordeal of the judicial combat which implied a direct appeal to God. Once the monarchy no longer allowed direct access to the Deity in this matter, but took on the entire responsibility of arbitrating the claims to honour, the court incurred the criticisms which arose from the conflict inherent in the notion, such as the popular opinion which regarded the honour of rustics as more worthy than that of courtiers,[4] or the wry comment of Voltaire who maintained, in answer to Montesquieu, that it is precisely at court that there is always least honour.[5]

The claim to excellence is relative. It is always implicitly the claim to excel over others. Hence honour is the basis of precedence. Hobbes, sternly ignoring the views of the moralists from Aristotle onwards, discusses honour in terms of this and formulates what I would call 'the pecking-order theory of honour'.[6] In a society of equals, such as a community of peasants, to attain the esteem of one's neighbours may be as high as honour can point and to establish hegemony over them would rather detract from that esteem by violating the premise of equality, but where we approach the pole where honour is established through the bestowal of honours, there must needs be competition for them. Where there is a hierarchy of honour, the person who submits to the precedence of others recognises his inferior status. He is dishonoured in the sense that he has disavowed his claim to the higher status to which he aspired. The superb mottoes of the aristocracy of Europe rub in the point: *Roi ne puis, duc ne daigne, Rohan suis*, or prouder still: *Después de Dios, la Casa de Quiros*. We can see the hierarchy of honour stretching from its source in God, through a King whose legitimacy depends upon divine sanction, through the ranks of the social structure down to those who had no honour at all, the heretics and the infamous. It is not only among the aristocracies, however, that honour has a competitive aspect, though the struggle for precedence may be more acute among them. The victor in any competition for honour finds his reputation enhanced by the humiliation of the vanquished. This is as true on the street-corner as in the lists. It was believed at one time in Italy by the common people that one who gave an insult thereby took to himself the reputation of which he deprived the other.[7] The Church of England hymn puts the point succinctly:

> Conquering kings their titles take
> From the foes they captive make

but the hymn goes on to contrast this principle of honour with the Christian ethic.

Since the treatises on honour first began to appear in the sixteenth century, Churchmen have stressed the basis of true honour in virtue and supported their thesis with the authority of Aristotle, yet they seem never to have convinced the protagonists in the struggle for honour, nor even for that matter all the writers on the subject. Nor do they appear to have persuaded the monarchs in whose gift honour lay who, in dispensing it, followed more often their personal whims or considerations of political expediency; honours have often been for sale by a sovereign with empty coffers. Yet if sovereigns have fallen short of the ideal of bestowing honour only on the virtuous, the same can be said of the *vox populi*. Respect and precedence are paid to those who claim it and are sufficiently powerful to enforce their claim. Just as possession is said to be nine-tenths of the law, so the *de facto* achievement of honour depends upon the ability to silence anyone who would dispute the title. The reputation of a dangerous man is liable to assure him precedence over a virtuous man; he may not be thought privately to be honourable, but while no one is prepared to question the matter, he is treated as though he were and granted the precedence which he claims. On the field of honour might is right.

There are reasons in the nature of honour itself which submit it to the shifts of power, and these will become clear if we examine how honour is recognised or impugned, and by whom. We should start by noting the intimate relation between honour and the physical person. The rituals by which honour is formally bestowed involve a ceremony which commonly centres upon the head of the protagonist whether it is the crowning of a monarch or the touch on the head with a book which confers academic degrees in the University of Oxford. As much may be said of many rites of passage and in fact we should regard honorific rituals as rites of passage. The payment of honour in daily life is accorded through the offering of precedence (so often expressed through an analogy with the head), and through the demonstrations of respect which are commonly associated with the head whether it is bowed, touched, uncovered or covered; while, again, the head of the person honoured is used to demonstrate his status whether it is adorned, dressed in a distinctive way, prohibited to be touched or even if it is chopped off.[8] It is worth observing in the latter case that the right to be executed in this way, even though the execution itself is a dishonour, preserves a recognition of the honourable status of the victim which derives from his birth and which the dishonourable personal conduct he was condemned for does not suffice to obliterate, since it is the concern not only of the individual but of his lineage. Decapitation recognised that there was something worth chopping off. Even where polite society has outlawed physical violence it retains the ritual slap on the face as a challenge to settle an affair of honour,[9] and it was commonly admitted that offences to honour could only be redeemed through blood. 'La lessive de l'honneur ne se coule qu'avec du sang.'[10]

Any form of physical affront implies an affront to honour since the 'ideal sphere' surrounding a person's honour of which Simmel speaks is defiled.[11] Moreover, the significance of the presence of a person is highly relevant to his honour. That which is an affront if said to his face may not dishonour if said behind his back. That which, if done in his presence, is offensive may not be so if he is not there to resent it. What is offensive is not the action in itself but the act of obliging the offended one to witness it. Thus in the villages of rural Andalusia a father cannot admit the presence of his daughter's suitor – custom imposes an avoidance between the two – yet he would be dishonoured if his daughter were to marry without being courted, not the contrary. In all these instances we can see that honour is exalted or desecrated through the physical person and through actions related to it which are not merely symbolic representations of a moral state of affairs, but *are* what we might otherwise infer they represent, that is to say, they are transactions of honour – not the bill of goods, but the goods themselves. Therefore, the act of resentment is the touchstone of honour, for a physical affront is a dishonour, regardless of the moral issues involved, and creates a situation in which the honour of the affronted person is in jeopardy and requires 'satisfaction' if it is to return to its normal condition. Indeed the language of the Spanish Theatre of the Golden Age treats honour almost as if it were a good, something which can be taken from one person by another and which may be owed and restituted. This satisfaction may be acquired through an apology which is a verbal act of self-humiliation or it may require, and if the apology is not forthcoming does require, avenging. To leave an affront unavenged is to leave one's honour in a state of desecration and this is therefore equivalent to cowardice. Hence the popularity among the mottoes of the aristocracy of the theme of *nemo me impune lacessit* (no man may harm me with impunity). The equation of honour with valour and cowardice with dishonour, apparent in this, derives directly from the structure of the notion, quite regardless of the historical explanations which have been offered of this fact.

We have not so far considered the question of intention at all, and have implied that it is subsidiary in cases of physical affront. Intentions are, however, all-important to the establishment of honour since they demonstrate the sentiment and character from which honour *qua* conduct derives. To show dishonourable intentions is to be dishonoured regardless of the result. To desire to run away in battle is dishonouring whether one succeeds in doing so or not, while honour – and in this case honour through the conduct which gives proof of proper sentiments is clearly meant – can still be saved when all else is lost. Moreover, intention is a necessary component of the competition for honour expressed in the challenge; the essence of an affront is that another should dare to affront one. Therefore, when apologies are offered they normally take the form of a denial of the intention to cause offence. By proclaiming it to be unintentional the offender reduces the gravity of the affront; it makes the apology easier to accept while it also reduces the humiliation of the apologiser and therefore makes it easier to give. Thus, one can see that while honour is established or impugned by physical behaviour this is because certain intentions are made manifest in it, are, as it were, necessarily implicit. To maintain that one did not intend what one did is to require a certain indulgence on the part of the listener – an indulgence which may not be granted if he has been seriously affronted; for actions speak plainer than words where honour is concerned. Yet words also have their value as actions and in this field the way things are said is more important than the substance of what is said. The apology which does not sound sincere aggravates the offence.

To sum up, both words and actions are significant within the code of honour because they are expressions of attitude which claim, accord or deny honour. Honour, however, is only irrevocably committed by attitudes expressed in the presence of witnesses, the representatives of public opinion. The problem of public knowledge as an essential ingredient of an affront has been stressed by various authors, and it has even been doubted that honour could be committed by words uttered in the absence of witnesses. On the other hand, a person can *feel* himself to be dishonoured even if the dishonour is not known. Yet there is no disagreement that the extent of the damage to reputation relates to the range of public opinion within which the damage is broadcast. This is the basis of the dilemma which faces the hero of Calderón's, *A secreto agravio, secreta venganza;* how to cleanse without publicising his dishonour. Public opinion forms therefore a tribunal before which the claims to honour are brought, 'the court of reputation' as it has been called, and against its judgements there is no redress. For this reason it is said that public ridicule kills.

Given that a man's honour is committed by his estimation of the intention of others, everything depends upon how an action is interpreted. Certain actions have a ritual significance which is conventionally recognised, others depend for their interpretation upon the nuances of manners. To affront ambiguously enables a man to attain his ends without perhaps having to face the response to his affront; he can at least put his antagonist to the test in such a way as to avoid the responsibility for the breach of the peace which ensues. The opening scene of *Romeo and Juliet* provides an illustration:

> 'Do you bite your thumb at us, sir?'
> 'No sir, I do not bite my thumb at you sir, but I bite my thumb.'

The intention, though denied, was plain enough to provoke a scrap. The ambiguous affront has the advantage also that it places the antagonist in a dilemma: if he responds, the affront can be denied and he can be declared touchy, quarrelsome and therefore ridiculous; if he does not respond, he can be made to appear cowardly and therefore dishonoured. If a man sees no insult and can be justified in seeing none, then his honour is not jeopardised. Hence the possibility of 'turning a blind eye'. But if he realises that he has been insulted (and others will usually help him to realise it), yet does nothing about it, then he is dishonoured. The ambiguous affront which provokes no reaction is therefore commonly followed by a more explicit one, if the intention is indeed to challenge. The victim of an affront is dishonoured at the point where he is forced to recognise that he has been. A man is therefore always the guardian and arbiter of his own honour, since it relates to his own consciousness and is too closely allied to his physical being, his will, and his judgement for anyone else to take responsibility for it.

When a person reacts to a slight upon the honour of another, it can only be because his own is involved. Thus, according to ancient French law,[12] a member of a slighted man's family or lineage could pick up the glove, or a man bound in liege to him, but no one else. The pact of brotherhood between knights referred to by Caro Baroja[13] created such a lien and, in *Romeo and Juliet*, Mercutio considered his friendship with Romeo a sufficient justification. The possibility of being represented by a champion in the judicial combat was restricted to those who were judged unable to defend their honour personally: women,[14] the aged or infirm, or persons of a social status which prohibited them from responding to a challenge, in particular, churchmen and, of course, royalty. It must otherwise always be an individual's own choice whether to maintain or abandon his claim to honour, whether to react to a slight and vindicate himself or to accept it and the dishonour which accompanies it. Thus a man is dishonoured if, when he is able to do so for himself, he allows another to pick up the glove for him. This remains true even though at certain periods the seconds were expected also to fight.

The ultimate vindication of honour lies in physical violence and when other means fail the obligation exists, not only in the formal code of honour but in social milieux which admit no such code, to revert to it. This is congruent with what has been said already about the relation between honour and the physical person. Within the formal code the duel displays the principles involved: the offended party, judging that his honour was impugned, issued a challenge by which he invoked the honour of his offender and demanded satisfaction. The offender was obliged then either to retract and offer apologies (a course of action which was incompatible with the conception which many men had of their own honour) or to accept. Yet 'satisfaction' is not synonymous with triumph, only with the opportunity to achieve it under conventionally defined conditions which imply a judgement of destiny. In this sense the duel shares with the judicial combat the nature of an ordeal, though the implication was manifest only in the case of the judicial combat which was ordained by the magistrates as a means of validating an oath. God would surely not protect a perjuror who had taken his name in vain. In this way the realities of power, be they no more than the hazards of the field of honour, were endowed with divine sanction. The fact of victory in the judicial combat was something more than hazard for it implied validation, and the satisfaction by which honour was restored was something more than personal satisfaction, for it was accorded by the appeal to the test of courage regardless of the outcome. The duel finished the matter; the quarrel could not honourably be prosecuted thereafter, either by the contestants or their partisans. On this account the duel and the judicial combat are to be distinguished from the feud which, even though it is inspired by similar sentiments, requires none of the formal equality of the duel nor its ceremonial setting and claims no judicial character for its outcome. Thus, unlike the jousting lists which promoted the competition for honour, the duel is rather the means of settling disputes with regard to it. It is not surprising then that it has tended to be frowned upon by the state which has frequently forbidden it, even during epochs when it remained the accepted custom of the aristocracy. (The Church, in keeping with its commitment in this regard, also prohibited it at the Council of Trent.)

The appeal to a private ordeal cuts out the 'fount of honour' from its role in determining the honourable status of its subjects. Like Shakespeare's Richard II, the state prefers to have the last word in such matters rather than remit them to the unpredictable hand of destiny. Yet seen from the individual's point of view, to have recourse to justice is to abnegate one's claim to settle one's debts of honour for oneself, the only way in which they can be settled. When challenged to fight, it is not honourable to demand police protection. Therefore, while the sovereign is the 'fount of honour' in one sense, he is also the enemy of honour in another, since he claims to arbitrate in regard to it. He takes over the functions of the Divinity thanks to his sacred character. The change from the period when the law prescribed the judicial combat to that when the duel was made illegal corresponds to an extension of the competence of the state in judicial matters. Yet no man of honour, least of all an aristocrat, was prepared to remit to the courts the settlement of his affairs of honour. Hence the inefficacy of the legislation against duelling.

The conflict between honour and legality is a fundamental one which persists to this day. For to go to law for redress is to confess publicly that you have been wronged and the demonstration of your vulnerability places your honour in jeopardy, a jeopardy from which the 'satisfaction' of legal compensation at the hands of a secular authority hardly redeems it. Moreover, it gives your offender the chance to humiliate you further by his attitude during all the delays of court procedure, which in fact can do nothing to restore your honour but merely advertises its plight. To request compensation or even to invite apologies are courses of action which involve risk to honour if they are not adopted with the implication that they cloak a demand for satisfaction. If someone steps on your toe inadvertently while getting on to a bus, you humiliate yourself by complaining, even if apologies are proffered. The man of honour in the sense of precedence says nothing at the time, but catches his offender a sharp one on the shin as he gets off; his honour is revealed to have been jeopardized only by the action which restores it to grace and he has circumvented the risks of placing it in foreign keeping. *Nemo me impune lacessit* therefore is not only a favourite motto of the aristocracy but of any group which values this conception of honour. The resemblance between the mores of the street-corner society and those of the aristocracy, both contemptuous of legality, derives from this: the aristocracy claims the right to honour = precedence by the tradition which makes them the leaders of society, arbiters rather than 'arbitrated' and therefore 'a law unto themselves'. The sacred quality of high status is demonstrated in freedom from the sanctions which apply to ordinary mortals. (The same principle explains the incest of the Gods.) On the other hand, street-corner society claims also to be a law unto itself, not because it is above the law but because it is outside it and because the concept of honour = virtue has no claim upon its aspirations.

When honour is impugned it can be vindicated. Yet the power to impugn the honour of another man depends also on the relative status of the contestants. An inferior is not deemed to possess sufficient honour to resent the affront of a superior. A superior can ignore the affront of an inferior, since his honour is not committed by it – though he may choose to punish an impudence. The combatants in a duel must recognize equality since they stand on equal terms in it. Montesquieu refers to the mediaeval laws[15] according to which a judicial combat could take place between a gentleman and a villein. Yet the former was bound to appear, then, without the symbols of his rank and to fight as a villein on foot. This disposition disappears from the code of honour of a later age. When Voltaire answered provocatively a discourtesy from the Chevalier de Rohan, the latter had his henchmen beat him and Voltaire's noble friends declined to take up his cause. In addition to his hurt he was covered in ridicule. He did not forgive the Duc de Sully at whose house the incident occurred. Yet the Chevalier was not apparently dishonoured in the eyes of his peers, even though he evaded the duel to which Voltaire attempted to challenge him by procurring his imprisonment and exile. A man is answerable for his honour only to his social equals, that is to say, to those with whom he can conceptually compete.

The intention of a person, we have said, is paramount in relation to his honour, but it is the intention evident in his actions rather than that expressed in his words. A man commits his honour only through his *sincere* intentions. Giving his word of honour, he asserts sincerity and stakes his honour upon the issue, be it a promise regarding the future or an assurance regarding past events. If his true will was not behind the promise or the assertion, then he is not dishonoured if he fails to fulfil the promise or turns out to have lied. If he intended to deceive, he is not dishonoured by the revelation that he did so, since he 'did not mean it', he 'had his fingers crossed', that is to say, he meant the opposite of what he said. Yet according to the rules of this puerile device for disengaging honour, the fingers must be held crossed while the words are spoken; they cannot be crossed afterwards. This fact demonstrates the essential truth that it is lack of steadfastness in intentions which is dishonouring, not misrepresentation of them.

We can explain now something which appears anomalous in the literature of honour: on the one hand honour demands keeping faith and to break one's word or to lie is the most dishonourable conduct, yet in fact a man is permitted to lie and to deceive without forfeiting his honour.[16] The formal vocabulary of challenges commonly bears the implication of oath-breaker or liar. The judicial combat was a means of proving which of the two contestants was a liar, while the word *mentita* (giving the lie) figures in the Italian codes of honour as the formal provocation which cannot easily be refused. In the Spanish drama *mentís* carried the same significance. On the other hand, King Ferdinand of Aragon boasted of the nine times he deceived the King of France, and Don Juan, in the play of Tirso de Molina, in spite of the deceptions he had perpetrated, declared himself a man of honour as he gripped the stone hand of the Comendador and gave this as his reason for accepting the predictable consequences.[17] It appears to me that critics of recent times like the dramatists who took up the theme have neglected to consider the fact that Don Juan is a man of honour. He is a rascal by their standards and indeed an offender against loyalty, hospitality, friendship and religion, as Professor Parker has noted.[18] But such a view neglects to examine the concept of honour which is displayed in the play and to say, like Professor Parker, that Don Juan is the negation of 'Caballerosidad' in every respect is to beg the question. Don Juan is a protagonist of the 'pecking-order theory of honour'. He is an affronter of other men, a humiliator and deceiver by design of both men and women, a scoffer at the moral and social orders and, in his sexual relations, a 'scalp-hunter', but not a voluptuary and not, be it noted, an adulterer; his four female victims are presumed virgins; he is not a man to grant precedence to another even in this.

To take an example from contemporary ethnography, the Greek peasants whose concern for their honour is very great, regard deception involving a lie as perfectly legitimate and honourable behaviour.[19]

The anomaly is therefore this: while to lie in order to deceive is quite honourable, to be called a liar in public is a grave affront. The explanation lies in the ambiguity as to whether the word given did in fact commit the honour of the liar, and this can only be established by a knowledge of his true intentions. If it did not, that is to say, if his intentions were misrepresented but not rescinded, then the person deceived, not the deceiver, is humiliated. If, however, the lie was told or the promise made because the liar did not dare to affront his antagonist, or if, having committed his honour to another man, he lacks steadfastness, then the liar is dishonoured. He has desecrated that which is sacred to him, his true self. The whole question hinges therefore on the moral commitment of the liar. To lie is to deny the truth to someone who has the right to be told it and this right exists only where respect is due. Children are taught to tell the truth to their elders who are under no reciprocal obligation, since it is they who decide what the children should be told. The duty to tell the truth curtails the personal autonomy of the man who may otherwise feel himself entitled, on account of his social pre-eminence, to represent reality as he pleases and offer no justification. The moral commitment to tell the truth derives then from the social commitment to persons to whom it is due. This is the meaning of the story of the emperor's cloak. At the same time, a man may not question the truth of an assertion made by one who does not owe it to him. The right to the truth and the right to withhold it both attach to honour and to contest these rights is to place honour in jeopardy.

A man of honour may not lie to someone whom he is not prepared to affront, for to deceive a person intentionally is to humiliate him, and this amounts to an insult to which the norms of the community define the modes of honourable response. Given the ambiguity of the interpretation of his action, the person thus offended is entitled to interpret the lie as an act of cowardice and to declare the liar dishonoured by it. The *mentita* therefore represents a counter insult which demands of the person accused as a liar that he demonstrate by his response that he did in fact intend to affront, under pain of being proved otherwise a coward. Yet if he responds to the challenge, he is not dishonoured (for it is not dishonouring to affront another man): he is only dishonoured as a liar if he fails to do so.[20]

Hence the importance of the oath in relation to honour. It commits the honour of the swearer just as 'crossed fingers' liberate it and aims to eliminate the ambiguity as to his true intentions. By invoking that which is sacred to him – his God, the bones of saints, his loyalty to his sovereign, the health of his mother or simply his own honour – he activates an implicit curse against himself in the eventuality of his failure to implement his oath or, at least, he assures that public opinion is entitled to judge him dishonoured. Moreover, he cannot impugn the honour of the person to whom he is bound by oath by deceiving him. The latter is untouched by his deceit. If he proves false, the dishonour is his alone; retribution can be left to public opinion or to the Gods.

Yet even an oath which is not made freely is not binding, nor is a word of honour which is not intended as such. The attempt to use ritual to commit the honour of a man comes up against the difficulty that no man *can* commit his honour against his will, since his honour is what he wills and the attempt to oblige him to do so invites him to 'cross his fingers'. The ritual of the oath, like the rites of the church, is invalid without the intention of the participant.

I have used the word 'sacred' in a colloquial sense which may well raise objections from anthropologists. Yet in saying that a man's honour is sacred to him I do no more than repeat what is stated in a host of contexts (including the American Declaration of Independence). It is literally more exact to say that a man's true self is blended with the sacred. In the oath, the sacred is invoked in order to commit honour in ways which indicate something more than a conditional curse: 'I swear by all that is sacred to me' presupposes such a close connection. We have noted also that the same forms of conduct demonstrate respect for persons of superior honour as for religious objects, while the position of the monarch as both the fount of human honour and appointed by the Grace of God brings a divine sanction to the social system. Indeed the King was literally sacred through the sacrament of coronation. Honour, in addition to connecting a man to others within the hierarchy of his society, connects him to his sovereign and to the Deity: 'A traitor to my God, my King and me' was the form of the indictment which expressed the challenge in *Richard II* (Act I, Scene 3).

Moreover, the notion, common in all the languages of Europe, that honour is susceptible of 'defilement' or 'stains' of which it requires to be purified entitles us to mark a resemblance to the customs of primitive societies whose chiefs are the object of prohibitions similar to those which circumscribe the man of honour. The early anthropologists might well, in fact, have translated the word *mana* as *honour*,[21] at least in the contexts in which it referred to persons, and noted that the Polynesian victor who acquired the *mana* of his slain foe by taking his name was behaving rather like the conquering kings of the hymn. But they became interested in the subject while studying magic and the 'primitive mind', and they therefore stressed the differences rather than the resemblances between the customs which they studied and their own. They could with difficulty envisage the 'savage' as having honour such as they themselves possessed and the age in which they wrote was disinclined to perceive the 'irrationality' of the primitive mind in its own attitudes to social status. The analogy between honour and *mana* is a matter I have discussed more fully elsewhere.[22]

We have so far discussed honour as a purely individual attribute. Now we must examine how it is related to social solidarities. Social groups possess a collective honour in which their members participate; the dishonourable conduct of one reflects upon the honour of all, while a member shares in the honour of his group. 'I am who I am' subsumes 'whom I am associated with'. 'Díme con quién andas y te diré quién eres' says the Spanish proverb (Tell me whom you associate with and I will tell you who you are). Honour pertains to social groups of any size, from the nuclear family whose head is responsible for the honour of all its members to the nation whose members' honour is bound up with their fidelity to their sovereign. In both the family and the monarchy a single person symbolises the group whose collective honour is vested in his person. The members owe obedience and respect of a kind which commits their individual honour without redress. Here intentions are irrelevant for, whatever his feelings about the matter the individual is born a son and a subject, he does not compete or contract in order to become so. Thus parricide and regicide are sacrilegious acts which homicide is not.

The idea that the honour of the group resides in its head was fundamental to the conception of aristocracy and assured the fidelity through the oath of the liegeman to his lord; the inferior in such a relationship participated in the honour of his chief and was therefore interested in defending it. Yet the principle holds beyond the ties of the feudal system; the system of patronage depends upon it, also. Hence the hubris of the tyrant's minion, the vicarious glory of the noble's servant.

Yet there exist other social groups whose leader is an elected representative and whose person, as opposed to his post, possesses none of this sacred quality. Here the tribunal of public opinion is sovereign: in trade-guilds, municipalities or republics.

This observation provided Montesquieu with his basic dichotomy: a distinction between the monarchy whose operative principle is honour, and the republic whose operative principle is virtue, by which he meant civic virtue, something rather like what is meant today by 'citizenship'. He encountered difficulty in making himself understood to those who showed themselves unwilling to adopt his usage.[23] The distinction was criticised by those who maintained that there was honour in a republic, by those who maintained that there was virtue in a monarchy, and by Voltaire whose opinion has already been given.

The difficulty of distinguishing between the two terms, honour and virtue, was responsible for those confusions, neither the first nor the last of their kind, which centre on the meanings of the word honour: honour which derives from virtuous conduct and that honour which situates an individual socially and determines his right to precedence. The two senses appear to be so far removed from one another that one may ask why they were, and still are, expressed by the same word, why the languages of Europe are so determined to avoid clarity in this matter.

The political significance of the sacred is that it arbitrates questions of value, lays the limits to what can be done or maintained without sacrilege and defines the unconditional allegiances of the members of a society. Authority as political power claims always to be moral authority, and the word therefore enjoys the same duality as honour from the moment that the legitimacy of the use of force is disputed. It cannot admit that its actions are devoid of legitimacy. In the same vein, no man of honour ever admits that his honour = precedence is not synonymous with his honour = virtue. To do so would be to admit himself dishonoured. For him there is only one concept, his honour. However far apart the abstract notions of precedence and virtue may be, they come together in the individual at the level of behaviour. Therefore, as we have seen in the instance of the lie, an action *may* be potentially dishonourable, but it is only when this action is publicly condemned that it dishonours. Hence, just as capital assures credit, so the possession of honour guarantees against dishonour, for the simple reason that it places a man (if he has enough of it) in a position in which he cannot be challenged or judged. The king cannot be dishonoured. What he *is* guarantees the evaluation of his actions. He is above criticism. This is what I call the principle of *Honi soit qui mal y pense*.[24] It is incorporated in the jurisprudence of honour in a provision, implicit throughout, which is expressed by Bryson in the following terms: 'Just as honouring one who was undeserving was a kind of contempt, and true honour dwelled rather in him who honoured, so an offence given to an honourable man stained only the offender. As for the offended party, he was still more worthy of honour if he bore the offence magnanimously.'[25]

At the level of political action, the concept of authority partakes of the same nature; the king can do no wrong because he is the king and therefore the arbiter of right. Reference to authority takes precedence over reference to privately reasoned evaluations. What God, King, Country, or Party says is right. *Lèse-majesté* is the sister of rebellion and criticism of established authority, beyond the limits which convention allows, is an act of disloyalty. In this sense, therefore, the respect felt for the monarch possesses something of the same power to render sacred as the reverence felt for the Divine: in paying this respect, we abnegate our right to question and bind ourselves to accept what might otherwise appear to us wrong. The arbitrary nature of sacred power extends beyond the frontiers of religion.[26]

The ritual and ceremonial aspects of honour assure not only the opportunity for those who feel respect to pay it, but they commit those who pay it even if they do not feel it. Regardless of private feelings they serve to establish the consensus of the society with regard to the order of precedence; they demonstrate what is acceptable by reference to what is accepted. If the honour felt by the individual becomes honour paid by the society, it is equally the case that the honour which is paid by the society sets the standards for what the individual should feel. Transactions of honour therefore serve these purposes: they not only provide, on the psychological side, a nexus between the ideals of society and their reproduction in the actions of individuals – honour commits men to act as they should (even if opinions differ as to how they should act) – but, on the social side, between the ideal order and the terrestrial order, validating the realities of power and making the sanctified order of precedence correspond to them. Thus, thanks to its duality, honour does something which the philosophers say they cannot do: derive an *ought* from an *is*; whatever *is* becomes *right*, the *de facto* is made *de jure*, the victor is crowned with laurels, the war-profiteer is knighted, the tyrant becomes the monarch, the bully, a chief. The reconciliation between the social order as we find it and the social order which we revere is accomplished thanks to the confusion which hinges upon the duality of honour and its associated concepts. It is a confusion which fulfils the function of social integration by ensuring the legitimation of established power.

I have attempted to discover the general structure of the notion of honour in the literature of Western Europe and have therefore overlooked the very considerable differences between countries and epochs;[27] I did not attempt to explain the variations in the frequency of duelling or the particular emphases which different periods placed upon the constituents of honour, religious, political, financial or sexual. However, such variations are also found within the culture of a single region and epoch and, while this has sometimes been taken to reflect differences between classes or factions in their struggles to impose their own evaluations upon their society,[28] it must be pointed out that this is not merely due to the emergence of new social forces which require the rules to be altered, as it were, if they are to gain power, but to the fact that different elements of a society behave in different ways and think in different ways, albeit within the framework of a common language.

A system of values is never a homogeneous code of abstract principles obeyed by all the participants in a given culture and able to be extracted from an informant with the aid of a set of hypothetical questions, but a collection of concepts which are related to one another and applied differentially by the different status-groups defined by age, sex, class, occupation, etc. in the different social (not merely linguistic) contexts in which they find their meanings. Like tropical fish whose radiant colours fade once they are taken from the water, the concepts which compose such a system retain their exact significance only within the environment of the society which nurtures them and which resolves, thanks to its internal structuring, their conflicts with each other. The variations in the components of the notion of honour in Andalusia reflect, in this way, the articulation of the social structure, and can only be studied in terms of it. This is what I shall now try to do.

2 Honour and social status in Andalusia

A certain bashfulness disguises the expression of attitudes concerning honour in our own society (perhaps because the word has acquired archaic overtones), but this is not so in the small town in the Sierra de Cádiz where I first investigated this theme.[1] Here questions of honour can be debated without causing embarrassment, and they loom large both in theoretical discussions regarding the propriety of conduct and also in the daily idiom of social intercourse: indeed, the honourable status of the members of the community is a matter of continual comment. Reputation is not only a matter of pride, but also of practical utility. Where free associations of a contractual kind govern the forms of cooperation and enterprise, a good name is the most valuable of assets. Moreover, the honour of a man has a legal status in Spanish, which it does not have in Anglo-Saxon, law.[2] The value attached to honour can also be seen in the custom of bargaining where intermediaries, reminiscent of seconds in a duel, are required for the successful negotiation. Attempts to damage reputation are constantly made and every quarrel, once inflamed, leads to imputations of acts and intentions which are totally dishonourable and which may well have nothing to do with the subject of the quarrel. The discussions of honour are not restricted to literal expression; circumlocutions are frequently used and the reputation of a person is more commonly attainted by implications than by direct statements.

The girl who discussed in literal terms whether or not it was dishonouring to recognise one's own nickname[3] was in no way exceptional in her preoccupation to reach a clear distinction between the conduct which dishonoured and that which did not, though in maintaining that she could without dishonour respond when it was mentioned in the street, she was going counter to the general opinion of the community. She herself admitted that it depended upon the nature of the nickname, since, while some nicknames, such as hers, derive from the surname of an ancestor or from a place of origin, others are unflatteringly personal. I put her thesis to the test when challenged one dark night upon the road and earned, first of all some astonished comments that I should announce myself as 'the Englishman', and when I asked why I should not do so, a homily on 'how we behave here'. The customs of the bull-ring and the music-hall whose heroes present themselves under the rubric of their nickname are not those of the *pueblo*. I had, in any case, overstated her thesis, for the girl denied that she would go so far as to announce herself by her nickname, and she held more conventional views regarding the other ways in which honour could be forfeited. These, as she saw them, were concerned entirely with the possibility of imputing an improper relationship with a member of the male sex.

Criticising people behind their back is one thing and treating them with contempt to their face is quite another. This society lays great emphasis on courtesy, and when people have quarrelled to the point that they are not prepared to behave with courtesy to one another, then they avoid entering each other's presence; it is recognised that the two 'do not speak', and others connive in avoiding situations where they might be forced to do so. There is, however, a certain class of person to whom courtesy is commonly denied, the 'shameless ones' (*los sin vergüenza*). These are people whose dishonourable reputation is established beyond all doubt through their habitual indulgence in conduct which is shameful: petty thieving, begging and promiscuity in the case of women. They are considered to be outside the moral pale, and, in this way, are associated with the gypsies who are thought to be, by nature, devoid of shame. Such persons are often addressed directly by their nickname without the Christian name and treated with open disdain (though fear of the magical power of gypsies usually affords them a certain respect from the unsophisticated). The fact that these people are prepared to put up with such treatment confirms their status as shameless.

The mores of Andalusia, like those of peasant Greece,[4] are indulgent towards conduct which we might regard as boastful, and the example is not lacking of one, Manuel 'el Conde', who, even by their light, was regarded as somewhat overbearing. A man of short stature and unimposing physique, he was a recognised agricultural expert (*perito*), that is to say, one whose opinion could be called upon by the syndical organisation. His opinion was given in fact, in not unforceful terms, upon any occasion when he thought it relevant. He was accustomed to boast of his ugliness, as though it were an embellishment to his other qualities, and to stake his claim to honour without quibbling:

'I have not much fortune,' he would say, and then, tapping his breast, 'but I have within me that which is worth more than fortune, my honour.'[5]

He was also fond of interjecting a pun into the conversation when the subject of partridges was mentioned:

> 'La perdí' dice Usted? No, señor, no la perdí!'
> ('The partridge, you say? No, sir, I have not lost it!')

That which he has not lost is his shame, for it is common practice to allude to this word by the pronoun without pronouncing it; to 'lose it' means to lose one's shame.

From Manuel's vainglorious pronouncements two points are to be gleaned: first, the close association between the notions of honour and shame, which appear synonymous in many contexts as in these, and secondly, that this quality, once lost, is irrecoverable.

The word which I have translated as 'shame' is *vergüenza*, but it both carries a heavier emphasis and covers a wider range of meaning than the English equivalent. In a previous discussion of the subject[6] I have defined it as a concern for repute, but it is both a sentiment and also the public recognition of that sentiment. It is what makes a person sensitive to the pressure exerted by public opinion but also the reputation earned in consequence. In these senses it is synonymous with honour, but the sentiment also finds expression in ways which are no longer so, such as shyness, blushing and the restraints which derive from emotional inhibition, the fear of exposing oneself to comment and criticism.

As the basis of repute, honour and shame are synonymous, since shamelessness is dishonourable; a person of good repute is taken to have both, one of evil repute is credited with neither. (This is so at least at the plebeian level which is all we are concerned with for the moment.) As such, they are the constituents of virtue. Yet while certain virtues are common to both sexes, such as honesty, loyalty, a concern for reputation which involves avoidance of moral turpitude in general, they are not all so. For the conduct which establishes repute depends upon the status of the person referred to. This is particularly evident in the differentiation of the sexes. The honour of a man and of a woman therefore imply quite different modes of conduct. This is so in any society. A woman is dishonoured, loses her *vergüenza*, with the tainting of her sexual purity, but a man does not. While certain conduct is honourable for both sexes, honour = shame requires conduct in other spheres, which is exclusively a virtue of one sex or the other. It obliges a man to defend his honour and that of his family, a woman to conserve her purity. Yet the concepts of honour and shame also extend to the point where they are no longer synonymous, and at this point they lose their ethical value. Shame, no longer equivalent to honour, as shyness, blushing and timidity is thought to be proper to women, even though it no longer constitutes virtue, while honour, no longer equivalent to shame, becomes an exclusively male attribute as the concern for precedence and the willingness to offend another man if provoked. At this point also these modes of conduct become dishonouring for the inappropriate sex: for a man, to show timidity or blush is likely to make him an object of ridicule, while a woman who takes to physical violence or attempts to usurp the male prerogative of authority or, very much more so, sexual freedom, forfeits her shame. Thus honour and shame, when they are not equivalent, are linked exclusively to one sex or the other and are opposed to one another.

There is however one further usage of the word *vergüenza* which is common to both sexes and this is the sense of 'to put to shame', literally 'to give shame' (*darle vergüenza*), or speaking about oneself, to feel shame, literally, 'to be given it'. It derives from the concern for repute, since one who is thus concerned is more easily put to shame than one who is not, but it is, so to speak, its negative counterpart. A person who *has vergüenza* is sensitive to his repute and therefore honourable, but if he *is given it*, he is humiliated, stripped of honour. By implication, if he had it already he would not have to be given it; and this is made clear in the usage of *darle vergüenza* to mean to punish a child. A person who possesses *vergüenza* already does not expose himself to the risk of humiliation. In accordance with the general structure of the notion of honour explained already in the first chapter, he is shamed (*avergonzado*) only at the point when he is forced to recognise that he has accepted humiliation. In this sense, as that which is not inherent in the person but is imposed from outside, shame is equivalent to dishonour. This explains the usage in the law of an earlier period of the punishment of *vergüenza pública*, the public dishonouring in the stocks. Honour is the aspiration and the validation of status, while *vergüenza*, opposed to honour, is the restraint of such an aspiration (timidity) and also the recognition of the loss of status. Thus, just as honour is at the same time honour felt, honour claimed and honour paid, so *vergüenza* is dishonour imposed, accepted and finally felt. Honour originates in the individual breast and comes to triumph in the social realm, *vergüenza* in this sense originates in the actions of others as the denial of honour, and is borne home in the individual. The concepts of honour or shame are therefore either, according to context, synonymous as virtue or contraries as precedence or humiliation.

We might express the relationship between the two concepts in the accompanying diagram.

It will be noted that the ethically neutral qualities which are exclusively either honour or shame are at the same time necessary ingredients of the qualities, linked to one sex or the other, which are ethically valued

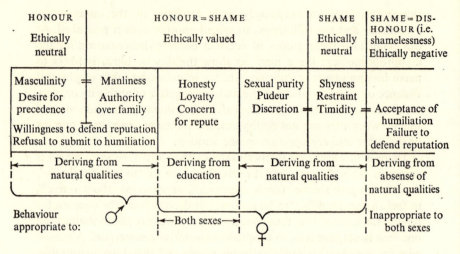

HONOUR Ethically neutral		HONOUR = SHAME Ethically valued			SHAME Ethically neutral	SHAME = DIS- HONOUR (i.e. shamelessness) Ethically negative
Masculinity = Manliness Desire for Authority precedence over family Willingness to defend reputation Refusal to submit to humiliation		Honesty Loyalty Concern for repute	Sexual purity Pudeur Discretion ⇥	Shyness Restraint Timidity ⇥		Acceptance of humiliation Failure to defend reputation
⟵ Deriving from ⟶ natural qualities		Deriving from education	⟵ Deriving from ⟶ natural qualities			Deriving from absense of natural qualities
Behaviour appropriate to: ♂		⟵—Both sexes—⟶ ♀				Inappropriate to both sexes

Fig. 1. Honour and shame in the value system of the Andalusian pueblo.
N.B. All the terms shown on this chart are either translations from the
Spanish of the pueblo or summaries which represent recognised categories of
behaviour, expressed in the evaluations which people make in the course of
living. Thus, while 'manliness' is a literal translation of *hombría*, 'concern for
repute' is derived from statements regarding *fama* and equally from expressions of concern regarding the *quedirán*, critical gossip. Female sexual purity
is expressed by either *honra* or *vergüenza*. The implication of honourability or
shamelessness associated with such statements is also made clear in a great
variety of ways which include gesture. An established vocabulary of gesture
exists in order to convey the meanings: 'hard face' (*cara dura*), which is a way
of saying shamelessness, financial dishonesty, homosexuality, cuckoldry and
of course that great desecratory gesture known as the *corte de manga* (cut of
the sleeve) which is used to dishonour another man entirely.

and are equivalent to both honour and shame. This is so because they
derive from natural qualities. Thus restraint is the natural basis of
sexual purity, just as masculinity is the natural basis of authority and
the defence of familial honour. The ideal of the honourable man is
expressed by the word *hombría*, 'manliness'. It subsumes both shame
and masculinity, yet it is possible to possess masculinity without shame
as well, for which reason it is placed under the title of ethical neutrality.
Masculinity means courage whether it is employed for moral or immoral ends. It is a term which is constantly heard in the *pueblo*, and the
concept is expressed as the physical sexual quintessence of the male
(*cojones*). The contrary notion is conveyed by the adjective *manso* which
means both tame and also castrated. Lacking the physiological basis,
the weaker sex cannot obviously be expected to possess it, and it is

excluded from the demands of female honour. On the other hand, female honour is not entirely without a physiological basis also (although this is not expressed with the same linguistic clarity), in that sexual purity relates to the maidenhead. The male, therefore, both lacks the physiological basis of sexual purity and risks the implication that his masculinity is in doubt if he maintains it; it comes to mean for him, despite the teachings of religion, an, as it were, self-imposed tameness = castration, and is therefore excluded from the popular concept of male honour. The natural qualities of sexual potency or purity and the moral qualities associated with them provide the conceptual framework on which the system is constructed.

This division of labour in the aspects of honour corresponds, as the reader would guess, to the division of roles within the nuclear family. It delegates the virtue expressed in sexual purity to the females and the duty of defending female virtue to the males. The honour of a man is involved therefore in the sexual purity of his mother, wife and daughters, and sisters, not in his own. *La mujer honrada, la pierna quebrada y en casa* (the honourable woman: locked in the house with a broken leg), the ancient and still popular saying goes, indicating the difficulties which male honour faces in this connection, for once the responsibility in this matter has been delegated, the woman remains with her own responsibility alleviated. The frailty of women is the inevitable correlate of this conceptualisation,[7] and the notion is not, perhaps, displeasing to the male who may see in it an encouragement for his hopes of sexual conquest. Thus, an honourable woman, born with the proper sentiment of shame, strives to avoid the human contacts which might expose her to dishonour; she cannot be expected to succeed in this ambition, unsupported by male authority. This fact gives justification to the usage which makes the deceived husband, not the adulterer, the object of ridicule and opprobrium according to the customs of southern Europe (and formerly, England and the whole of Europe).

I have described the symbolism of cuckoldry previously[8] which I summarise now as follows: the cuckold, *cabrón*, literally the billy-goat, is said to 'have horns'. The horns, a phallic symbol, are also the insignia of the Devil, the enemy of virtue, whose associates possess other symbols of a phallic nature, such as can be seen in the famous prints of Goya. Yet male sexuality is essential to the foundation of the family, as well as necessary, in its associated aspect as courage, to its defence. As well as potentially evil, it is also, when combined with shame as manliness, good. The manliness of a husband must be exerted above all in the defence of the honour of his wife on which his own depends. Therefore her adultery represents not only an infringement of his rights but the demonstration of his failure in his duty. He has betrayed the values of the family, bringing dishonour to all the social groups who are involved reciprocally in his honour: his family and his community. His manliness is defiled, for he has fallen under the domination of the Devil and must wear his symbol as the stigma of this betrayal. The responsibility is his, not the adulterer's, for the latter was only acting in accordance with his male nature. The pander, not the libertine, is the prototype of male dishonour,[9] for the latter may be assumed to defend these values when he is called upon to do so, that is to say, when *his* honour is at stake. The transfer of the horns from the adulterer to the victim of the adultery concords with the moral indeterminacy of the quality of masculinity and the positive value of manliness.

The adulterer may not be regarded as dishonourable – and we shall see that opinions vary in this regard according to social status – but this does not save him from committing a sin in the eyes of the Church. The idea that the punishment for a breach of rights should be visited by custom on the victim not the perpetrator may still perhaps strike us as anomalous, but this is only if we view this as an instance of a legal mechanism, a punitive sanction, and this is not in fact the framework within which it is to be interpreted.

The code of honour derives, as has been said, from a sacred quality of persons, not from ethical or juridical provisions, and we have seen how in European history it has conflicted with the law of the Church and the law of the land. If we view the adulterer and the cuckold, not in terms of right and wrong, but in terms of sanctity or defilement, we can see why the latter, the defiled one, should be the object of contempt, not the defiler. Through his defilement he becomes ritually dangerous and the horns represent not a punishment but a state of desecration.[10] In contrast, the adulterer is a sinner and, technically, in Spanish law, a criminal.

We have pointed out that where the concepts of shame and honour overlap they are equivalent to virtue, but the ethics of the community are not exhausted by this category. There remain the fields of conduct which contribute little or nothing to reputation but face only the individual conscience which, again, may not respond to all the injunctions of Catholic teaching. It is noteworthy that religion does not define adultery in the same way as urban custom nor the penal code, which exonerates *discreet* male marital infidelity by defining a husband's dalliance as adultery only if it takes place in the conjugal home or with notoriety.

Though the penal code of Spain defines offences against honour, proceedings are instituted only at the demand of the injured party.

Other than as an ideological statement, the legal provisions serve also to validate the rights of individuals whose conduct, indicted in other ways, may be justified by reference to their honour. The sanctions which maintain the code of honour in the *pueblo* are popular and are based upon the idea of ridicule, *burla*. *Burla* is the destroyer of reputation, whether it is employed by one individual against another in an act of defiance (as the Burlador de Sevilla employed it against the men and women whom it amused him to dishonour), or as a sanction exercised by the collectivity in the form of public ridicule. I have previously given a description of the institutions which exert the collective sanctions: the giving of a nickname whose significance in regard to honour is discussed in chapter four, the popular ballads, especially those which were formerly sung by the masked figures of the Carnival, or the institution of the *vito* (elsewhere referred to as the *cencerrada*, the charivari), with its cow-horns, bells, strings of tins, catcalls and obscene songs.

If we examined the incidents which provoked these sanctions we may divide them according to the nature of the transgression. Of the damaging nicknames, a few relate to economic behaviour and a few to sexual behaviour, though the majority ridicule a person on account of a specific incident which appealed to the collective imagination or of a physical or cultural deficiency. Some songs of Carnival publicised acts of dishonesty, but many were concerned with sexual offences and in particular, infidelity to husband or fiancé. The marital misfortunes of shepherds, those 'sailors of the wavy sierras', as Gerald Brenan has called them,[11] whose long spans of absence from the *pueblo* make their wives subject to suspicion, were high among them. The justification given for singing these songs was that it was necessary to warn the husband or prospective husband of the condition of his honour, though the nature of the rhymes themselves show that this duty was undertaken with glee rather than compassion for the victim of such a betrayal. The *vitos* were aimed at publicising scandalously, and thereby prohibiting, a living scandal.

The folklore has defined the traditional occasion for the charivari as the remarriage of a widowed person. There had once been such a *vito* in the distant past. Since the *vito* is against the law, it no longer takes place within any *pueblo* where there is a detachment of civil guards. There was one more recent case involving a young widow who had gone to live with a widower upon his parent's farm, but the majority of cases recorded, and the most violent ones, were provoked by the action of a man who was not widowed but had abandoned his wife in order to take up with another woman (and such a woman was necessarily shameless in the popular view). He was not, that is to say, a cuckold, but an unfaithful husband. However, the nature of the proceedings and the words of the songs left no doubt that he was endowed with the symbols of the cuckold, and this fact is reinforced by the usage of the *pueblo* which applies to such a person the word *cabrón*, which to the educated means only a cuckold. In the same vein, it is significant that, following the quarrel between Manuel el Conde and the carpenter,[12] the latter should have attacked his reputation by saying that he was cruel to his daughter, his only child, and that he intended to abandon his wife and go off with another woman, not that *his wife* had unfaithful intentions.

It would appear then that the theory of cuckoldry which we have outlined requires further explanation in order to cover this extended sense. This can be given without doing violence to that already offered.

To begin with, the *vito* is concerned uniquely with the behaviour of married persons. For the plebeians, in contrast to the middle classes, the rites of the Church are not essential to marriage and many common law marriages exist. The Anarchist movement which formerly had great influence here rejected all religious teaching and ceremonies, and in spite of a certain amount of proselytising by the Catholic Action committee, the poorer people very often do not marry until they have a child. Therefore when unmarried people set up house together they are regarded as a young married couple by the community, and it is in fact quite likely that they will get married within a year or two. On the other hand if a person who is already considered to be married goes to live with another, not his spouse, this is, by the same logic, equivalent to bigamy, since the fact of cohabitation rather than the Church rite is the criterion of marriage.

It is accepted that young people who face opposition to their marriage from the girl's father may force the father's hand by running away to spend the night together. After this, their recognition as a married couple, their marriage for preference, is the only way in which his honour can be retrieved. There were no fewer than six such escapades during a single year. But in one of these cases the father failed to react in the expected fashion. His daughter was a minor and had fine prospects of inheritance since he was a well-to-do farmer. The young man had been employed upon the farm and hoped, so it was thought, to become through marriage its heir. The father's immediate reaction, in this case, was to have him arrested and thrown into jail on the charge of violation of a minor.

In no instance recorded in this town was the *vito* put on for a married woman who had left her husband to live with another man, though there have been cases elsewhere. It seems most improbable in a town of this size, three thousand inhabitants, that such a couple would remain in the place. Women who 'go off the rails' go off them elsewhere, and thereby they justify the countryman's cherished belief in the iniquity of the city. There are, nevertheless, a number of unmarried or abandoned mothers who remain in the *pueblo* with their family.[13] Their disgrace is clearly recognised, but they are not treated as shameless. Their status is somewhat similar to that of a young widow. Their prospects of remarriage are very poor, since the man who wished to marry such a girl would be dishonoured – honour requires that one marry a virgin, since otherwise one becomes a retroactive cuckold – yet if their conduct gives no cause for scandal, they are distinguished from the loose women who come within the category of the shameless and who are sometimes designated by the word *deshonradas*, dishonoured.

It is said that the *vito* would formerly have been put on for any marital infidelity in the *pueblo*, though in fact the transient adventure and the discreetly-conducted affair always appear to have escaped. This may be due, in part, to reasons of practical organisation: the assemblage of young men with the equipment of horns and cowbells and the composition of the songs, all take time – and the *vito* must catch the couple together. Unlike the songs of Carnival which recount past events, the *vito* cannot relate to what is no longer happening.

There are however two categories of person who escape the *vito* altogether. These are the shameless ones and the *señoritos*, the upper class of the town. The shameless escape for the obvious reason that people who have no honour cannot be stripped of it. The *señoritos* escape because they are not part of the plebeian community, and their actions do not therefore affront its standards of conduct in the same way. It is recognised that they are different. The elderly lawyer who maintained a widow as his mistress was not thought to be a candidate for the *vito*, even though her daughter was also subsequently credited with that title, nor was a *vito* ever put on for the sake of that rich man who took as mistress the wife of a plebeian, though the latter was celebrated by the nickname of 'the horn of gold'. The *señoritos* did not, however, escape mention in the popular ballads. Given that the desecration symbolised by the horns relates to the dishonour of a man through his failure as a defender of his family, it follows that this carries different implications whether he is plebeian or *señorito*. The upper class husband can maintain two establishments and divide his time between them, but this is not possible for the plebeian who has neither the time nor the resources; if he takes a mistress to live with him this can only mean a rejection of his family. Therefore the word *cabrón* carries a different connotation in the plebeian community; the implications of conduct are different. The plebeian adulterer desecrates his family by taking a mistress, the *señorito* demonstrates his superior masculinity by doing so. In fact it is common to find men of the wealthier class in the cities who maintain a second household, and though this is resented by their wives, they are not subject to general opprobrium. This was not found in any of the towns where I studied, all of them of a few thousand inhabitants only. Nevertheless the case was reported to me, from a town of no more than sixteen thousand inhabitants, of a man of wealth and high consideration who, childless in his marriage, maintained no fewer than three illegitimate families within the precincts of the town. His relations with these households were conducted with great discretion, though the facts were widely known, and he was never seen entering the house of one of his mistresses during the daytime. He gave his numerous sons a professional education and for this reason was regarded as a very good father and a good man.

The association of male honour with the family and the qualities necessary to defend it, rather than with the morality, religious or not, of sexual conduct does not mean that the latter has no hold upon the men of Andalusia. Yet it is curious that this aspect of Christian morality is given more weight by the plebeians (who are mostly anti-clerical and rather irreligious), than by the middle and upper classes who are pillars of the Church and often profoundly religious. There is, in fact, a plebeian preoccupation with the notion of vice which is freely applied to any form of sensual over-indulgence, in particular women and wine, and this is thought of as something approaching a monopoly of the outside world and of the rich who maintain connections with it. This view of 'vice' expresses a social reality: it is only possible to escape the sanctions of popular opinion by going away. The shame which is bound up with the collective honour of the *pueblo* is opposed to the shamelessness of the cities, since vice implies shamelessness. Such a view also implies that the rich are shameless, and this is quite often said. This conception of honour, associated with shame as we have seen, is similar to that of the Christian moralists whose criticism of the code of honour has been mentioned. Indeed, and in more ways than in this, the views of the *pueblo* echo those of the moralists of an earlier age.

I have defined shame in its social aspect as a sensitivity to the opinion of others and this includes, even for the *señoritos*, a consciousness of the public opinion and judgement of the whole community. One finds therefore a rather different attitude towards sexual promiscuity among the *señoritos* of the small town than among those of the cities, an attitude which expresses itself in the idea that male marital infidelity is dishonourable because it is an act of disrespect towards the wife. The husband who respects his wife is not promiscuous. I have the impression that this notion is less important in more sophisticated places.

Yet if the judgement of the *pueblo* brings its weight to bear upon the mores of its upper class, it is equally true that the influences of the outside world pervade the *pueblo*. Moreover, the 'puritanism' of the *pueblo* does not suffice to obliterate a consciousness of the value of sexual conquest as a justification of masculinity. A conflict of values is therefore implicit between the male pride which expresses itself in gallantry towards the female sex, and that which reposes upon a firm attachment to the duties of the family man. Manuel el Conde, the protagonist of honour, furnishes an illustration. At a fiesta held in the valley one of the local belles walked past him with her head high, ignoring his presence. Manuel was piqued.

'If it were not,' he said, 'for the ring upon this finger, I would not let that girl pass by me as she has.' Manuel thus recoups upon the hypothetical level the masculinity which he sacrifices in reality to his familial honour. He eats his cake and has it, albeit in fantasy.

There is another way in which plebeian honour departs from that of the upper classes. Honour is an hereditary quality; the shame of the mother is transmitted to the children and a person's lack of it may be attributed to his birth, a consideration that explains the power of the insults, the most powerful of all, which relate to the purity of the mother. After this, the greatest dishonour of a man derives from the impurity of his wife. On the other hand, if his own conduct is recognised as dishonourable, then the honour of his family has no protector. Therefore, in its aspect as equivalent to shame, the nuclear family shares a common honour. The children not only inherit their shame, their own actions reflect upon that of their parents. The purity of the daughter reflects that of her mother, and thereby, the honour of her father. Her brothers, participants in a common heritage, are equally attainted by the dishonour of any member of their elementary family.

Social status is inherited primarily from the father whose patrilineal first surname a son inherits and will transmit to his descendants. The economic status of the family depends upon the father's ability to maintain or to improve its wealth. Therefore, in its aspect as right to precedence, honour derives predominantly from the father, whereas in its aspect of shame it derives predominantly from the mother. The distinction concords with the fact that precedence is something which can be gained through action – male enterprise, whereas shame cannot be gained, can only be maintained through avoiding the conduct which would destroy it – female restraint. An earlier period of Spanish history conceptualized these notions with more clarity than today as we learn from Caro Baroja's discussion of the descent of rank and purity of blood, concepts which represent quite clearly the notions of honour as precedence, and shame, respectively.[14]

The *pueblo* is envisaged as a community of equals amongst whom economic differences do not amount to differences of social class, even though they are considerable. All address their age-mates in the second person, even the employee his plebeian employer. From this community the *señoritos* are excluded; they are accorded, as a title of respect, the prefix 'Don' to their Christian name which indicates their superior status, in contrast to the title, 'Señor' which is given to the respected members of the *pueblo* who have reached the age of retirement. The status of respected elder in a community of conceptual equals is as high as any member of the *pueblo* can normally aspire. Such positions of authority as exist between members of the *pueblo* derive from power delegated from the upper classes in a particular post, not from the quality of the person. Therefore there are no occasions when an order of precedence is ever required. The rule of 'first come, first served' governs all the contexts of ordering persons whether in the market or at the town-hall. This is not so among the *señoritos* who possess a concept of social status which differentiates them from the plebeians and involves an order of ranking, however unclear the ranking order may be, and however loath they are to make it explicit in their treatment of their fellows. There are, nevertheless, degrees of deference paid according to their relative status even in the context of the *pueblo*, and there is at least one family which conserves documents from the eighteenth century to prove its superior origins. Though they mix freely in everyday life, occasions arise when it is necessary to separate the sheep from the goats, and persons whose claim to status is well-established from those whose claim is less secure: the reunions with the summer visitors (who are persons of superior status to any in the *pueblo*), the visit of an important outsider or the marriage of a daughter of a leading family. On all these occasions personal attachments to the host cut across any objective criterion of ranking, yet the ranking is clearly implied.

A situation when a stratified order of precedence was required occurred when the image of Our Lady of Fatima visited the town and places were reserved in the church for the leading citizens and their wives. This gave rise to disputes, and for understandable reasons. First of all, seating in the church is normally quite informal and irregular; the men separate from the women and stand at the back, if indeed they attend the same mass as their wives. Other religious fiestas are organised by the church brotherhood of the particular cult, but there is no value attached to the order in which a procession is followed, and *señoritos* and plebieans attend in a haphazard manner. There was no precedent which could be followed in the order of seating. On this occasion, it was decided that, since the church was likely to be overcrowded, seats would be reserved. Proximity to the image therefore became a criterion of precedence in an entirely novel setting. But how was it to be accorded? The question of precedence could not be decided by the mayor on the basis of official posts, as on the occasion of the governor's visit, since the privileged were to include more than the officials and his authority was irrelevant since this was a religious occasion. The reception committee which had been specially formed for the event possessed no authority to enforce their ruling, and the priest wisely preferred to have nothing to do with such details. As a result, many felt that they had not been given the honour which was their due, and a series of quarrels ensued regarding their placing, which conflicted with the spirit of the occasion.

The nearer we move to the centre of national society and the higher in the hierarchy of status, the greater the importance of precedence, since the greater the number of contexts in which it is required and the greater the need for criteria by which it may be established. It follows therefore that the importance of honour = precedence increases with social status until we reach the aristocracy and the members of official organisations whose precedence is regulated by protocol, and among whom the concern for precedence is increasingly vital.

In the *pueblo* the ideal of equality in honour reigns and precedence deriving from birth and associated with status is missing. When conflicts threaten, the personal attribute of masculinity comes to the fore to determine the pre-eminence of one man over another and the word *cojones* is heard. It is a term which expresses unqualified admiration for the protagonist, quite regardless whether his behaviour is from other points of view admirable. It is to be noted that it is seldom used or understood in the literal sense.[15]

Physical violence is not thought to be a legitimate way to attain one's ends, yet when his rights are infringed, a man is forced to stand up for himself under pain of appearing a coward. So when violence occurs, it is characteristic that both parties believe themselves to be on the defensive, merely protecting their rightful pride. On festive occasions it is expected that people will forget their animosities and meet in a spirit of amity. Nevertheless, much wine is drunk then and fighting not uncommonly occurs among the young men, not so much as a defence of rights but as an expression of rivalry. Such an incident took place at a fiesta in the valley on the eve of St John. It was attended by the sons of El Cateto and also by those of La Castaña against whom the former had an antipathy of long standing. Before the end of the evening, Juan el Cateto was declaiming that he had more masculinity than all the Castaños put together. In the fight which ensued between the male youth of the two families, no damage was done since the combatants were on the whole more drunk than the public to whom it fell to hold back the assailants. Such incidents serve to show how the struggle for prestige is subdued in daily life by the conception of a community of equals which ordains that a man may not humiliate another. It is not dishonouring to avoid a person with whom one has quarrelled, but on the occasion of a fiesta each is entitled to think that it is the duty of the other to avoid him. This view of the town as a community of honourable men concords with the notion, expressed in the Fuero de los Españoles, that every individual has the right to honour. The competition for prestige finds its limits in the obligation to respect the pride of others, and this is true at any level of the social structure. Both the Catetos and the Castaños were criticised for their 'ugly' behaviour which spoiled the fiesta. There is no conception of sportsmanship which permits men to accept humiliation with dignity or to inflict it rightfully within the limits of a defined context. The existence of the sport of boxing in other countries and in Madrid, which is known thanks to the newspapers, is regarded as proof of the barbarity of foreigners and the corruption of the great city.

The collective honour of the *pueblo* is expressed in rivalry between *pueblos* which furnishes a body of rhymes in which each is epitomised by its neighbours in the most disobliging terms, implying dishonour in a rich variety of ways of which the most outspoken concern the purity of their women. The collections of folklore abound in examples. This collective honour is not usually expressed, however, in a hostile attitude towards individual outsiders. The individual stranger presents on the contrary an occasion to demonstrate the honourability of the *pueblo*, and every member becomes potentially a bearer of its honour. How the visitor is received depends upon the context in which he confronts the community. If he is recognised as a person of status, if he comes alone and with friendly intent it is important that he be received in accordance with the principle of hospitality towards strangers; they alone can validate the collective image. Yet in order to do so the visitor must be a person worthy of respect. The higher his status, the more important it is that he be favourably impressed, for he does honour to the *pueblo* by coming. It is above all to the visitor of the *señorito* class that the traditional courtesies of Andalusia are shown. The plebeian visitor still requires to be favourably impressed but more suspicion attaches to his visit. He may have come for reasons which do the *pueblo* no honour;

those who come to seek work are potential blacklegs; those who come for commercial reasons may have come to cheat. Both have come seeking their own interest and while they should be favourably impressed, they should also be watched. Boys who come from neighbouring towns to court a girl are treated traditionally with hostility, if not actually with violence, by the young men of the *pueblo* whose collective honour is challenged by their presence.

Visitors who come in large numbers during the fiesta offer a problem; by swelling the attendance at the fiesta they do the *pueblo* honour, for the number of people who attend gives a measure to its importance, yet it may transpire that they have come with the intention of inflicting humiliation. A visiting football team, for example, does honour only so long as it is defeated, but if it wins it inflicts humiliation. If it succeeds in imposing its superiority, then it is liable to be resisted as in Ubrique where the *pueblo* defended their honour against humiliation by a more expert team from Cortes de la Frontera which scored two goals in the first five minutes, yet failed to win the match. Unprepared to submit to such treatment, the infuriated public drove the visitors off the field and out of the town in a hailstorm of stones, and their bus was sent after them to pick them up and take them away.

In all situations of challenge a man's honour is what obliges him to respond by resenting the affront, yet a challenge is something which can only be given by a conceptual equal; the force of an affront lies in the fact that it is an attempt to establish superiority over the affronted person. If this is not the case then there is no challenge. This may be demonstrated by a fact that appeared to me at first curious. The farm of Pegujál has an only son and he is mentally deranged. He lives there with his widowed mother and keeps a small flock of sheep. These he takes out to pasture wherever he wishes, often beyond the frontiers of his land, in disregard of the land rights of the valley. The owners or lessees of pasture may find him any day encroaching upon their property, and if any reproach is made to him he merely utters oaths and throws rocks. Encroachment upon pasture is one of the causes of quarrels in which the honour of both parties becomes involved, but in this case it is not so. His lunacy places him outside the community of normal men and he is therefore unable to affront. People take no direct steps to restrain him and, if he turns up on their land, they shrug their shoulders. His actions cannot constitute a challenge, since he is mad.

Equally, if there is already a difference in social status between the two parties, then actions which might otherwise be an affront cease to be so. The man who has the right to authority over others does not affront them in exercising that right. It is not humiliating to obey the com-

mands of a person entitled to give them. This fact is crucial to understanding how honour is effective in relations within the hierarchy of this
society. To receive protection from someone not recognised as a
superior is humiliating, but from the moment that protection is accepted
superiority is admitted, and it is no longer humiliating to serve such a
person. Service and protection are the reciprocal links which hold a
system of patronage together. At the same time the patron increases his
prestige through the possession of clients, while the client participates
in the glory of his patron. The two are linked together by a personal tie
which gives each diffuse rights over the other: service when it is required,
assistance when it is needed. The system is reinforced through the
institution of ritual kinship and expressed in its idiom. The terms
padrino, apadrinar, compadre (godfather, to sponsor, co-parent) have
extensions far beyond the literal sense. *El que tiene padrinos se bautiza,*
the saying goes. (He who has godparents gets baptised.) In the struggle
for life success depends in reality upon the ability, much less to defend
one's rights against equals, than to attract the favour of the powerful.

The social class of the *señoritos* is defined by their way of life, but
their prestige relates to their ability to operate a system of tacit reci-
procities: to possess clients who owe them fidelity and respect, *compadres* with whom to exchange favours, and equally, patrons of whom
they in their turn can demand favours, not only for themselves but for
their clients. Thus they build up the reputation for beneficence which
is an aspect of honour. But such beneficence requires economic power.
Let us see, therefore, how the notion of honour relates to money.

Financial honesty (*honradez*) is associated with honour in the sense
that it is dishonourable to defraud. Yet the circumstances need to be
defined since to outwit is permissible, even mandatory in the context of
bargaining. As Don Candido, the *juez* (magistrate) of Zahara once
warned me, 'In your country it may be different but here a bargain is
not a bargain unless you have told forty lies.' Rather than a matter of
abstract principle, the obligation to deal honestly is, in fact, a personal
one. You owe honesty in defined situations, as loyalty to a particular
person. To persons with whom you have or wish to form ties, to kin,
friends, or to employers, particularly if they are also godparents; to
abstract entities such as limited companies less, and to the state not at
all, since these latter categories, not being persons, cannot offer the
reciprocity required in the system of patronage. Within the community
of the *pueblo* there is an obligation to honour one's undertakings, and
complaints about those who have failed to do so both stress this as a
norm of conduct and also demonstrate that it is not always obeyed. In
fact, men learn whom they can trust little by little, testing each other as

they go along. In the case of default they have at least recourse to the tribunal of public opinion before whom they can impugn the reputation of the other, as well as the more cumbrous and distrusted mechanisms of the law. The tribunal of public opinion is not of much use when dealing with people from another town or from the city, and the law is less effective also, so the distrust towards outsiders seems sensible enough. For the same reason the outsider has less control over the sanctions which enforce honesty towards him.

There is a tendency to presume upon the favour of a patron when he is the employer, and servants and bailiffs frequently regard it as their due to take financial advantage of their situation. For these reasons the absentee landowner, even though he turns up at harvest time, seldom avoids being cheated. *El ojo del amo engorda el caballo.* (It is the eye of the master which fattens the horse.) Moreover, persons of high social status tend to be lenient towards the peccadillos of their trusted employees as long as they 'don't go too far'. To be penny-pinching does not go with the ideal of aristocratic behaviour.

The ability to pay is an essential part of honorific behaviour, whether in the context of hospitality towards strangers, or in asserting preeminence among equals or bestowing protection upon inferiors. Paying is a privilege which goes to the man of precedence since to be paid for places a man in a situation of inferiority, so disputes about paying the bill occur whenever there is no clearly defined superior who can claim the right to do so. (In such a situation a man must put up a good fight in order to defend his honour even though he may be delighted to lose.) There are barmen in establishments frequented by gentlemen of honour who have amassed a tidy fortune simply by giving way to all those who claimed the privilege of paying. The humiliation of being paid for is still very real, even though it may no longer go so far as in the days of George Borrow who tells of a nobleman who ran his friend through with his sword at the end of a drinking-bout, because the latter insisted on footing the bill.

The show of beneficence forbids one to appear grasping or concerned with money. Yet on the other hand, the man who takes no care to preserve or augment his resources may lack the wherewithal to validate his honour on the morrow. There are many spendthrifts in the cities to whom the attraction of honorific behaviour in the present outweighs their concern for the future. Such people are often more involved in display and competition with equals than in meeting their obligation to dependents.

There is no subject upon which more contradictory opinions have been put forward than 'the Spanish attitude to money'. They range from

Don Ramón Menendez Pidal's assertion that 'it is a natural trait in the Spaniard not to allow any calculation of gains and losses to prevail over considerations of another order',[16] to the sly jibe of Cortés that he and his companions suffered from a disease of the heart which could be cured only with gold. Foreign observers have brought their testimony to bear at both extremes, some praising the disinterestedness of the Spanish character, others, perpetrators of the Black Legend in the Spanish view, asserting the opposite. Such a contradiction can only be reconciled through an appeal to context. By translating the ideal of beneficence into the reality of behaviour we can see that it implies a concern in acquisition, on the one hand, with a view to gaining honour through disposing generously of that which has been acquired, on the other. To give a thing away one must first of all get hold of it. The same concern in acquiring honour, through the act of beneficence rather than, as in the Anglo-Saxon countries, through the fact of possession, explains these extreme views. For Mediterranean honour derives from the domination of persons, rather than things, and this is the goal which distinguishes the acquisitive values of Andalusia. It is, needless to say, a goal which is inimical to capitalist accumulation.

It appears to me that the question of the nature and implications of honour has been neglected in the discussions of the origin of capitalism: the Puritans' rejection of the flamboyant conception of honour which still reigns in southern Europe and centres upon patronage and women was bound up with their particular notion of egalitarianism, their condemnation of sensuality and their thrift. Within such a complex of values possession, stripped of its significance as a means to enhance their honour by establishing domination over others, became an end in itself as a sign of Grace and aimed thenceforth at accumulation rather than conversion into prestige through redistribution. The conflict between honour = precedence and honour = virtue was resolved in favour of the latter and honour was felt as religious conscience and manifest in financial solvency; earned no longer, so to speak, with lance in hand but with cheque-book in pocket. All their attitudes: to display, to women, to cuckoldry, to courage, to violence, to rank and privilege, to legality, to lying, to literacy, even to Time, are to be explained simply as an inversion of the aristocratic equation of honour = precedence. The resemblance, noted by various authors, between the Andalusian anarchists and the Protestant revolutionaries of the seventeenth century can be related first of all to this. The differences can be related also to the differences between the social structures involved in the comparison.

The concept of honour presents itself to the individual in a different contextual framework according to his place in the social structure, and the differing value attached to its various aspects can be explained by this. Its relation to economic and political power is not seen in the same light by those who possess such power and by those who do not. Those who have no possibility of playing the role of patron do not compete with their equals in the same terms, while their prestige relates, as we have seen, to a public opinion which recognises virtue rather than precedence as the basis of honour.

At the same time their lives are circumscribed by a community which is a territorial unit and proximity makes the moral sanctions of the *pueblo* effective. This is not the case with the upper classes whose social superiority places their honour in a sheltered position with regard to those sanctions. Their effectiveness varies with the size of the community, so that a distinction must be made not only between different classes but also between the community of a few thousand souls in which public opinion represents a homogeneous body of knowledge and comes to bear upon every member, and those where only the eminent are known to everyone. The urban parish possesses a certain social identity, a network of neighbourly relations through which social control is exerted which likens it to a limited extent to a rural community,[17] yet the possibility of a relative anonymity is open to the man who moves from one district to another, and the force of public opinion is diminished when it is no longer omniscient. The diminished concern with the ethical aspect of honour in the large towns must surely be related to this fact.

The situation of the *señoritos* is also different in the two environments. In the *pueblo* they form a small group who meet each other every day and whose every action is common knowledge to the entire community. They constitute its upper class. In the city this is no longer the case; people of equivalent occupation and wealth form a middle, not an upper, class, and they accept the leadership of persons of greater wealth and wider horizons. They are therefore simultaneously less subject to the sanctions of the *pueblo* and more subject to the influence of the upper class. The *señoritos* of the small town appear fine figures at home, but when they come into the city, they shrink in stature, and seem no more than the uncouth country cousins of the urban middle class. *Señorito de pueblo* is a term of denigration in the mouths of city folk.

We must consider the honour of the aristocracy. The Andalusian aristocracy is largely dependent upon landed estates in whose administration they take a varying interest. They maintain their ancient palaces in the cities of Andalusia though many spend much of their time in Madrid. They form the nucleus of so-called 'society' which includes persons of wealth or eminence who do not belong by birth to the aristocracy. This is what I refer to as the upper class. While its various elements mix freely and intermarry, a fundamental prestige attaches to birth which modifies, but does not obliterate, consideration of wealth.

The moral sanctions of the *pueblo* have only a limited importance for the middle class and none for the upper. It is no doubt a satisfaction to them to feel that they are appreciated by their dependents and admired by the populace, but their reputation looks to their equals for validation, not to their inferiors. Their lives possess far more privacy than the *pueblo*, and though they appear as public figures, their intimacy is confined to the circles of their dependents and their peer-group. Gossip indeed exists and tends to be relayed over a wide range, so that a person of the upper class possesses a public character, but his social position is a matter of birth and wealth, and it is therefore, in a sense, impregnable to gossip. If he is disliked by his peers he may be avoided, but his honour is very rarely publicly affronted. He is dishonoured only by being ostracised by his social equals.

The sanctions of honour=virtue therefore play a less conspicuous part than in the plebeian milieu, or for that matter in an earlier period of history. Those who have been ostracised have been so because of their political behaviour during the Civil War or their financial unreliability, rather than their sexual behaviour.[18] However, between plebeian and upper class honour there is, in addition to the difference already noted which was seen in the conception of the cuckold, a further difference. A man's sexual honour is attained not only through the purity of his womenfolk but through his commitment to any other woman in whom he has invested his pride. The infidelity of his mistress leaves him a cuckold also. Thus on one occasion a lady of the upper classes whom gossip had credited with a clandestine lover over a number of years transferred her favours to a fresh admirer. Shortly afterwards her abandoned lover was seen lunching with her husband and the comment was made: 'There go the two cuckolds!' The abandoned lover was equated with the infelicitous husband.

This usage no longer submits to the explanation which I have given of the symbolism of the horns in the plebeian community, that they stigmatise the failure to defend familial obligations. It is here the lover's honour=precedence, not his honour=shame which is at stake for he has no rights over the woman in question. He is humiliated only in that he has lost to another the 'right' to her favours,[19] the title of *amant en titre*. The fact that this usage does not conform to the definition given above does not invalidate it. The point, precisely, was that the plebeian conception is not the same as that of the educated classes. The difference corresponds to the relative emphasis placed upon honour as deriving from virtue rather than from precedence. If the former meaning is taken as a basis, then this extended sense must be regarded as a figurative form. On the other hand, if the usage of the educated is adopted, as one who fails to assert his sexual claims, then the plebeian usage must be regarded as, in part, figurative. The two senses overlap, but they do not coincide. Both must be regarded as figurative from the point of view of the brief definition of the *Diccionario de la Academia* quoted above.[20]

The greater sexual freedom of men of the middle classes corresponds to the fact that they are less constrained by the social control of public opinion, due to their greater freedom of movement and material possibilities. But it is also influenced by the fact that, whereas in the plebeian class the woman is the financial administrator of the family – she remains in the *pueblo* when the man goes away to work and therefore she keeps the key to the family chest – in the middle class the woman has relatively less importance in the question of the financial resources of the family, since the husband is not a manual worker but an office worker, rentier, businessman, professional or administrator. She enjoys relatively less liberty of action since she has servants who perform the tasks which take the plebeian housewife out to the fountain or the market. She is seen in public much less, spends her day in her house, or in visiting hers or her husband's female relatives or in church or occupied by church affairs. Outside her family circle she spends little time in mixed company. Her husband goes alone to the casino or the *tertulia*, the group of friends who meet habitually for conversation. The middle class wife is noticeably more restrained in behaviour than the plebeian, her husband more authoritative and more jealous.

When we reach the upper classes, however, this tendency is reversed, and we find women enjoying much the same independence as in the upper classes of the other countries of Europe. They are subject to less, not more restraint. They smoke and drink in public places frequented by their class, attend social engagements with their husbands, drive automobiles, travel alone and exercise authority in ways which are not allowed the wives of the middle classes. All these activities imply, of course, a higher standard of living. Moreover, gossip credits them with a sexual freedom which is not attributed to the wives of the middle class, and since we are concerned with honour as reputation it is gossip rather than the truth which is relevant. Nevertheless, the number who live separated from their husbands is much greater than among the middle classes, where this is very rare.

If we take the paradigm of plebeian honour and shame shown on page 22 and compare it with the values of the upper class, we can see certain significant variations. Rather than variations in the structure of the concepts, it is a matter of emphases upon their different properties. Thus it appears that shame and honour are less often synonymous with one another. Shame is above all an emotional condition which relates to a given situation in which the individual is put to shame. It can even be experienced vicariously. The word is still used as a personal quality, and one who affronts public opinion is said to have lost it, but self-respect would be a more appropriate translation here; its aspect as hereditary and natural is no longer taken literally. Children are expected to resemble their parents in character, but the shamelessness of one person does not imply that of his family as clearly as in the pueblo.

Physical courage for the male and unwillingness to accept humiliation for both sexes, are essentials of honour, and financial honesty also, since the contrary implies, apart from everything else, a base concern in money which is unaristocratic. Honour is a question of class honour and personal precedence, power and the capacity to patronise which of course requires wealth, while sexual behaviour which dominates honour in the *pueblo* appears somewhat less important. Sexual conduct is a matter of conscience and is the subject of religious sanctions. It exposes a person's self-esteem rather than his honour.

Therefore a paradox confronts us which the remainder of this essay will be devoted to clarifying: those whose claim to honour is greatest, and also most dependent upon lineal descent, are most careless of their sexual honour. It is the counterpart, in the sphere of sexual behaviour, of the paradox noted by Voltaire, that there is always least honour to be found surrounding the king. It is far from being particular to Spain; on the contrary, it is perhaps more marked in other countries. However, we shall restrict our consideration of it to the Spanish social scene.

An obvious explanation presents itself: the concept of honour varies from age to age and its importance appears much diminished in modern urban society. The disappearance of the duel in modern times is a testimony of this, though the existence of the duel far from sufficed to make aristocratic honour safe in the eighteenth century, and in the most recent period in which it was prevalent it was not much concerned with the defence of sexual honour.[21] An upper class is always more amenable to foreign influence, and thereby to change, and the ideas of the twentieth century have tended towards, not only a diminution of the concern for honour, but also a greater freedom of action for the married woman. Moreover, there has been a great change in the last three decades in Spain in this regard, not only among the upper class but among the urban middle class. The paradox might be regarded then simply as a fortuitious product of the 'folk–urban continuum';[22] sexual jealousy is going out of fashion and rustic society is behind the times – an assertion for which there is some evidence, as we shall see. It is also true that the aristocracy is much more subject to foreign influence: English nannies, German Fräuleins, foreign universities and visits to Paris to buy clothes.

However, it appears to me from an admittedly inadequate knowledge of the historical records that the greater independence of women of the aristocracy antedates by a long way the disappearance of the duel and the influence, such as it may have been, of the movement for the emancipation of women, if indeed it is not rather a permanent feature of aristocratic society.

There is always a tendency to attribute that which one disapproves of to foreign influence and in this, Spanish critics have not been exceptional, whether Don Gregorio Marañon who attributed foreign origins to Don Juan,[23] or, two centuries earlier, Fray Joseph Haro who blamed the custom of the *Chichisveo* (*sic*)[24] on the Italians. Father Haro, writing at the beginning of the Bourbon period, was certainly correct in attributing changes in custom to foreign influence. Yet his complaints regarding the looseness of morals, in particular of the upper classes, have a very traditional ring to them. Father Haro understood the word *chichisveo* in a rather different sense to the Italian (where it means simply the person of the *cavalière sirvente*) as the institution of chivalrous, he thought culpable, friendship between a married person and a member of the opposite sex. His explanation why the rich were the worst offenders was an economic one: that a gentleman is expected to make costly gifts in order to maintain such a friendship. Certain resources are perhaps necessary, but this does not explain why the lady's husband should accept that his wife should receive such an admirer. Economic reasons may be cited to explain why the poor did not indulge in the *chichisveo*, but not why the rich did.

If Father Haro gives a time-depth to the paradox he does not resolve it. There is no doubt that the customs of the aristocracy were changing in the early Bourbon period in this regard. Even though neither the theatre of honour nor the picaresque satires against honour can be taken as literal testimony, they at least indicate a popular preoccupation in the earlier period. Yet the desperation of the aristocratic heroes of the theatre of honour in defending their vulnerability through women implies, unless they are all to be taken as paranoids, that their womenfolk gave them reasons for anxiety. (The fact that the women were often innocent of any infidelity scarcely detracts from the point since that is what makes the plot a tragedy.) The behaviour of the protagonists implies that they were acting according to expectations which, over-optimistic or pessimistic as the case may be, had some foundation in reality: the husband that his wife might be seduced, the gallant that he might succeed in his suit. The existence of the institution of the Celestina alone implies that the danger to marital honour was a real one. Traffic-lights are not found where there are no automobiles. Lope de Vega's thesis[25] that the only security of a man's honour lies in the virtue of his womenfolk, which appeals to our modern standards by its reasonable-ness, suggests a new approach to the problem, not that the problem did not exist.

I conclude therefore that this is only partially a modern phenomenon to be attributed to foreign influence and will try to give a more funda-mental explanation.

The paradox should be rephrased in accordance with the distinctions already made: the class which possesses by birthright most honour = precedence is most vulnerable in its honour = shame. When we say 'the upper class', we must distinguish between male and female honour, since the carelessness of women relates to their own reputation, while that of men to the steps which they take to cover their vulnerability through women. The obligation for men to avenge their sexual honour is what has varied, above all, from the age in which vengeance is represented as a duty to that in which such acts of vengeance are not only effectively punished by the law but regarded in sophisticated society as barbarous and atavistic. Since the conventions of modern upper class society repudiate any means of responding overtly to such an affront (save through legal action which only aggravates the dis-honour by publicising it), there is little that a man can do about his tarnished honour other than impose the best interpretation of events he can, or cut his losses and renounce his responsibility by an act of separation, which itself is somewhat dishonouring.

It has already been pointed out that the upper classes are hardly susceptible to plebeian sanctions and the development of modern urban society and the segregation of classes which goes with it makes them even less so. Just as the liar is only dishonoured when, impugned as a liar, he fails to vindicate his honour, so the cuckold is only dishonoured when public recognition is given to the fact that 'the horns have been put on him'. The *pueblo* does this, and the smaller the community the more effectively; the upper class does not. Therefore the situation tends to remain ambiguous and to allow alternative interpretations.

The alternative interpretations which can be placed upon the same behaviour are seen clearly in the ambiguity which surrounded the institution of the *cicisbeo*. The *cavalière sirvente* appears in the first instance as the guarantor of the husband's honour, who accompanies his wife on occasions when the husband is not able to do so. Since the husband allows it, *honi soit qui mal y pense*. But the sanctioned guarantee becomes, in the eyes of the sceptical, a cover-plan.[26] Whether or not this scepticism is allowed expression depends upon the status of those concerned and the social position of the critic. Father Haro, as a churchman, was in a position to voice his scepticism. In his view, the occasion is all that is needed and 'la carne hace su oficio' (the flesh knows its business); he ridiculed the idea that such a relationship could remain innocent. (He belongs to the school of thought which maintains that female honour is only safe if the lady is locked in with a broken leg.) Yet the idea that women not subjected to male authority are a danger is a fundamental one in the writing of the moralists from the Archpriest of Talavera to Padre Haro, and it is echoed in the modern Andalusian *pueblo*.[27] It is bound up with the fear of ungoverned female sexuality which has been an integral element of European folklore ever since prudent Odysseus lashed himself to the mast to escape the sirens. It is through their sex that women acquire power over men, and 'women have naturally the ambition to attain command and liberty, and they wish to invert the order of nature, attempting (even though it may involve the greatest cruelties) to dominate men'.[28] This then is the traditional way of thinking, but it is no longer that of the educated classes if indeed it ever was.

However, we must look at it from the woman's point of view. Status derived from birth is not uniquely a male attribute. A woman is granted the status of her husband, but she does not thereby forfeit that which she received by birth. Legally she retains her maiden name, merely adding her husband's to it, and she passes it on to her children as their second surname. Moreover, unlike most English titles, but like the British monarchy, Spanish titles pass through the female line in default of a male heir in the same degree of kinship. The result is that they frequently pass through women, changing from one patriline to another. A daughter, in default of sons, bears the title and her husband takes it by courtesy, as her consort. There is no lack of examples in the literature of anthropology of women who take on a social attribute of men, becoming substitutes for them, whether, for example, for the purpose of marrying a wife in the lineage systems of Africa, or of continuing a feud in Montenegro. Yet the point to be retained is that a Spanish woman of high birth is able to transmit her patrilineal status to her children.

Even though woman's shame in the plebeian sense is visualised as a positive attribute, something which can be lost, it cannot be won like precedence, nor is it inherent like status. It is preserved by refraining from actions which are proper to men, and this is possible and necessary, according to the division of labour, because women are under the tutelage of men. Legal independence is a male prerogative, and a woman acquires it only when she leaves the tutelage of her father (until recently at the age of twenty-three). If she has married before then, which is commonly the case, she has already passed under the tutelage of her husband. Had she already acquired legal independence, she would lose it on marriage. As a young unmarried woman she is not *socially* independent, since her honour still concerns her family and her marriage prospects. In view of the length of courtships she may well not marry before coming legally of age and until her marriage or the day when she is finally relegated to spinsterhood her reputation requires to be defended with all the constraints upon her that this implies. Only as a widow does she acquire real independence, act for herself and her under-age children in legal and business matters and very often she must support them. Though her honour is bequeathed to her children she does not pass under the authority of her sons, but rather respect demands that they should heed her wishes. She accedes in fact to the resposibilities and status of a man. The Andalusian widow often takes on the duties of her independence with enthusiasm and makes up for the years she has spent in subservience to the male sex.

In the beliefs of the *pueblo*, the same association is made in this case between the male role and aggressive sexual activity, and this is seen in the fact that widows are commonly believed, even in cases of apparent implausibility, to be sexually predatory upon the young men. It follows from the basic premises of thought upon this matter that a woman whose shame is not in the keeping of a man is sexually aggressive and dangerous. The association reaches its extreme representation in the figure of the witch, the unsubjected female who rides upon a broomstick to subvert the social order sanctified by religion. She is a woman who has foregone the moral qualities of her sex and become the consort of the he-goat. Both in the beliefs regarding the sexuality of widows (whose remarriage, it will be remembered, is given the same treatment as the *cabrón*), and regarding the supernatural practices of witches, the same assumption is displayed: once the sexual division of labour breaks down, women become men and where this occurs there can be neither honour nor shame. The point is expanded in chapter four.

Father Haro viewed the matter in these terms and attributed the deplorable state of sexual morality which he strove to reform to the fact that the sexes were abandoning their 'natural' roles in their dress and in their customs. Men were sitting on the floor like women, and women were getting up on to stools. Sodom and Gomorrah all over again! The inevitable result was the *chichisveo* in which all honour was irretrievably lost.

Another writer of the previous century had already demonstrated the thesis in a different way. La Pícara Justina tells the story of a girl who is robbed of her purity by a young man and left dishonoured.[29] She therefore disguises herself as a man and joins the criminal underworld. When finally she finds her betrayer and forces him to marry her (thereby restoring her honour), she reverts to female dress. The parable could not be clearer: a woman stripped of her honour becomes a man. Her honour restored, she reverts to her true sex. Moreover it is anything but an unique example.[30]

The popular beliefs regarding widows and witches, the ancient churchmen, moralist and novelist, give us a clue to the interpretation of the conceptual chart, not an ethnography. It provides the moral basis for the oppositions associated with the division of labour, so that such a chart now enables us to see coherence in the judgements passed in situations in which *honra, hombría* and *vergüenza* are invoked, why the conduct which is honourable for one sex may be the opposite of that which is honourable for the other; why women who adopt male behaviour prejudice their shame, while those who have abandoned their claim to shame are no longer submitted to the sanctions which control the behaviour of honourable women. Such women can behave as men do, attend functions from which honourable women are excluded, and use their sexuality to dominate men, as Father Haro believed all women desired to do. Yet by the same token they also forfeit their hold upon the honour of men. It also entitles us to see the victim of the *vito* as an Odysseus who failed to make himself fast and succumbed to the sirens. It is the pollution of his status as a community member rather than his immorality which calls down the wrath of the excommunicatory rite.

We are now in a position to resolve the paradox regarding the women of the aristocracy. Not only are they free of the sanctions which enforce the plebeian code of honour, their status marks them off from the duty to respond to its precepts, not like the shameless whose failure to respond established their dishonourable status, but because by the principle of *honi soit* their honour is impregnable and does not therefore depend upon male protection. Thus the lady of the upper class can command men without inverting the social order, since her power derives from her rank, not from her sexuality. It is not humiliating for a male inferior to obey her orders. She escapes the restraints which weigh upon middle-class wives, since, whatever her conduct, she possesses a status which cannot be forfeited. Her religious duty and her conscience require her to be virtuous and obey her husband, but if she does not do so, she is wicked, she is not dishonoured. She cannot then be stripped of her honour and become a man in the sense in which the plebeian can, thereby threatening the 'natural order', for the natural order for the aristocracy does not depend upon the same conceptualisation of the division of labour and the opposition of honour and shame associated with it, and it is not therefore threatened when women escape from the tutelage of men. It has been suggested that male slaves, on account of their inferior status, lack the social personality of men. By an analogous reasoning, women of high birth are accorded on that account a right to the kind of pride which is a male attribute, an element of masculine honour. They do not thereby forfeit their femininity, any more than the slave acquires a feminine status through being denied a masculine one; they acquire in addition some of the moral attributes of the male. Sexual and class status come together to qualify the rules of conduct which apply to their behaviour.

I have examined the conceptions of honour which are held by different classes in Andalusia, plebeian, *señorito* and aristocratic, and the ways in which these are modified by the fact of living in a small isolated township or a big city. Small-town plebeian honour stood at one extreme and aristocratic honour at the other. In the former, in many of its aspects, honour was allied to shame and equated with virtue; in the latter the yardstick of honour was precedence. The difference was explained, in the same manner as the difference within the *pueblo* between the honour of males or females, by the place of the individual within the social structure.

The dual nature of honour as honour aspired to and honour validated reflects the duality of the aspiration to a role and its attainment. To be dishonoured is to be rejected from the role to which one aspired. 'I am who I am' is answered: 'You are not who you think you are.' The search for identity expressed in these attitudes is the search for a role and the transactions of honour are the means whereby individuals find their role within the social organisation. Yet, in a complex society, the structure of common understandings, like the structure of roles, is complex; the criteria of conduct vary, and with them, the meanings attached to the concept of honour. So we can see that, on the one hand, the need for common understandings and the mechanisms of social integration (such as the acceptance of the usage of the upper classes) tend to unify its conceptualisation, on the other, the demands of social organisation promote differentiation.

It was suggested initially at the end of chapter one that the confusion of the meanings honour = precedence and honour = virtue
served the function of social integration by crediting the rulers with a
claim to esteem and a charter to rule. But it is a function which is ful-
filled only as long as the confusion is not recognised as such, and we
have seen that this is far from being always the case. Once it is realised
that 'honour has gone to the village', there is room for polemic, a
polemic which has been carried on for centuries (particularly between
the Church and the aristocracy) and of which the disagreement between
Montesquieu and Voltaire is only one of a whole number, one which
opposed the realism of the noble jurist to the moralism of the bourgeois
poet,[31] the 'is' view of honour to the 'ought' view.

The social struggle is visible behind the semantic battle; in a sense,
the sense which Speier suggested, it is fought out in words. The rebellion
of the agrarian masses of Andalusia was promoted by a concept which
illustrates this, '*señoritismo*'; *señorito*, the term of respect towards a
member of the ruling class became extended in *señoritismo* to mean the
rule of corruption and social injustice. The vocabulary of honour was
subverted by the failure of the *señoritos* to satisfy the claims upon their
image. The confusion of precedence and virtue broke down and new
attitudes emerged, represented by the anarchist leaders and expressed
in a new vocabulary, which stood in direct contradiction to the traditional values of Andalusia. But the battle over words is fought out only
perhaps to start afresh as the operative pressures of social organisation
impose themselves and the need resurges to sanctify a new established
order. The 'is' becomes 'ought' once more and authority is re-endowed
with *mana*.[32] Behind the new order of precedence and the redefined
honour the same principles can be seen at work, for if, as Durkheim
suggested, 'the idea of force is of religious origin',[33] it is also true that
the reality of force possesses the power to command the reverence due
to religion in order to sanctify itself.

The conceptual systems which relate to honour provide, when each
is taken in its totality and in its varied contexts, a mechanism which
distributes power and determines who shall fill the roles of command
and dictate the ideal image which people hold of their society. At the
ultimate level of analysis honour is the clearing-house for the conflicts
in the social structure, the conciliatory nexus between the sacred and
the secular, between the individual and society and between systems of
ideology and systems of action.

3   Spiritual kinship in Andalusia

The institution of the *compadrazgo* or co-parentship, 'a complex of formalized friendships and fictional kinship',[1] as it has been called, has been studied extensively in a number of New World cultures and has been the subject of a learned article devoted to its development in European society in earlier centuries[2] and of another comparing its form and function in Spain and in Spanish America.[3]

Yet the descriptions of it in Europe are few despite the great importance of the figurative uses of its terms in the social life and even in the political theory of Spain. Much more has been written and said about *compadrazgo* as a system of personal alliances in politics than about the institution from which the analogy was drawn. Here my concern is to examine its morphology and significance in the Andalusia that I studied a quarter of a century ago.[4]

Most anthropological writings on the subject have been content to consider it only from the viewpoint of its practical aspect, rather than from that of its religious significance – which I would maintain is essential to an understanding of its social significance – and have thus in effect given preference to the derived forms over the complex of ideas on which it was founded.[5] This is due, in part at least, to the fact that it first attracted the notice of anthropologists in Latin America where the elaboration of its social forms went far further than in Spain. Leaving the figurative usages of the word on one side, the bond of *compadrazgo* is established in Spain exclusively through a ritual relationship centred on the baptism of a child. For this reason, if its foundations in the font are primordial, it can nevertheless make sense as a social institution only in relation to the framework of kinship within which it is enclosed.

Morphology

Every Spaniard has one Christian name and two surnames. It is true that the children of the wealthy are sometimes baptised with several Christian names but this is not the plebeian custom in Andalusia. The surnames are the first surname of the father and, added to it, the first surname of the mother, that is to say, the patronyms of the two grandfathers. Putting it in another way, a man passes on his surname to his grandchildren through his daughters as well as through his sons. But if it passes through his daughters to his grandchildren it will go no further, for at each generation the maternal patronym of a man is replaced in his children's name by that of his wife, their mother. This loss of the line when it passes through women matters little to people who live above all in the present and value living contacts more than any identification with ancestors. The tombs of forebears, in contrast to those of many peoples of much simpler culture, and also of other parts of Spain, play little part in their lives and for the bulk of the population they are not even purchased but rented for a period of nine years, the bare term necessary for the decay of the physical corpse, before a fresh tenant takes possession. Knowledge of the past is limited to that which has been experienced personally by the living.

At the same time the wife does not change her surname to her husband's on marriage but retains her own, adding with the prefix 'de' her husband's surname. Needless to say these three surnames are never employed together except in very formal contexts. In general usage they constitute alternative ways of referring to the person: either by her own name or as the wife of so-and-so.

The same principles are to be found in the transmission of property as in the transmission of names. The rights of inheritance of all children of a marriage are equal regardless of primogeniture and regardless of sex. By law, one-third of the property of a testator remains in his free gift and when this option is exercised it is said that the recipient of the extra third, one of the children, has been 'mejorado' (advantaged). But this is not common practice in Alcalá de la Sierra, and should it occur under normal circumstances it is the prelude if not, as is more likely, the result of an unassuageable quarrel. 'The proper thing to do' is to leave the inheritance to the children *in toto* and let them decide whether they will continue to hold it undivided or to split it up between them. This 'régime de partage obligatoire' as LePlay called it,[6] is the indigenous custom of Andalusia and not, as in certain parts of Spain and France, the law which has been imposed by a central power against ancient local tradition of primogeniture.

It can be seen, then, that just as the grandfathers transmit their patronym, so they transmit their property. Yet this transmission is not properly regarded as lineal since the idea of conserving anything in a lineage is lacking. In contrast to the peasant communities of the north of Spain, its significance in Andalusia is rather that it establishes ties only within the structure of the family. Wealth inherited from the four grandparents is concentrated in the parental household, and in due course distributed once more among its offspring. There is no general preference attached to male children 'to carry on the line' or 'to bear the name' and fathers tend to prefer their daughters to their sons and to collaborate more closely with their daughters' husbands than with their own progeny. The customs of plebeian Andalusia differ in regard to inheritance from the traditions of the aristocracy whose titles pass preferentially by primogeniture in the male line and whose economic position was formerly protected by a system of entailments. Yet as has been noted, even among the nobility whose notions of descent are much more developed, titles pass through a daughter in default of a male heir.

The family comes into existence when a man and woman desert the household to which they formerly belonged in order to become the principals of a new household. The extended family is found only as a rare and rather unrespectable anomaly. The legal and religious celebration of marriage is sometimes retarded or dispensed with altogether, but in the eyes of the community the creation of a new household constitutes a marriage. Indeed, in the absence of any concept of the family as a land-holding or as a lineage, this is what the family must be. A separate dwelling is regarded as essential to a married couple and people will not marry until they can have one.

There is no system of dowry and the financial transactions involved in marriage consist only in the expenses involved in the celebration and in the money ('*pa' la cama*') handed over some weeks before the ceremony by the groom to his bride for the equipment of the new home. The inheritance of either partner of a marriage remains his own property though it enters into the community of goods of the marriage as long as both parties remain alive. There is a distinction in Spanish law between inherited wealth and wealth acquired during the course of the marriage and this latter belongs by right in equal parts to husband and wife. The essential equality of the two parties of a marriage reflects the equality of the sexes in inheritance. However, since the community of goods is no more than the extension into property law of a conception which exists already in the dogma of the Church, namely the unity of the married couple, the single legal personality created by this unity vests its financial direction in the husband. Subject to his wife's signature where her own possessions are involved, the husband controls the wealth of the whole family. A woman only recovers her full legal personality on becoming a widow, if indeed she does not acquire it then for the first time, having married before she came of age at twenty-three years old. This is the legal situation. The conception of the household as a single legal entity is also expressed in the term '*cabeza de familia*' (head of a family) a category which once provided the basis of municipal voting and taxation, and is still today in use.

Considered as an economic unit, the family is quite independent. Where the majority are day-labourers and where some go away to find work for weeks at a stretch the men do not cooperate in the production of the livelihood of the household. Each member contributes his earnings, but only in the spending of the family income is the household a single unit. Therefore, in contrast to the legal situation, in practice the finances of the family are handled by the wife, since to her the task of provisioning the household falls. Moreover, when, in the marriage ceremony, the groom hands his bride the 'arras', the thirteen pieces of silver, it is interpreted as a promise that he will hand over the totality of his wages to her. These facts make plainer the determination of every housewife to have her own house. Upon the farms where married sons or sons-in-law are employed they are paid a daily wage like any other employee. In certain instances, unmarried sons who live upon the farm with their parents are paid a daily wage in order to enable them to amass the funds they need in order to get married. In all these provisions it can be seen that the individual is conceived as such, and as such he belongs to a nuclear family, but there are no larger units of importance until we reach the community which is composed conceptually of households.

The terminology of kinship corresponds to that used in England with certain small divergencies. A distinction is made between first cousins ('primos hermanos' – brother-cousins) and cousins in general ('primos'). The terms for uncle and aunt are also used *à la mode de Bretagne*, as it is said in French, to designate the first cousins of parents, and the terms for nephew and niece the children of first cousins. Affinal kin may be distinguished by the addition of the adjective *politico/a*, but there are separate terms for affinal kin in the first degree: brother/sister-in-law, son/daughter-in-law, and father/mother/parents-in-law. The latter, *suegro*, is extended into a kinship term which has no equivalent in English: *consuegros*, the parents-in-law of one's children. Since each is *suegro* to the others' child the term is reciprocal. The form of address '*compadre*' is occasionally used between *consuegros*, for they are parents together of the married couple, and it is said that *consuegros* are *compadres*, but the term *compadre* is normally reserved for the relationship between the corporal and spiritual parent within the *compadrazgo*. This relationship is initiated by the fact that one has become *padrino*, godparent, to the other's child.

It is characteristic of the institutions of spiritual kinship that the importance attached to them varies according to place, social standing,

3

family tradition and individual character. So a whole spectrum of forms, varying in significance, can be discovered within a single area. Yet, in addition, there are a number of frivolous derivative forms both of *padrinazgo* and also of *compadrazgo*. Thus, *compadres de carnaval*, are a boy and girl who team up for the duration of the festival, *madrina de guerra* is the girl or woman who knits socks for a soldier away at the war, etc. The seconds of a duel are *padrinos*, and so are the proposer and seconder in a club election. There is also the slang use of '*compadrazgo*' to mean a system of exchange of favours among the politically influential, while the word '*padrino*' can be used of anyone who acts as a patron. '*Tener buenos padrinos*' means to be in a position to 'pull strings'. There is also the use of '*comadre*' and '*comadreo*', the person and the activity, represented by the English word 'gossip', whose etymology ('God-sib') shows it to be derived from a similar institution. The term '*compadre*' and '*comadre*' are used loosely in certain circles to give an impression of bonhomie and this usage has become today the prerogative of the '*Andalucía de pandereta*' (tambourine Andalusia), of the music-hall stage and of those who model their behaviour upon it. These figurative uses are confined to people amongst whom the institution has ceased to have any serious social significance. Mintz and Wolf[7] conclude that '*Compadrazgo* survives most actively in present-day Europe within the areas of lesser industrial development' and this conclusion is quite correct regarding Andalusia, but when[8] it is suggested that its function:

> was to solidify social relationships horizontally among members of the same rural neighbourhood, it is expressed in linguistic terms in the widening of the meaning of the word *compadre* to include the term 'neighbour'. In Andalusia, for example, the term *compadre* is easily extended to cover any acquaintance and even strangers

it is clear that the authors have been led astray by the imprecision of their lexicographical sources.[9] For such extended use is typical of certain social elements in Seville, but not at all of the rural environment where the institution remains most serious. A summer visitor to Alcalá who favoured this mode of address, so far from solidifying his relationship with the rustics only convinced them that he did not know how to behave, that he was 'fresco' (fresh). In the ambience of modern Spanish city life the institutions of spiritual affinity have little significance outside the liturgical, whereas the terminology derived from them is much used in a figurative sense. On the other hand, among people of the country the institutions retain their pristine form and such figurative uses are not employed. However, this essay is concerned first of all only with the pure and proper forms.

Of these the *padrinazgo* possesses two distinct variants. *Padrinazgo de boda* (of marriage) and *padrinazgo de pila* or *de bautismo* (of font or baptism). The *padrinos de boda* are the sponsors at a wedding. There is no spiritual significance in their role in the marriage ceremony and it is perfectly possible to be married without *padrinos* from the religious point of view. The tradition of many Catalan towns excludes them altogether. The *padrino's* chief function is to pay (a) for the religious ceremony, and (b) for some of the entertainment. The *padrinazgo de boda* creates no *compadres*. Nor does the ceremony of confirmation which requires a godfather in the eyes of the Church but has little social significance otherwise.

The choice of the *padrinos de boda* is a matter largely regulated by custom. An enquiry into local customary law organised by the Ateneo de Madrid in 1900 sent questionnaires to correspondents all over Spain and the subjects treated included the *padrinazgo*. It would appear from this that there are several main systems which predominate in different areas. But it is characteristic of the Spanish *pueblos* that each adheres to a distinct customary tradition and therefore any attempt to reach general conclusions is bound to aim only at approximations. In addition, there are variations in custom according to the social status of those concerned and how far this was taken into account by the recipients of the questionnaire it is hard to say. It has for some time been the fashion among the educated to have as *padrinos de boda* the mother of the groom and the father of the bride and isolated instances of such an arrangement appear in the Ateneo's report for different parts of Spain. In the region of Santander it is the groom's father and the bride's mother. In the North-West of Spain and also in an area of the East coast the *padrinos* are the groom's baptismal godfather and the bride's baptismal godmother. In between these areas the general tendency is for the groom's elder brother and his wife to be *padrinos*. There is a rough reciprocity in this arrangement where brothers must, as in Alcalá, get married in order of age. The younger brother has had to wait for the elder to marry and for the family to accumulate the necessary money to do so. In return the elder pays for his junior's wedding. There is a general tendency throughout the South for the *padrinos* to come in any case from the groom's side of the alliance and this tendency finds expression in a *refrán* from the province of Caceres:

> En la boda de malos aliños
> De parte de la novia son los padrinos

(In the ill-spiced wedding
The Godparents come from the bride's side)

Among poor families the problem often reduces itself to finding a friend or member of the family willing to make the required disbursements. The report records for the province of Cordoba that the *padrino* is the employer or a politically influential person. Today in Alcalá it is common for the landlord to stand as *padrino* to his tenant's son or to his employee's. Wealthier people sometimes offer to pay for the ceremony of a poor couple who wish to regularise their union with the rites of the Church and thereby become technically their *padrinos*.

It would seem unnecessary to insist on describing the ritual of baptism.[10] Nevertheless, certain points of significance require to be set forth. The rite of baptism marks the acceptance of a soul into the Church; 'cristianar' (to make Christian) is an alternative word for 'to baptise', to 'christen' in English. It accords the remission of sins and in particular, of Original Sin; as a result of which its soul will, if a child should die, go straight to Heaven. Should it die unbaptised, it will go to limbo, if not to Hell. The term '*angelito*' (a little angel) is used in Andalusia to describe a deceased child baptised but not yet arrived at the age of moral responsibility at which it can be said to have formed a sinful intention. For its death the church bell is not tolled ('*doblado*') but a quickly repeated note is rung upon the small bell ('*repique*') to announce its happy and immediate union with the Almighty. Baptism is the rite in which the child receives its Christian name which is the name of the saint under whose patronage it makes its entry into the Christian community. This name is given to it by its *padrinos de pila* who receive it from the font and who make on its behalf the vows necessary for its acceptance.

The *padrino* cannot be a parent; neither father nor mother can stand as sponsor to their own child. There exists an explanation of the interdiction on a purely practical level. A woman must wait forty days after childbirth before going to church for the ceremony of purification, and since the child must be christened as soon as possible lest it die unbaptised, it follows that the ceremony must take place without her. Regardless of the age of the child it is however the plebeian custom of Andalusia for the parents not to attend the baptism of their offspring, and it becomes clear that the necessity to baptise before the mother can attend is a redundant explanation. The interdiction for a parent to stand as sponsor was formally laid down by the Council of Mainz in the ninth century and the disjunction of the two personalities of parent and godparent was thenceforth complete. The juxtaposition of the ideal of natural paternity through which the Sin of Adam was transmitted and spiritual paternity in the rite through which it is washed away gives a theological justification to the prohibition, and the contrast is often subsequently made in theoretical writings between corporal generation and spiritual regeneration. But the argument which determined its imposition was one relating to the concept of spiritual affinity. The spiritual affinity established through the ceremony of baptism renders a sexual relationship incestuous, and constitutes an impediment to marriage. Already three centuries before the Council of Mainz, the Code of Justinian had declared illegal the marriage of a godfather with the mother of his godchild, while the Council of Trullo (Constantinople) in A.D. 692 had maintained spiritual affinity to be greater than that which proceeds from bodily union[11] and had ordained that those who had married the widowed mother of their godchild should separate forthwith and do penance for fornication. The Council of Mainz laid down that spiritual affinity existed between godfather and godmother and consequently forbade that a man and his wife should stand as godparents to the same child. This prohibition seems not to have been respected everywhere and the modern custom of Andalusia and many other regions of Spain is precisely to the contrary. But the rule was sufficient at the time to effect the disjunction between the two roles, for if spiritual affinity were created between husband and wife their marital relations would become incestuous. This was the dogmatic justification for the prohibition. From that period onwards spiritual affinity was discussed and expanded until an impediment to marriage existed even between the child of the *padrino* and the brothers or sisters of the baptised. Since during the Renaissance the political utility of the *padrinazgo* was exploited by the nobility of Europe and hence the fashion demanded numerous *padrinos*, the prohibitions of marriage became so complex that it was difficult to observe them and the Council of Trent put the matter right by limiting the number of *padrinos*. It also reduced the degrees of spiritual affinity which prohibited marriage to the following which pertained till 1918: godparent–godchild; baptiser (who in cases of emergency need not necessarily be a priest and was often in fact the midwife) and baptised; and *compadres*, that is to say godparent and parent. There is a certain confusion in many texts as to whether the term *compadre* refers to the persons who are both spiritual parents of the same child or whether it is the relationship of spiritual parent to natural parent. Subsequent to the Council of Trent only the latter involved an impediment to marriage though popular imagination continued to maintain that a parent could not in emergency baptise his own child for fear of contracting a spiritual affinity with his spouse 'quae matrimonii usum impediat'.[12] From here onward I use the term *compadre* to refer to the relationship between spiritual and natural parent. This is the popular usage of Andalusia.

Today in Andalusia it is an understood thing that a *padrino* is someone who cannot contract either marriage or sexual relations either with his godchild or with a parent of his godchild and this is a self-evident truth which devolves from the conception of *what the padrinazgo is* and not from any theoretical knowledge of the nature of spiritual affinity in Church doctrine.

To summarise what the *padrino* is in the view of what one might term 'popular theology', he is the person who acts as substitute for the parent – (a current designation in the middle ages was 'propatres') – in that relationship to the child from which the parent is excluded and in those rites which custom forbids the parent to attend. It may be noted that, at any rate in the plebeian tradition of Alcalá de la Sierra, the definition holds good for the *padrinos de boda*, for the parents do not attend the wedding ceremony of their children either.

Padrinos de pila are chosen or accepted by the parents. They may either be invited to be *padrinos* or they may offer themselves. But there are certain preferential rules and these are as various and as ill-defined as those which govern the selection of the *padrinos de boda*. The rules apply only to the first-born in the great majority of instances.

Once more the questionnaire of the Ateneo de Madrid provides a picture of the distribution of the various systems. These are for the main part two in number. That in which *the padrinos are grandparents*, which is found in the East, Catalonia, Aragon and the Basque provinces, and in the West, Galicia and Extremadura. The other system is that in which the *padrinos* are the *padrinos de boda*. This is found in the remainder of Spain and also in parts of Galicia and in Extremadura.

There is, clearly, the possibility of a logical connection between the systems for selecting the two varieties of *padrino*. For example, the rule which prescribes the *padrino de pila* of the bride or groom as the *padrino de boda* cannot be followed in every case in conjunction with the rule which designates the *padrino de boda* as the *padrino de pila* of the first child or the same *padrinos* would continue for ever. On the other hand, where the *padrinos de boda* are parents of the couple, it follows that they will be the child's grandparents and this is precisely what another rule says they should be. Yet such deductive conclusions are not borne out by the distribution shown in the Ateneo's report and it becomes evident that these rules are simply preferential customs. No sanction enforces them. Those who do not get on with their elder brother choose somebody else, whatever the rule says. Preferential rules delineate an ideal type of the institution whose nature may well be embodied in a number of different forms. The rules are therefore alternatives of which one or another is favoured by one particular community at one particular time. And there is no reason to suppose that in this matter fashions do not change. The rule will be determined by the consistency found not between one preferential rule and another but between the conception of what a *padrino* is and what a *compadre* is, on the one hand, and on the other the conception of what is a brother, cousin, grandparent, father-in-law or whatever category of kin is selected as the preferred one. It is this which determines the appropriateness of the choice at the general level.

The first facts to observe about the *padrinazgo* in Alcalá are:

That the *padrinos* are in principle a married couple, or possibly a betrothed couple.

That the *padrinos de boda* should be *padrinos de pila* to the first child.

There is little agreement among the people of Alcalá regarding the choice of the *padrinos de boda*, but traditionally-minded people appear to follow one of two rules.

One is that whereby the groom's elder brother is *padrino de boda* with his wife and subsequently the couple are *padrinos de pila* to the firstborn. The reception on the first day is given by the bride's family in her house. That of the second day is given by the *padrinos*. In this way there is a sharing of expenses between the two families.

The other rule searches for balance in another quarter. There is a formal rule regarding the naming of children which is observed by all. The children are named after their grandparents in the following order: first son after paternal grandfather, first daughter after paternal grandmother; second son after maternal grandfather, second daughter after maternal grandmother. In this way the children are associated once more with their grandparents. In the choice of *padrinos* a further refinement occurs. The *padrinos de boda* are, in this case, from the bride's family and in consequence the first child will get its Christian name from its paternal family and its *padrinos* who were *padrinos* of the marriage from its maternal family. The *padrinos* of subsequent children are chosen with regard to the same principle, that is, that its *padrinos* come from the opposite side to its Christian name. Within such a system, the child is linked to its grandparents on one side by its name and on the other by its godparents who give it that name.

In those instances where there is no preferential rule to follow for the choice of the *padrino*, he is simply a close friend, a relative for preference it would seem, or less commonly an influential person who is prepared to patronise the family. The essential thing is that he, or rather they, should be close friends ('*de confianza*') of the parents. And the importance of their feelings towards one another is particularly great in view of the relationship of *compadrazgo* in which they are henceforth to stand.

Being a *compadre* imposes certain forms of behaviour upon the participants. In explaining what a *compadre* is people say: 'He is one of the family', meaning that he is received as if he were of the family, a mode of behaviour facilitated by the existence of the incest-barrier, and they also explain: 'You cannot refuse your *compadre* anything which he asks. Anything which is yours is his.' By implication anything which is his is yours for the relationship is totally reciprocal. No difference either in behaviour, in obligations or in form of address distinguishes the natural from the spiritual *compadre*. It is a relationship of absolute trust and it involves the self-esteem of the participants in the highest degree. You can quarrel with your family but not with your *compadre*. Therefore while it frequently overlays a relationship of kin it is not the same in kind as natural kinship.[13] Fate determines who are one's kin and one's obligations toward them are defined by custom and by law. But one *chooses* one's *compadres* and one's obligations towards them depend only upon their personal wishes.

Custom is explicit only upon one point. *Compadres* must address one another in the third person. And this usage is the more remarkable within a community where persons of the same age always speak in the second person. So that two men who have spoken together all their lives in the familiar form adopt, from the day they become *compadres*, the formal '*Usted*'. Once more the degree of seriousness with which the relationship is treated influences the extent to which this custom is observed. Persons who are already related as members of the same elementary family retain the use of the second person, their relationship as kin taking precedence over their relationship as *compadres*. Yet I have recorded instances of '*tío*' politico and '*sobrina*' and also of father and son-in-law who spoke together in the third person since becoming *compadres*. The reason for this custom is always given that: '*compadres* respect one another'. This does not imply that their behaviour becomes any more distant or unfriendly. Children speak to their parents in the third person for the same reason, and spouses 'respect' each other. A bullfighter can be fined for 'lack of respect for the public'. 'Respect' means maintaining a proper regard for a person; it means the avoidance of the 'laissez-aller' which is the idiom between equals within the community; it means the recognition of dependence upon the good opinion of the other.

To sum up the two institutions – or should one say the two types of social relationship created by the institution of baptism? – the *padrinazgo* is a ritual relationship between a child and its substitute parents concerned with the personal destiny, religious and material, of the child, while the *compadrazgo* is an individual relationship in which the child provides the pretext for establishing a unique bond between two equal adult persons and their wives.

At different periods of history and in different countries and classes one or other of these two aspects has predominated. In some parts of Hispanic America the value attached to the *compadrazgo* is such that the pretexts for establishing such a relationship provided by baptisms are insufficient and additional occasions are furnished by other religious and lay ceremonies.[14] The desire to provide offspring with powerful patrons appears, on the other hand, to have been the motive for the multiplication of *padrinos* which the Church opposed during the epoch of the Renaissance. In Andalusia today, even though the institution remains constricted for the most part within the circle of family and close friends, one finds both forms in existence. That in which the *padrinazgo* is the important relationship, for example, when a landowner takes on the duties of *padrino* for the child of someone in his service and pays for the education of his godson without in fact changing in any noticeable way his relationship to the child's father. And that in which the child's baptism is the occasion to inaugurate the *compadrazgo* between two old friends; the first case insists on the unequal relationship between godparent and godchild; the second upon the equality between *compadres*.

Interpretation

Turning to daily life to see how, within a living community, the institutions of kinship and spiritual kinship interrelate, one must try first of all to evaluate the system of naming.

Everyone is addressed and known within the community by his Christian name, and if any title of respect is accorded on account of status or age it is prefixed to the Christian name. Few people other than those concerned with administration know more than a handful of surnames. Christian names qualified by nicknames suffice for daily use. The use of the surname is confined to the realms of letters and the law. All dealings of an official character employ surnames and whenever a person is addressed in writing as opposed to speech it is by his surname, for nicknames are considered 'ugly' and people are ashamed to use them in the presence of those who do not belong to the community; they are never written down. The Spanish word for surname 'apellido' derives from a word meaning a call to arms and originates in the demands which the political authority made upon each household, demands of taxation and military service. The surname may be said, then, to define a person to the outside world, to define him as a member of the nation, as the son of a certain household, the heir to his two grandparental families.

A nickname is never mentioned in the presence of its owner and he is supposed not to know of its existence.[15] It is often a purely descriptive term which serves simply to identify him, and it may be used in conjunction with prefixes of respect, but it is also the vehicle of satirical criticism and as such it has particular importance in the service of the institutions of public mockery, the 'vito' and formerly, Carnival. It is more often than not inherited and it is used collectively for households and particularly for sets of siblings. It defines a person then, to the community, as the community sees him behind his back, either as a member of a certain household or as a personality outstanding enough to earn an individual nickname.

The Christian name is usually required in conjunction with either the surname or the nickname. The 'impersonal' form of address 'Señor So-and-so' is something which belongs to the urban milieu or to relations with strangers. In the rural community everyone knows everyone else. The outsider, from the moment that he is accepted within the community, is called by his Christian name and is given a nickname, usually one referring to his origin, or to his profession if he belongs to the professional classes. But the use of a nickname by itself implies a degree of disrespect, particularly if it is a satirical one. It is significant that the recognised 'shameless persons' are addressed by their nicknames and that in the songs of the 'vito' and Carnival the victims are addressed by their nicknames without the Christian name. By depriving them of their Christian name the community excommunicates them. The Christian name is the name with which personal relations are conducted.

It is the first name which its owner learns to recognise himself by, for it is the name which distinguishes him within the family. (He comes to learn his surnames only later when he goes to school). It is individual and not generic and its whole significance can be derived from this fact. In matters of inheritance siblings are equivalent. They bear the same surnames and usually the same generic nickname. Their Christian names distinguish them as individuals.

'Christian name' is an English expression which in Spanish is merely 'name' ('*nombre*'), but it is the name with which the child becomes a Christian at baptism, that is to say, becomes a member of the community. For the word 'Christian' has a popular parlance nothing to do with religious faith. It is not the atheists nor the anarchists who are excluded from the category but the gypsies and the Moors across the straits ni Africa – though gypsies do in fact profess the Christian faith. 'Christians' is a term which is contrasted with 'Moors', that is to say, with the enemies which the townships of Andalusia were mostly founded to repel, or with gypsies, those beings who, though they live there, are excluded from the moral community.

The ritual acquisition of a Christian name marks the beginning of the social personality of the individual and the rite which accords it is carried out under the auspices of the *padrinos*, not of the parents. In the language of the Alcalareños, to stand as *padrino* to a child at baptism is said 'to baptise' ('*bautizar*') as though it were the *padrino*, not the priest, who performed the ceremony. The name which is given in this way is the name of a saint under whose special patronage the infant enters the Christian community. From the religious point of view the relationship between the individual and his saint is of little importance but the idea of supernatural patronage is one which is general throughout Spain. Ships are launched, townships were founded under the protection of a specific saint to whom they were dedicated. But the Christian name also creates ties in the social sphere. The individual's yearly festival is not the anniversary of his birth but the feast of his saint. This means that all those who are called by the same name celebrate their personal feast upon the same day. This creates a particular relationship between them which is expressed in the word '*tocayo*'. This is not only a descriptive term but it is also used as a form of address. *Tocayos* greet each other and get together upon their feast day.

The significance of the Christian name may be illustrated in another way. Domestic animals are never called by a saint's name because this would be thought improper both towards the saint and also towards the other bearers of that name. How would one like to be *tocayo* with one's neighbor's mule? By the same logic people were very shocked when a member of the community (of old anarchist stock) called his daughter Diana. They complained that this was a name for a dog, not for a Christian soul. The little girl was not made to suffer for her parents' unfortunate choice. She was called Anita like any other girl whose name is Ana.

Among the countryman's phrases there is a way of asking the *nombre* (Christian name) of a person: '*Cual es su gracia*?' (what is your grace?) This usage strikes the foreign ear as curious and to understand it fully it is necessary to review the semantics of the word. To translate it as 'grace' is far from adequate. The essence of its meaning is a free gift, something which requires no justification and which is not to be reciprocated, an inherent and personal quality. This is the sense which is common to all its meanings, whether in its use as the ability to make people laugh, or as the magical power to cure by touch: as a favour or in the plural form as the idiomatic way of acknowledging a favour, i.e., 'thanks'. It is something which cannot be exchanged for money or material advantage. (If you pay for a thing you owe no thanks). It is said that a '*sabia*' who demanded payment for her cures would lose her grace, for it is a gift of God which cannot be trafficked with. It is by Divine Grace, according to the theologians, that original sin is remitted through the rite of baptism. From this use of '*Gracia*' to mean name is formed another name for the *padrinos* – '*padres de gracia*'.

The Christian name then, in opposition to the surname, defines the individual within the family, defines him in his personal relations within the community, defines him in relation to God, links him with a saint, and through that saint with *tocayos* who may be anything else, but not his siblings, and in many cases links him with a grandparent. It represents a man's personal, in-group, '*gemeinschaft*' self in contrast to his legal, exterior, '*gesellschaft*' self represented by his surnames. Indeed, the distinction between the person as himself and the person as a social cypher is one which is ever-present in this society which by tradition offers to a percentage of its population the opportunity of stepping outside the social system altogether into the surnameless seclusion of a religious order. The idea of a dual purpose in the system of naming, i.e. to define a person in formal terms and at the same time as an individual personality, may, if one wishes, be seen displayed in the conventional phrase with which the people of Andalusia give their name 'para servirle a usted y a Dios' (at your service and at God's).

Armed with this conception of Andalusian personality, the juxtaposition of kinship and spiritual kinship appears no longer simply a matter of theology and enters the realm of social structure. Its structural significance can be traced throughout the whole length of the life cycle.

The child goes to its baptism with members of its family and its godparents who make the necessary vows on its behalf, but without its parents. It is received from the font by the godparents. They pay for the ceremony and they make the child certain presents which vary according to the financial circumstances of those involved. At the least, they must give it the cross or the religious medallion (usually the Virgin) which it will wear always from then on and which is believed to be an effective protection against the Evil Eye as well as against general misfortunes. It is thought proper to give also an article of clothing for the occasion. Later a boy's first pair of shoes should be given him by his godparents, who again are responsible for providing the elaborate dress for the girl's first communion. Subsequently, the godparent is expected to do favours for the child particularly in helping him to 'get a start in life' and in general, to indulge his personal desires, and should he die in childhood the godfather pays for the coffin. The contrast between parent and godparent in relation to the child is evident. The parents are responsible for the child as a member of the family, must teach it how to behave, must punish it 'to give it shame', must be respected by it in a number of established customs. For example, a son may not drink or smoke in the presence of his father. Parents and children are bound together by mutual responsibilities and reciprocal duties which will last the whole length of their lives. But the gifts of the godparent are free gifts, requiring no return.

In fact, the godchild's relationship with his *padrinos* depends very much upon the personal relations of his family; if the parents value the tie with their *compadres*, then the *padrino* plays a more important part in the child's life, but regardless of this the *padrinazgo* loses importance once the godchild becomes an adult. For the *padrinazgo* is the relationship between an adult and a child, not between two grown men, the fathers of families. Between two equals the tie of spiritual kinship is that of the *compadrazgo*. Thus, there is an instance in which two friends who call each other '*compadre*' and speak in the third person turn out not to be *compadres* but to be the *compadre* and nephew of a man now dead by whom the nephew was brought up. While to quote an instance of an adaptation of the terminology in the other direction, it is said of a wealthy landowner: 'He is *padrino* (not *compadre*) of the So-and-So's, his tenants, because he has 'baptised' one of their children.' And indeed he continues to speak to his tenants in the second person.

In contrast to the peasantry of Europe as they are generally described, the Andalusians are extremely romantic in their choice of a spouse. The marriage arranged by the parents for considerations of property are rare and are regarded ill. Courting begins at an early age without any definite obligation to marry. It takes place in the evenings at the door[16] of the house of the girl's family and the obligation develops only with time. Courting normally goes on for several years at the least. And during that time the privacy of the young couple is protected by custom. The future son-in-law who comes to the door of the house to court is never spoken to by the family. He must, himself, maintain a strict line of conduct in relation to the father of the girl who, in theory, must not be allowed to become aware that his daughter is being courted. When the father appears the lovers separate. He pretends not to notice them. An attitude of aloofness and hostility characterises the behaviour of the other members of the family, and continues until the young couple decide to get married. The groom's mother, sometimes his parents, are persuaded to pay a formal visit on their son's behalf in order to ask for the girl's hand. At first her father will hear none of it but at last he is persuaded by his wife. From this time forward the marriage becomes virtually certain. The ceremony is fixed for some three or four months ahead. The future groom is invited at last to enter the house upon whose threshold he has stood for years. During this time the money for setting up house is paid by the groom to his betrothed. The *padrinos de boda* are chosen. The romantic period comes to a close. The new link is forged, the attitudes affected must alter.

This does not always happen easily. Sometimes the father disapproves genuinely and will not give his consent. Sometimes the lovers wish to hurry matters. Sometimes they have a reason for this. At this juncture there is only one solution: elopement. The lovers run away together and make the situation which they desire a *fait accompli*. If they live in the town they run away to the country. Sometimes from the home in the valley they run away to the town. The essential act is to spend the night together. Once that has been done the girl cannot marry someone else. Her father is forced to approve. To one couple who had run away to a farm where they spent the night, the parents' emissaries were sent to beg the daughter to return. When they knocked on the door she came out onto the balcony leading her lover and told them: 'Go back and tell my father that I am his wife now.' The father normally acquiesces, indeed an ancient custom in some parts of Andalusia is said to have required that the father should never give his consent until the daughter has forced it from him by eloping. Yet his acquiescence cannot be regarded as a certainty. An employee, aiming it was thought at material advantage, eloped with the sixteen-year-old daughter of the farmer for whom he worked. But the farmer had the Civil Guard sent after him and he was clapped into jail to await trial for seduction of a minor.

When the day of the ceremony arrives, the groom goes with the *padrinos de boda* to the bride's house and from there they set out for the church accompanied only by the bride's unmarried friends. None of the parents go to the church and indeed the *padrinos* are the only married people who attend the ceremony. The married guests wait for them outside the church or at the festal house, to welcome them into their new status. With the creation of the new unit of society relations alter in every direction. The romantic wooer becomes the head of a family. He no longer begs for his fiancée's favour. On the contrary he now has the right to administer her property. She has the new responsibility of running her house, of raising her family. The days of '*pelando la pava*', of courtship in the doorway, are over. Mutual concern regarding the state of the heart is replaced by common concern regarding the state of the household. The change is symbolised by the changed relationship with their *padrinos de boda.* When the first child is born they may become its *padrinos de pila.* To its parents they are now no longer *padrinos* but *compadres,* persons between whom there are reciprocal responsibilities.

Once the marriage has taken place the attitude of the wife's family to the husband alters fundamentally. No longer a threat to the family's honour, he becomes himself bound up with it, and a person who has his say in the family's affairs. It is noticeable that he usually gets on very well with them, and is frequently employed by his father-in-law in preference to a son. On the other hand, the wife normally knows her family-in-law much less well and is liked by them much less. The woman is the centre of the household and it is in the house, not out at work that frictions tend to take place. Once more the legal situation is reversed in practical life. While in legal terms the husband has authority over the wife, he becomes in fact far more fully a member of her family group than she becomes of his.

Another change is foreshadowed in the marriage. The parental couple are deserted one by one by their children who marry and move to another house until the day comes when they remain alone. Sometimes they are lent a grandchild to give them a hand; sometimes they employ a girl from a too-numerous family. But the time approaches when they will become the dependents of their children, when they can no longer work their land nor go out for work. They are no longer parents but grandparents, minor members, like their grandchildren, of the household, contributing the 'durillo' (five pesetas) of their old-age pension as once they contributed their daily wage or the money they earned washing or carrying water. Many hold out against this move and prefer to remain in their own house, but when one of them dies then the widowed one must choose which of their children to go to live with. In the majority of cases they choose a daughter in preference to a son.

When one considers the family in this society one can see that both the moral and also the economic bases for its extension are lacking. A family is never conceptually more than the two spouses who have chosen each other for reasons of personal inclination, and their growing children. The independence and authority of the married couple are such that no form of coexistence with another married couple is possible within the familial organisation. Where circumstances such as the distance of a farm from other habitations or the common ownership of property require the cooperation of several related families there are often quarrels. The family may be said, then, to be formed through the break-up of the parental family and to be destroyed through the formation of the filial family.

Within the total social structure, marriage effects precisely this passage from one to the other. Given this, it is logical that the major structural tensions should be found in the relationships which lie closest to the elementary family and should manifest themselves in the processes of its formation and destruction, that is to say, birth, marriage, and retirement.

In the case of ascendant–descendant relationships, the *padrinazgo* appears as an institutional avoidance between parents and children whereby the conflict between the old family and the new is insulated. The disjunction of the parental figures into natural parents and spiritual parents corresponds to the delegation, upon the occasions of the *rites de passage* of the children, of that side of parenthood which conflicts with the responsibility for the integration of the household. The guardianship of the individuality of the child, his Christian-self, is transferred to *padrinos* who have no concern in the structural destiny of the parental family. One can perceive a certain analogy between the role of *padrino* and the role of mother's brother in certain patrilineal societies. And indeed the analogy is supported from a source which owes nothing to the analyses of social anthropology. '*En Mingrélie*', says the Abbé Corblet,[17] '*l'affinité spirituelle égale le parrain au frère de la mère, en sorte qu'il peut, en tout temps, entrer chez elle comme dans sa propre maison.*' The ideal person to fill this role of *padrino* is a member of the close kin of the parents who may be expected in any case to feel for the child the kind of indulgence proper to a godparent, that is to say, a grandparent, or a father's or mother's brother or sister.

In the case of collateral kin, a similar explanation is valid. To begin with, the tensions are more obvious. Collateral kin are people who belong or will belong to different families. Shared participation in a common family is their tie. But in every instance this participation establishes them in rivalry, not in cooperation. Between *consuegros* relations are usually distant and jealous. They have not usually chosen to be so related to one another and their equality in relation to their common grandchildren draws them no nearer together. The conventional rules which balance their claims in matters of Christian names and *compadrazgo* reflect their jealousy. The equality among siblings also inspires jealousy. A sibling is someone with whom one must share one's inheritance and he is also someone who must share with one the duties and expenses of caring for aged parents. Siblings who are not on speaking terms with one another are no great rarity in Alcalá, and siblings who do not speak with their brother- or sister-in-law are even less so. The secondary meaning of the word '*primo*' (cousin), reminiscent of the usage of Elizabethan England, is a fool or simpleton, and this implies that he who puts confidence in kinship ties in the second generation is likely to be deceived. Only mutual affection and shared affections keep them together. In many instances an inheritance is put on the market for no better reason than that the sibling group cannot agree regarding its exploitation. A negative example reinforces the point. Several families exist in Alcalá in which the children have never married but have preferred to remain together in the same household where they live in happy concord as an example, one might think, to married siblings. But the community does not see them in this light but rather as odd and faintly ridiculous.

Upon these ambiguous relationships the *compadrazgo* is superimposed with its obligation of absolute trust. Disregarding any conventional rule of selection, a *compadre* is first of all a person with whom there exists a mutual desire for such alliance. Thereafter the prescription which demands compliance with the wishes of the other guards against jealousy and restrictive feelings, that which ordains the third person guards against the familiarity which might breed contempt. This trust and this respect for the other's dignity are irrevocable. One cannot renounce *compadrazgo*. A man who quarrels with the spiritual parent of his own child or the *natural* parents of his godchild desecrates his own personality. One man who missed the potatoes from the bottom of his garden with regularity decided to lie in wait with a big stick and catch the thief. He found that he was his *compadre* so he did nothing. But next night he took a basket and dug up some of his *compadre's* vegetables and left the basket outside his door with an envelope which had his name on it as if it had fallen into the basket by accident, in order that the thieving *compadre* might know that he had been discovered. Those who heard this story were very shocked to think that any man could steal from his *compadre*. The self-esteem of each man is committed in this relationship in such a way that each is in the other's power. For this reason the *compadre* is, as in America, the person par excellence from whom money is borrowed. He cannot refuse to lend, nor can he refuse to pay back. For the *compadrazgo* imposes the duty of cooperation in a way that kinship alone does not. It imposes a restraint in conduct, language and feeling which is not to be derived from any other relationship. By delegating the spiritual parenthood of his child he binds himself to his chosen friend who thereby champions the threat which the child's growing up represents to the integration of his family, yet between these two there is at the same time created a relationship within which no reproach is possible. The statement, therefore, that the *compadrazgo* is used to 'intensify' the bonds of kinship[18] would be misleading if applied to Andalusia (or anywhere else). For we have seen that spiritual affinity and kinship are different in nature. I would say, rather, that the preferential rules which designate a member of the family as *padrino* serve the purpose of exorcising from kin relationships the jealousies which are inherent in them. They establish the tie of *compadrazgo* between affinal kin whose relationship becomes cemented precisely through the birth of the child. The elder brother who 'baptises' his nephew may in so doing attach his indulgent concern to the child who will be his own son's *primo*, but he also becomes with his wife *compadres* with their sister-in-law. The *primo* who became *compadre* is no longer the potential 'muggins' but the sacred friend. Thanks to the '*gracia*' which is the essence of spiritual kinship the *compadrazgo* preserves natural kinship from its all too natural consequences.

In this essay, I have attempted to see the *compadrazgo* (and *padrinazgo*) only in relation to the family system, in contrast to Foster who is chiefly concerned with its importance 'in stabilising and integrating communal life'[19] and Mintz and Wolf who 'especially emphasise its functions in furthering social solidarity'.[20] In consequence this analysis cannot claim to be of any but the most indirect help in disentangling the problems of its dissemination and transformation in the New World. The institutional forms of spiritual kinship have been shown to be easily adapted to uses which have nothing to do with either kinship or religion, even within Andalusia. How to evaluate the content of a social institution is as delicate a matter as distinguishing between the literal and figurative uses of its terminology. Indeed it is characteristic of complex societies that the same word may have a different signification for different elements of the society. Thus there is no reason to suppose that the aristocracy has ever given the same signification to the *compadrazgo* as the peasantry, and in view of the different laws of inheritance and their different customs of family life, it seems likely that they did not. This supposition would support both its extension during the Renaissance among the aristocracy as a mechanism of worldly patronage, and also explain why, once the Church insisted that spiritual affinity should be taken seriously, it declined into the figurative forms current among the upper classes today. It would also explain some of the curiously misleading definitions given in dictionaries, from that of Covarrubias onwards.[21]

However it is not merely in differences in the customs of different classes that the explanation of the variety of its functions lies, for the conceptual opposition between spiritual and natural kinship does not prevent the former from being exploited for the sake of political or economic ends which appear to contradict the idea of its spiritual nature. Custom in many places, especially in Italy, attempts to guard against this by explicitly forbidding economic involvement between *compadres*. Though it has not been my concern here to show how it is in fact put to political use within the structure of patronage, this is implicit in the rule which the Report of the Ateneo found, especially in the Province of Cordoba where it is stated that the *padrino* of a child should be the landowner and this custom is also common upon the haciendas of Latin America. The conceptual equality between *compadres* makes it particularly effective as a bond between persons who are anything but equal socially, whether their inequality is a matter of class difference or political power, and it is in this vertical sense that it is found 'furthering social solidarity' rather than in the sense that Mintz and Wolf conjectured. The problem of the adaptation of the *compadrazgo* to political ends is a matter I have examined elsewhere.[22]

Yet it is important to recognise that it owes its political efficacy to its spiritual function which makes it intimate, personal and irrevocable, in a word sacred, and sets it apart from utilitarian contractual relationships. In a sphere where trust is vital yet uncertain it guarantees that trust. Where rivalry is rampant it prohibits competition. In an agonistic society the *compadrazgo* creates a realm apart where peace reigns. Where class hostility is great it provides a basis for alliance between members of different classes and hence a moral justification for patronage. Thanks to the moral equality of the *compadrazgo* the social inequality of the *compadres* is acceptable. For, as the analysis of honour explained, there is a certain ambivalence in the notion of service as so often elsewhere in the domain of honour: it is humiliating to be subjected to the commands of others, but on the other hand one may share in the superior honour of a person to whom one is attached. A man is bound in sacred duty to his *compadre*, therefore it is not a restriction of his personal autonomy to comply with his wishes; he is not dishonoured by being a client but on the contrary he gains in honour through the bond of intimacy with a powerful patron. Moreover, quite apart from the possible advancement he may owe to his preferential tie with such a person, advantages may accrue to his child, the godson of his *compadre*. In the popular stories of Alcalá the benign patron is frequently figured paying for the 'career' of his godson, that is to say the education necessary for his entry into the professional classes – particularly when he has no children of his own. The favours granted to a godchild are deeds of particular virtue, since they are demonstrations of grace and therefore morally superior to the 'natural' desire to help one's own children in life. Hence people boast not only of the high status of their *padrino*, but also of the number of their godchildren.

The opposition between spiritual and natural kinship makes it possible for a relationship of subordination upon the mundane level to be shorn of its dishonouring implications through the spiritual equivalence of the *compadres*. Yet this spiritual equivalence hides a fact that is never stated yet is easily observed: where the *compadres* are socially unequal the superior is always the spiritual, never the natural, parent; one does not 'baptise' the child of a social superior, for if *compadres* are ideally equal, godparent and godchild are not. The sponsor must be at least the social equal of his spiritual child. Such a principle is implied by the nature of honour, for it is not only personal sentiment and aspiration but also recognised status, and these two aspects correspond to the distinction already made between the Christian-name self and the surname self. His familial honour he inherits with his surname, if 'he bears an honourable name', but if he is to increase the honour attaching to that name he will earn it through his personal qualities 'with lance in hand'. Any new accretion of honour must come from the destiny of the individual, which is in the care of the godfather rather than the father, who merely transmits what has already been accumulated. It is thus appropriate that the Christian name should be given by a sponsor superior in honour, since he is sponsor not only of the spiritual destiny of the child but of his worldly fate.

4   The moral foundations of the family

Ever since the days when primitive matriarchy was an accepted supposition the family has occupied a central place in anthropological theory.
Its functions and formation have been scrutinised and the rules for the
choice of a spouse or the systems of succession have provided the subject of many a learned thesis. The rights and duties attaching to familial
roles have been placed in their relation to the wider network of kinship
ties and patterns of residence have been invoked as an essential con-
tingency of these. Matriarchy as a concept did not long survive and its
place was taken by more modest and more precise notions expressed in
adjectives such as matrilineal, matri-lateral, -local, -focal, etc. which
aimed to describe the ethnography of the present or at least one small
part of it rather than explain the whole history of mankind. Precision
led to distinctions and distinctions to qualifications. The one simple
generality that remains (and not without a few exotic exceptions) is that
the nuclear family is a basic moral and residential unity. This *must* be so
since the members of a society are the product of the union of one man
and one woman; the biological division of labour is, then, in its dynamic
aspect the point of departure of every social system in the sense that
none could exist which did not meet the conditions necessary for the
production of successors and these conditions impose the limits to the
forms which the family can take. They require that children be not
merely born but nourished, protected and educated, and they make of
this institution everywhere the first collectivity to which an individual
belongs. For this reason the family relates in its implications to every
aspect of social life and finds a place therefore in the purview of all the
social sciences. The anthropologist's chief preoccupation, however, has
mostly been to examine how the family fitted into the kinship system or
how the members of kin groups were recruited, since it is precisely in this
way that cultures differ most from one another. Ignoring certain attempts
to derive the basic personality structure of a given culture from the mode
of rearing children one might say that whether the kin are regarded as an
extension of the family or the family is viewed as a function of the kinship system, its connection with kinship has provided the main focus of
its theoretical space within anthropology.

It is certainly well advised to examine this connection and I would not suggest that, even where the ideology of modern individualism banishes the notion of kinship from the realm of conscious concern, the nuclear family can be treated *in vacuo* without regard for its implications in the realm of kinship, yet there is still something to be said about the structure of the family in its relation to the general categories of sex and age, for this is where the sexes and the ages are most significantly related. The connection between the family and kinship is not in any case of the same order nor as evident where people decide upon the choice of a spouse for themselves rather than marry in accordance with the decision of their parents or a prescriptive rule and this is largely the case on the northern shore of the Mediterranean with which this essay is mainly concerned. This relative autonomy of the nuclear family – together with the absence of a clear rule of marriage – has made the Mediterranean an area of little interest to the theoreticians of kinship, if one excludes the purely 'tribal' peoples. Even in the lands beyond Europe where, among the Arabs, a certain tendency to patrilineal endogamy has been discerned and where kinship has attracted the attention of anthropologists ever since Robertson Smith, kinship theory has not prospered, for where women are not exchanged between the groups in which they are born, but marriages are determined by political and economic considerations, it fails to provide a discrete field of study.[1]

Mediterranean Europe is a region where from earliest known times women were preferably kept within the patriline rather than exchanged. Here, early on, people decided *against* foreign affines.[2] In addition among the peasants and townsmen who constitute the very great majority of the population there are today few areas where large kin-based *groups* are found and while kinship has often provided the ties which bind factions together, these are not based directly on the criterion of kin, but rather on networks of ties established by individual familial links – a fact that is virtually implied by the bilateral nature of Mediterranean kinship, which recognises the priority of the patriline in the bestowal of the surname but not in kinship terminology nor in the succession to property. Kinship has therefore been tangential to the formation of solidary groups and the family has been treated, if at all, without regard to its connection with the structure of the whole society and the mechanisms of political power, as though public and private or domestic life were two quite different things which should not be spoken of in the same breath. This is indeed our own ethnocentric feeling about how both should be conducted and those who fail to respect their separation are condemned as guilty of 'nepotism', a word which would hardly have any meaning outside Western civilisation, so self-evident is the moral obligation to help one's close kin in politics.[3]

It is worth observing that each of the nations of Europe believes the others to be guilty of nepotism to a far greater degree than themselves: the British are convinced that the French, Spaniards and Italians are more concerned in the advancement of their close kin than in the common weal, while the rest of Europe knows that England has traditionally been governed by a handful of noble families and their affines – a view confirmed by a perusal of the kin ties within the Conservative Party and the testimony of Hilaire Belloc's rhymes. In the continental view only their remarkable propensity for hypocrisy enables the English to deny this self-evident truth. In fact each nation fails to recognise the legitimacy of the particular compromise which another nation effects between the demands of familial ties and the requirements of the national political system. The conflict is common to them all; the compromise is the product of each national culture. Hence the accusation of nepotism[4] is bandied around as freely as, in earlier centuries, the responsibility for the pox. Yet, if this all too natural concern for the advancement of close kin is found to conflict with the ideal of an abstract justice and an ideological conception of politics, is it not simply that kinship here fails to provide the basis for the regulation of social relations and must therefore be set apart and hidden from the public domain?

One might sum up the Mediterranean as a region in which marriage is not made for the sake of kinship but rather the reverse; kinship, such as it is here, is derived from the links of marriage, which is made for love, sex, friendship, land, money, ostentation, social mobility or, like the Duke of St Simon, in order to acquire helpful relatives at court, but not in accordance with any structure of kinship. For this reason the nuclear family, the prime unit of Mediterranean society, 'the social isolate moving in a field of common values',[5] needs to be placed in a somewhat different framework from that which traditional anthropologists usually envisage for it. Let us seek this framework not within the kinship system, but within the value system of Mediterranean society and focus our attention first of all upon relations between the sexes in general before examining how they come together within the household. For the sake of exposition we start with the significance of their status as men and women before considering the consequences of their union for their relatives, for their status depends upon the recognition of certain values, vested in one sex or the other, which determine the ideals towards which they strive, the modes of conduct they adopt and the pressures that exert force in forming their conduct. Such values also lie at the basis of the interpretation of the customs of another culture. So it is not surprising if the sexual mores of the Latin peoples have often been criticised by Anglo-Saxon authors, particularly with regard to the status and treatment of women. A phrase, heavy with the tones of reprobation, 'a double standard of sexual morality', is frequently heard.[6] It is not clear what this phrase means, nor that it always has the same meaning, but it always suggests that those cultures that contain 'double standards' are somehow not morally respectable; decent English-speaking people, it is implied, have single standards. The contexts in which this phrase occurs show it to have two alternative senses: in the first case the 'double standard' refers to different standards for *ego* and for *alter*. Here it attaches to the fact that a man may think it perfectly right to seduce someone else's wife or daughter, yet think it very immoral if someone else seduces his. (This inconsistency of conduct and opinion has been exploited by dramatic authors over and over again.)[7] Such a man is applying a double standard, one for himself and a different one for others. In the second case the 'double standard' refers to the fact that different standards of conduct are demanded of men and women.

Taking the first meaning first: if this is a double standard then there are double standards wherever there is competition and rivalry. In this case there is competition for the favours of women because they are a source of prestige as well as of personal satisfaction and the competition is only keener if the rarity of these favours is ensured by the value attached to female purity. (The special glamour accorded by seventeenth-century gallants to the seduction of nuns surely derives from this scarcity-value among other things.) But one might as well talk about a double standard wherever a man would like to buy at a lower price than he would be prepared to accept and sell at a higher price than he would be prepared to give. If double economic standards were disallowed it would be the end of commerce just as the phrase, applied to sexual morality, condemns promiscuity altogether. I would not wish to be thought to be opposed to marital fidelity nor to prenuptial virginity, nor to sexual freedom for both sexes either, nor blind to the arcadian charms of the subsistence economy, my objection is only against the use of this phrase, for it expresses no more than the attitude of the speaker towards the values of an alien culture. The difference of values between the Mediterraneans and the heirs to the Puritan Revolution is founded upon different conceptions of honour, which differ as to whether men should or should not compete for the favours of women, whether, i.e. their honour is inflated or defiled by obtaining the favours of women over whom they have no rights. The Puritans believed that women should be distributed equally in accordance with the Christian ideal of monogamy, and so does the Catholic Church, but in the Catholic countries of the Mediterranean, as we know from the remarkable proliferation of dramatic works on the theme of Don Juan, this ideal has not gone unchallenged at the profane level. The kind of honour attaching to personal preeminence and the possession of women runs counter to the Christian ideal. Yet be it noted that both codes accept the same initial premise: that, whether honourably or not, men *do* compete for the favours of women. Women do not compete, at least overtly, for the favours of men but for their protection.

The second sense of the 'double standard' is also based upon a premise of moral equality, but this time it is not among men, but between men and women. It condemns the view that sexual promiscuity is a prerogative of the male sex, and that a woman should be heavily penalised for doing what would be a moral peccadillo and a source of prestige if she were a man. (The legal codes of several Mediterranean countries are founded upon this premise which is evident in their definition of adultery.) In fact there is no society in which the status of a man and a woman are identical, nor could there be, given the physical division of labour. Hence whatever may be said in favour of or against the traditional mores of the Mediterranean, it is not the fact that the standard is 'double' that is at fault, since all standards of sexual morality are double in this sense. Moral unisex has yet to come.

I believe a more satisfactory way to view this problem is this: every society differentiates between masculine and feminine roles. These are not unconnected with physical differences though they are not to be attributed uniquely to them. Even in the economic division of labour which places certain tasks in the hands of women and others in those of men, only a few are clearly determined by physical factors: apart from the nursing and care of children, obviously a female task, and certain masculine tasks requiring physical strength and weight, most attributions of role are to be explained by social consideration.

In fact the social division of labour between the sexes was thought to be 'natural' and therefore incontrovertible everywhere until the present age, no matter how it differed from place to place, because it related to the basic unquestioned concepts of male and female nature. This aspect of social differentiation I call the '*moral* division of labour', for it determines the way in which moral qualities are distributed between the sexes and hence what behaviour is regarded as proper or conceivable for each. The moral division of labour provides, as it were, the cultural premises on which each social structure is founded. The distribution of authority is obviously related to the different spheres regarded as the preserve of one sex or the other, but powers of a more occult nature are equally specific as to sex in many societies. Hence, in some, witchcraft is uniquely a male attribute, in others it is uniquely female. In some it is indifferently one or the other and in others yet again certain forms of supernatural power are credited to men while others are thought to be vested in women.

The Abelam of New Guinea studied by Forge[8] are a case in point but I might equally cite as an example the Andalusia where I worked myself. Here the distinction in powers relates clearly to the moral division of labour which is visible in every context, and especially in those where the physical person, the human body, is the centre of attention. Thus methods of curing are clearly defined as to sex; those employing practical techniques and acquired skill, the bone-setters and manipulators, are always men. Those requiring *natural* knowledge, herbalists, are indifferently men or women, while all magical cures are effectuated by women since they depend upon the quality of 'grace' which is a female attribute uniquely. This moral division of labour is reproduced, as one might expect, in the realms of witchcraft. Men bewitch by using a book of magic and invoking thereby the Devil, evil spirits and poltergeists, to effect their ends. The phrase is to 'read for somebody' and this is done from a distance, usually from another village. Female witchcraft operates in quite another way; through, as it were, a negative use of grace assisted by charms and spells which are not written down. And in the realms of magic, menstruation plays a large part, and the evil eye is here a uniquely female attribute which is not the case in some other parts of the Mediterranean. On the other hand, another mysterious source of evil, the *roba-niños*, or baby-stealer, is always a man, for he is thought to be natural, not supernatural, and to come always from a distance. The distinction elaborated by Mary Douglas between witchcraft from inside and witchcraft from outside[9] might seem applicable here, though I cannot see how 'the accusation reaffirms group boundaries and solidarity' when it is directed outside nor when it is aimed within does it bear any relation to factions, but it is certainly the case, as she suggested,[10] that the distinction between male and female witchcraft 'enters into the definition of the sexes'. If 'reading for somebody' is always done from another community it is also true that it is commonly done against a cousin towards whom jealousy is felt on account of shared inheritance and if it is always done by a man the victim was, in the several cases recorded, always a woman. Moreover female witchcraft and magic were often directed against men. The distinction appears to correspond to the role of the sexes in relation to the inside or outside of the community, for the values of contiguity on which the community as a moral entity depends are represented by the women who remain in the town (while the men go out to work for the most part) and who constitute the network of gossip; on the other hand the political and legal system is wielded by men who are associated with power emanating

from outside and 'above'; men operate by virtue of their relationship to
the world outside the community while women derive their power from
the world within, that is to say, from within the house or even within
their bodies. The written word is associated with state education and
legal documents and newspapers from the city containing news about
other places; moreover books, including books of magic, are bought in
the city. But the female witch keeps her charms locked in a cupboard in
the depths of her house and female power for evil as for good emanates
from within the female body: her eye and her sexuality are potential
sources of danger and if a woman cures she does so by virtue of 'the
grace in her hand' and the orations which she knows by heart, that is to
say, 'the grace in her tongue'. When she cures she draws the pain into
her own body and suffers it herself for several hours. This dichotomy
with regard to witchcraft and curing does no more, then, than reflect the
domestic division of labour which defines the interior of the house as the
sphere of women and all that is exterior to the house as that of men.[11]
One might sum the matter up by saying as has been said before[12] that
the sphere of culture is in the hands of men and that of nature in the
hands of women.

The family is the smallest social unit to contain members of both
sexes and must by definition contain them. Hence we find them differentiated here in starkest contrast. Their moral attributes like their
physiologies are complementary. It is also here that we find the other
basic social category which is morally differentiated: age. The household therefore contains all the elements of the moral division of labour
which is realised at the level of that unit in the first place. The conduct
expected of a person depends upon his sex and age and the norms
applicable to the different categories of sex and age are common to the
society as a whole, however they may be qualified in extra-familial contexts by considerations of occupation, social status or the nature of the
occasion. The shared intimacy of the household and mutual dependency
within it provide, at the same time, the internal bonds that are represented in relation to the exterior as common interests and a common
identity and reputation.

This unity is expressed in the notion of a common honour which
draws together the disparate criteria of evaluation proceeding from the
moral division of labour. Honour therefore is not a single value but a
complex of values united at the level of social relations rather than at the
conceptual level of ethics.

There is a general similarity in this regard throughout the Mediterranean, but there is also a considerable degree of variation in the
circumstances surrounding the notion of honour and even in the notion

itself, according to the ethnographic area. Variations are found in Andalusia between the rural and urban milieu and between different social classes, but here I am concerned rather with the similarities and with possible explanations of their common foundation. This resides in the fact that, in contrast to many other codes of honour including that of modern northern Europe – and perhaps ancient northern Europe also – men are responsible for the honour of their women which is associated with sexual purity and their own honour derives in large measure from the way they discharge this responsibility.

There is a near-paradox in the fact that while honour is a collective attribute shared by the nuclear family it is also personal and dependent upon the will of the individual; individual honour derives from individual conduct but produces consequences for others who share collective honour with this individual. The moral differentiation already referred to relates, of course, to the practical differentiation of function within the family, so that different standards of conduct are enjoined according to sex and age and these are complementary as the active and passive manifestations of the same principle: fortitude in young men and sexual shame in young women are the moral qualities of greatest significance in this regard and they become somewhat less so with advancing age. But they are combined in the global concept of honour attaching to the whole family which derives in different ways from the conduct of different members. The preoccupation with the sexual purity of women and its protection relates to the belief in the transmission of moral qualities through physical inheritance. Lack of chastity in women places in jeopardy the family honour accumulated by forbears, whereas in men it destroys the honour of *other* families. Once more it may be said that male honour faces the outside, female honour the inside or that male honour is aggressive, female honour vulnerable. These conceptions display the moral division of labour, but they are aspects of honour manifested by either sex rather than opposed concepts of honour, for they are united in the family honour of which they are the external and internal facets. As such they imply each other in the sense that female honour undefended can be taken not to exist while in its absence male honour cannot be transmitted. I have named these facets honour = precedence and honour = virtue, though I might more simply, if less precisely, have called them 'social honour' and 'ethical honour'.

Each nuclear family possesses both and it is thought that they are or ought to be associated even if in the individual instance they appear not to be, for honour in the end depends upon being able to impose a claim to it, so that the sanctions deriving from the moral judgements of the communityare not exerted against those whose power places them above a concern for their reputation in its eyes. On the other hand those who cannot claim such invulnerability are liable to suffer in their social standing from the stigma of dishonour conveyed by their womenfolk. Conversely, those families of least precedence in the community, those to whom no respect is due, are denied all reputation for virtue and their women, regardless of their actual conduct, get no credit for purity, nor is the defilement of their sexual honour regarded as a serious offence to their menfolk. It is as though they were deemed to have lost nothing since they had nothing to lose. Hence however different the referents by which male and female honour are established in terms of individual conduct they are amalgamated in the nuclear family to which the individuals belong, producing a unitary judgement which applies to all its members. This was explained in chapter two.

The distinction is recognised however in the rules that govern the transmission of honour from one generation to the next: the aspect of honour relating to social position descends through the male line in preference to the female and honour deriving from sexual shame is transmitted by females. This is only to be expected, since the quality associated with the other sex cannot be displayed in the conduct expected of a person or it receives a negative evaluation, but a man's sexual promiscuity, though it may be deplored, does not contaminate his family's honour any more than a woman's lack of fortitude. In each marriage therefore, two different strains of honour come together in order to provide the honour of the nuclear family thus formed. The sexual purity of the women is protected politically by the men. Men think themselves responsible for the behaviour of their women because this is where the essence of *their* moral honour resides and moral honour is the essence of honour because it is connected with the sacred in a way that political and social honour are not. This is clearly visible in a fact which would otherwise appear anomalous: that the gravest insults that can be addressed to a man refer not to himself at all but to his female kin, especially his mother, also his sister, and, in a somewhat different way, his wife. It is as though honour outside the house were to some extent exonerated from moral obligations which remain the preserve of the inner or feminine aspect of life and are therefore to be discovered only in the conduct of women. Hence men claim authority over their wives, daughters and sisters, requiring of them moral qualities which they do not expect of themselves – after all, a man cannot afford to have too fine a moral conscience or he would not be able to meet his obligations to his family in the struggle for existence, but a woman having no such responsibilities, can be the epitome of moral worth. Moreover sacred values centre in the house over which she reigns. Campbell speaks of it as a 'sanctuary' and stresses the sacred associations of the house and women in contrast to the profane associations of men.[13] For this reason also women are expected to be more assiduous in their religious duties than a man. A woman's place is in the home or in the church, where it is felt moreover the honour of the family will be safe. Hence finally women are thought to be 'inferior' to men in many ways but superior in certain others, those connected with the sacred and with the values of the heart.

'Men are all shameless' (i.e. dishonourable) women sometimes say, emphasising the concept of female honour and men are sometimes prepared jokingly to concede the point, for they know that the women's view is not the whole story. But they are quite sincere when they concede the ethical and emotional superiority of women, an attitude explicit in their attachment to their mother, their adoration of the Holy Virgin, and the way they speak about their parents: the mother is always thought to have been good, but the moral qualities of the father are seldom mentioned.

On account of this division of labour men, though they are the focus of authority within the family, are forced to give way to their women in certain situations. Feminine power is not overt, but, due to their participation in the familial honour (as the repositories of its moral and sacred aspects) women hold in their hands the power not merely to put pressure on their menfolk but actually to 'ruin' them. The fear of female sexuality which inspires much of Europe's popular literature and beliefs runs parallel to a much more realistic fear of female sociability. It is only too easy to understand then that men, conscious and resentful of their vulnerability through the actions of their womenfolk, should be eager to credit them with the faults of character that are, however ill-founded, commonplace in the literature of the Mediterranean, faults which justify their exclusion from the political sphere and the authority of their menfolk over them. This is the cultural justification for what has been called the 'double standard' and its internal logic.

Only in widowhood do women attain any position of overt power and this is not uniformly the case throughout the Mediterranean. Yet they do, at least on the European shore, accede to a position of authority over their children once their husband is gone. The authoritarian Spanish widow, once past the age of child-bearing, like certain hen birds of the pheasant family who in old age put on the plumage of the cock, becomes tougher in business than ever her husband was and keeps all the male members of her family trembling. It is curious to observe how many businesses in Spain are entitled 'vidua de . . .' (widow of so and so). They are much more numerous than in France where Veuve Clicquot almost alone keeps the standard of matriarchy flying, but there appears to be no English equivalent at all. Moreover this disparity cannot be attributed simply to the disappearance in England of the petty businesses that are a widow's only recourse, as might be suggested, for the Spanish businesses which bear that title are frequently very considerable and include a famous ranch of fighting bulls. Nor have I ever heard it commented on humorously that this supreme symbolic representation of masculinity should belong to a widow. The implication of the anomaly passes unrecognised.

Once past the age of sexual activity women are no longer a threat to the honour of their menfolk and at the same time they enjoy the deference which is due to age as well as the attachment and esteem of their children whose honour is owed to them. They become therefore in a sense surrogate males. This is not the only sense in which it is possible for them to become so, for in law the status of household head, *vecino*, devolves upon a woman in default of an adult male member. Thus a widow with no grown-up son living in the house possesses a masculine legal status.

There is, moreover, a strong likelihood that a woman will end her life as a widow since the life expectancy of women is greater than of men and women are on average several years younger than their spouse. As age reduces the energy and activity of the husband he is likely to depend increasingly upon his wife and often she has come to assume command of the family affairs before she has been widowed, so that widowhood brings no more than formal recognition to a situation that already exists. This development is not confined to any particular class, though one might expect it to apply particularly in the case of the peasants, whose women, in contrast to the middle classes, always enjoy a greater degree of responsibility for the financial direction of the family unit. But it is equally the case in the middle and upper classes who furnished even more spectacular examples of matriarchy among those that I recorded in my field notes. The prevalence of widows in that period was perhaps exceptional in that the end of the civil war some ten years earlier had left a much larger number than would otherwise have been the case and had also provided conditions in which only too many had been forced to recognise the necessity for struggle in order to survive, but there is no doubt that in assuming male prerogatives they were merely conforming to a more ancient tradition already recorded in the novels of Benito Perez Galdos, of which *Tristana* is the best-known example.

The widow as a surrogate male does not have it all her own way. The respect owed her by her children ensures their obedience and support, but her authority is often resented by other men who are subject to it, who commonly believe that a woman is not competent to exercise powers of command. Those employed upon agricultural properties owned and exploited by women were quick to point to the failings of their employers and if the olive orchard is said to be the ideal property for a widow it is because it supposedly requires very little direction. In fact I found little objective evidence to support the thesis that properties directed by women were less well run than those directed by men either as agricultural exploitations, commercial enterprises or peasant holdings. But men seem to be troubled and resentful at the political power of old women and I take this sentiment to be responsible for the extraordinary reputation for sexual rapacity which is accorded to widows in many Andalusian villages. It is a matter of popular consensus that women uncontrolled by men will throw caution to the winds and indulge in the most abandoned love-affairs; no matter how improbable on account of her age, the widow, it is thought, is likely to take on the predatory male attitude towards sexual promiscuity. I have often been astounded by the amatory conquests credited to septuagenarian peasant ladies. There was not one who employed a man upon her farm who was not thought to have taken him on as a lover and this popular belief clearly added to the resentment that men felt at being thus employed, since it reflected discreditably upon their honour in making them subject sexually to a woman, i.e. not the one who mounts ('pisar', literally to tread on) but the one who is mounted. In crediting such an appetite and proficiency in this regard to widows, popular gossip is of course reproducing the syndrome of the witch, who is pictured as a woman usually elderly, ideally a widow, endowed with male symbolic attributes and with a predatory sexual attitude. The witch is a woman who has become a man thanks to her occult powers and she inverts the basic premise of society, which is the moral division of labour. The broomstick upon which she rides, normally a symbol of her female domestic role, becomes once she sits astride it leaving the house the most impressively male symbol imaginable. While she uses the broom in her house for domestic purposes she holds it with the handle towards her body, but mounted astride it her relation to it is inverted: the stick protrudes from her loins and the hairy head of the broom occupies a position in relation to her person that corresponds in the male to that repository of the mystical force of masculinity, *cojones*. By inverting her relationship to her broom she becomes in her moral attributes supremely male; her place within the moral division of labour has become inverted, and stripped of female honour she has become male.

The explanation given for the prevalence of widows among the ranks of the witches in the sixteenth century, viz. that they were indigent and therefore a threat to the moral conscience of the community which salved its feeling of guilt in that regard by accusing them of magical malpractice,[14] is not invalidated by this point, but only weakened to the extent that a more direct explanation may be offered where this interpretation of widowhood holds. The frequency with which widows were accused of witchcraft is then related to the fact that they were widows by, as it were, a mechanical connection – they were witches because they were widows – rather than by a statistical connection deriving from the circumstance that, having no man to support them they *tended* to be indigent. In fact those accused of witchcraft were not always either widows or indigent or both, but they appear to me, from an admittedly inadequate knowledge of the sources, to be usually women who have in some way escaped from proper male authority. If this is indeed the case then perhaps they resembled the witches of modern Andalusia who, if they are not always widows, are commonly credited with making their husbands mad or stupid or impotent or at least blind to their nefarious or adulterine activities, that is to say, with dominating them. This explanation clearly could not account for accusations of witchcraft levelled at men, but it is not clear to me that the maleficent activities of men were of the same order save in the imagination of the witch-hunters who did not necessarily understand any more about the peasant's beliefs than do the middle classes of today. If not the dominated accomplice of their wife with whom they were accused, it is possible that they may have been, as in modern Andalusia, malefactors of a different nature. MacFarlane's observation that in sixteenth-century Essex men were accused of divination rather than maleficence leans at any rate in that direction, but the difficulty of controlling the *origins* of the witchcraft accusations of the past when the only records are those conserved by the courts who subscribed to a different theory of witchcraft than the populace is such that it may be well nigh impossible to establish to what extent the popular beliefs of sixteenth-century England resembled, if at all, those of the modern Mediterranean. My speculations in that regard claim only to suggest that the vexed problem of the sex of the witch is not to be resolved without regard for the moral attributes of the sexes as such.

II

Moral values are best examined through the sanctions that operate against their violation and honour is most clearly defined at the moment when it is lost. The Spanish literary tradition repeats *ad nauseam* that honour is like glass – once broken it cannot be mended – and the folklore justifies this view by celebrating not honour but the lapse from honour. The sanctions of popular opinion are manifest in a number of customs which all aim to commemorate the dishonour of an offender against its code: the songs of carnival, the *cencerrada* (charivari) which also involved the composition and singing of offensive songs under the window of the victim, but above all the nickname.[15]

The nickname represents the honourable standing of a member of the community. Like the attribution of an animal spirit in Central America it portrays an individual's social personality, but unlike the animal spirit and unlike the nickname of more northerly regions,[16] it is not purely individual but frequently attaches to a whole household whose common identity and honour are expressed in it. In this way it comes to be transmitted via the children to future generations, so that it can define a person either as himself on account of his individual characteristics or as the offspring of a given family. One can distinguish then first of all between individual and collective nicknames.

The nickname is always in origin an individual creation. The rules governing its attribution are not formulated by the people themselves but are dependent upon popular fancy. 'Dice la gente "el Panadero", "el Panadero", "el Panadero" y se le pega' – (People say 'the Baker', 'the Baker', 'the Baker' and it sticks). Then they start calling the children 'los Panaderos'. Yet it is possible to discover by observation the principles which govern its bestowal. It is owed first of all to some personal quality which serves to mark a person in the eyes of public opinion: his place of birth or residence, his occupation or some detail of his physical appearance or some eccentricity of behaviour. As a description it serves to identify him in a community where surnames are not used by anyone save in official communications and are known for the most part only to recognised kin. But it does more than distinguish an individual from others, it typifies him.

When a person is an immigrant to the community his town of origin is almost certain to provide him with his nickname. Place of birth possesses a mystical and legal importance in the lands of the *jus soli*. His nature derives from his birth-place and he remains always a son of his natal township, a notion evident in the usage of the word '*naturaleza*' to mean place of birth. But, at a more practical level, in a land where municipal communities are distinguished by their style of speech, accent and vocabulary, a man's place of origin is normally apparent in his speech. Within the community birth on an outlying farm, or even residence there at a subsequent date, may also provide him with a nickname. The great majority of the population lives in a town however and within the urban conclave the commonest form of nickname relates to occupation so that it is hard to say when the Baker is being referred to by a simple description and when by his nickname. The nickname may be used by itself but it may also be appended to the Christian name so that one might surmise that in the latter case it is thought of as an appellation rather than as a description, while when used alone it may refer to the social function rather than the man. Such a surmise is all the more reasonable if the baker in question happens to have another nickname by which he is more commonly known.

The distinction between category noun and proper name which has so often preoccupied philosophers is difficult to make in this case for every nickname starts as a descriptive device qualifying a Christian name and remains, if it succeeds in passing on to the next generation, as a dynastic attribute classifying the bearer not according to his own characteristics but to those of a forebear whose social personality was once epitomised in this fashion. When the Baker no longer bakes but cobbles and the Cobbler bakes the nickname has moved from description to nomination, from the individual to the collective form and its point of reference from the present to the past. Nor is there any surprise in this transition for those who recall *The Savage Mind* of Claude Lévi-Strauss, whose fifth chapter discusses with the perception and subtlety to which we are accustomed precisely how proper names can become common nouns and vice versa. Lévi-Strauss concludes[17] that there is no fundamental difference between the two, but rather that proper names lie upon the margin of classificatory systems, marking their limits, but ready to augment or diminish their semantic load as the circumstances require. The Andalusian nickname loses its semantic load as the circumstances in which it was invented recede into the past – and a small number had become so completely separated from their origin that no one could provide any explanation of them. But something remains to be said about the social significance of those circumstances in connection with the loss and transmission of honour.

Nicknames derived from occupation indicate little with regard to honour save in so far as it is connected with social status. Nevertheless some occupations are regarded as less honourable than others, even if not as unequivocally as in the days of Don Alfonso the Wise whose *Siete Partidas* list the occupations classed as dishonourable. In particular those practised by gypsies (who are regarded as totally without honour) can be opposed to the 'honest hard work' that gypsies refuse to do whether it takes the form of wage-labour or agricultural exploitation. Employment as a shepherd is not in itself dishonourable, though it implies poverty and lack of refinement on account of its association with the wilds, but the prolonged absence from the pueblo which it entails lays the shepherds open to suspicions as regards their marital honour.

Nicknames derived from physical characteristics are more aggressively disrespectful, since the individual is not classed, but singled out as an object of comment and submitted to the judgement of others – 'it's rude to pass personal remarks', as we were told as children, and such nicknames are rude for the same reason. In fact such nicknames almost always characterise a person by some physical *defect* which is not shared by the rest of humanity such as lameness, baldness, blindness, squinting, ugliness, toothlessness, shortness or tallness. It is referred to either directly or by analogy or implication and very frequently, in sarcasm, by its contrary. The possibility of using satire, mockery or condemnation increase enormously once the nickname applies to an individual rather than a class of persons and those which refer not to his appearance but to his characteristics of speech by imitating them are clearly a form of mockery. Thus the nickname 'el Gorrino' (the Piglet) was said to derive from a forebear who was accustomed to say slapping his stomach when he had eaten well 'ya me he puesto como un gorrino' (I've guzzled like a piglet) and other figures of speech have been used in the same fashion to provide nicknames. The mockery is evident in those nicknames that chastise social pretensions: the King, the Count, the Marquesita, etc.

Much more damaging yet to reputation are those nicknames which refer to moral character. They do so by commemorating events which reflect discreditably upon the honour of the participant. A long list takes us from comparatively innocuous commentary to the celebration of drunkenness, physical incontinence, cheating, prostitution, cuckoldry, sexual looseness, masturbation, bestiality. I will spare the reader the ethnographical detail.

The majority of people enjoy harmless nicknames and in default of any striking characteristic and any lapse from grace which might define them as themselves they are defined by their family of origin. The nickname received by a child when it was too young to have any identity other than as its parents' offspring is retained afterwards for life and transmitted in due course to the grandchildren, so that in certain cases a nickname is shared by people so distantly related that they no longer recognise that they are kin. From this we can see that the holders of a common nickname are not in any sense a group but are connected only by the fortuitous retention of the same nickname in a series of individual links constituted by a succession of nuclear families, that is to say, by the same process of transmission as honour. At this point it is possible to explain the apparent anomaly in the comparison with the animal spirits of Central America which are uniquely individual and are not transmitted to children even though the society is dominated by the notion of descent groups. Both animal spirit and nickname depict the social personality of the individual holder, but whereas the animal spirit is purely individual and relates to spiritual power in the celestial realm, here there are no descent groups and the nickname refers to social standing in *this* world where it proliferates attaching individuals to the past by means of no general principle of grouping but thanks to the contribution made to social standing by descent among people who are profoundly individualist in that they recognise no common identity beyond the nuclear family.

In fact I was able to observe that the holders of such common nicknames were amongst the most traditional and conventionally-minded persons and if they had inherited their nickname from so long ago (as is implied by its multiplication) it was because their ascendants in the intervening generations had given no occasion for the creation of a new one. This explanation is confirmed by the observation that the two largest nickname classes, the 'Condes' and the 'Gorrinos' which each numbered about fifty people were all very much of the same kind, small tenant or owner farmers of roughly similar status. In a few instances a person bearing such a traditional nickname had acquired an individual appellation subsequently. Thus José-Maria el Conde was generally known as Tío Bigote but since his children were already grown-up and living elsewhere when he grew the moustache which gave rise to this nickname they continued as Conde. I surmise that had he acquired such a nickname earlier (and it would not then have been prefixed with Tio which means uncle or old fellow) he might well have founded a new dynasty of '*los Bigote*' and their connection with the Condes would subsequently be lost. For a nickname tends to apply to the whole household. This is usually, but not always, the husband's but where the wife is the more imposing character she may furnish the children with their identity. She usually retains her natal nickname or she may acquire a personal one without transmitting it or she may be referred to by it when thought of apart from her family and included in the collective nickname when regarded as a member of the household or she may be called the wife of a man named by his nickname, e.g. 'Isabel la del Choro'. People sometimes acquire a supplementary nickname which co-exists with a dynastic nickname. Which one is used on what occasion depends in part upon the generation of the speaker or on the degree of contempt or friendliness felt towards the person in question. The niece of a man called 'el Peo' (the fart) assured me that his nickname was really 'el Sacristán' which was clearly much more complimentary.

The most derisive and obscene nicknames remain purely individual and are not transmitted to any other members of the household who possess, as it were, enough standing in their own right to be distinguished from their parent who earned the opprobrious epithet. Yet this does not mean that it does not affect the honourable standing of the whole family, for in order to humiliate them it can be recalled obliquely in such a way as to bring to mind, without explicitly referring to it, the incident that provided the damaging appellation. The body of nicknames therefore furnished the armoury of weapons available to the community in the daily encounters in which the honour of a household is impugned or modified. It is precisely because honour is established through such encounters that the powerful are able to translate their power into honour. For who will speak dishonourably about a person whose patronage they hoped for or whose ill-will they have reason to fear? The masks of carnival concealed the identity of the singers but carnival was disallowed by the government following the civil war.

The fact that a nickname is given merely by popular consent leaves the system open to adaptation. The nickname of a family changes with its honourable status. A fresh event that fires the public fancy is soon celebrated by the invention of a new nickname which attaches at first to the individual but may subsequently be extended to his household if it is decided to place them all in the same boat. The system in any case offers here a choice in that a nuclear family is formed by the marriage of two persons who have each a nickname. There is always therefore some doubt as to which will be passed on to the children. Now it is significant that in some cases the nickname is transmitted bilineally: that of the mother passes to the daughters, that of the father to the sons. This is not because the nickname is itself necessarily masculine or feminine, for a version can always be adapted to serve for the other sex. Thus Señor Pedro 'Zarzales' (brambles) gave his name to his descendants and his daughter was called la Zarzala which does not exist in Spanish and 'la Parrala' (the flirt) gave hers to her sons who were called 'los Parralos'. From the moment that a nickname has gained established currency it becomes detached from its origin and leads a life of its own. Thus the female members of the dynasty of los Condes (the counts) were not called la Condesa as in Spanish (as everyone perfectly well knew) but la Conda, that is to say they were not thought of as countesses but as daughters of a man called 'el Conde'. The semantic content is emptied by the fact that the word has become a proper name; through habitual usage nicknames are in Lévi-Strauss' phrase 'partially freed of their signifying function' and able to become, despite their derogatory sense of origin, something to be proud of. Once imbued with the sacredness of tradition, they become honorific like the names of the British political parties Tory and Whig. One might say then of the nickname which starts as an expression of contempt that familiarity breeds respect.

If the most violently obscene nicknames cannot be transmitted it is, I suggest, because they cannot be stripped of their signifying function. For the converse reason the nickname presents no problem in regard to the sex of the person by whom a nickname is inherited, for once this happens it no longer signifies an object of specific sex but simply membership of a given household. However, as has been said, the kind of honour transmitted through the male or female links is different and it seems therefore more appropriate to associate a woman with her mother than with her father, since the honorific qualities expected of her are feminine ones, and vice versa. Yet be it noted that this is the exception rather than the rule and that just as people inherit a component of their honour from both parents so they can inherit the nickname of either.

The usage of a nickname is disrespectful in itself and therefore it cannot with decorum be mentioned in the presence of its owner who is supposed to ignore it. There are however a few individuals who are openly addressed by their nicknames and this is because they are recognisedly shameless, moral outcasts to whom no respect is due under any circumstances. Nicknames are however sometimes shouted among young people in the street within earshot of the owner somewhat in the spirit of carnival. The owner is expected to turn a deaf ear refusing to recognise whom it refers to. A person humiliates himself by admitting that he knows he has a nickname. In this the mores of the pueblo differ from the usage of the bull-ring and the flamenco stage whose champions, frequently gypsy, are announced under the title of a nickname such as 'Gitanillo el de Triana' or 'Manitas de Plata'. It is worth recalling that 'those who fight with wild beasts for money' were among the statutorily infamous in the *Siete Partidas* and that stage performers were so regarded throughout Europe until much more recently.

In the analysis of the nickname we find a plan of the dimensions of honour in the community which are individual, collective or hereditary in varying degrees and according to circumstances. They could best be assessed perhaps – if measurement were possible – in the amount of respect accorded by popular opinion to a person, but it should be stressed that it is *popular* opinion in every sense of the phrase, i.e. both specific to a community and also plebeian: every system of nicknames is particular to a given place and it does not include the summer visitors, nor professional visitors nor the upper class who are known only by their profession if they have one. Disrespect also implies a certain intimacy (as we know from the usage of terms of disrespect to express affection) and such people are felt to be too distant to be granted a nickname. A person loses his nickname when he leaves his natal community and is almost certain to be known elsewhere only by his community of origin. It is therefore something of a tribute to the force of personality of the mother who bestowed her nickname 'la Parrala' on her sons that she should have earned it in the first place, since the whole family was from a nearby town and had up till that time borne the collective nickname of their native pueblo.

My interest in the subject of nicknames inevitably encountered the barrier of discretion and I sometimes caused embarrassment in asking people to discuss with me an institution thought by many to be uncouth. Within the plebeian community this was not hard to overcome, since to begin with there was no way to identify people other than by their nicknames. But I was surprised by the violence of the reaction of some members of the middle class who explained to me that the nickname was the shame of Spain which would not escape from barbarism until it were stamped out. This attitude might be thought to relate to their personal sufferings at the hands of popular satire, yet as has been stated such people were given no nicknames. This hostility is to be attributed rather to the feeling that in the nickname the pueblo expresses its aspirations to autonomy by judging people and events by its own lights and ignoring the standards of decorum of the middle class and the laws of the state. As such it preserves the moral independence of the popular community against the culture of the middle classes who sense in it a challenge to their authority. It is inspired by the same spirit as the anarchism which flourished here for fifty years prior to the Civil War, and though this observation was never made to me, it is perhaps significant that the anarchist leaders in the village are remembered only by their nicknames.

Since honour is hereditary as well as earned and hereditary in both lines, it comes to bear its full weight in the determination of marriage which may be viewed here rather than as an exchange of women, as a fusion of the honour of two nuclear families from which the honourable status of their grandchildren is derived. Hence, unlike marriage within elementary structures which is decided according to rules of kinship, Mediterranean marriage is determined by a market principle involving evaluation rather than prescription and evaluated in terms of the competitive aspect of honour: the parties to the marriage should be equal in honour if one or other is not to be deemed to have made a regrettable choice. A 'bad' marriage, that is to say, one made with a spouse inferior in honour, may be better than no marriage at all, but it is still regrettable from the point of view of the grandparents whose grandchildren are inferior to them either in terms of their precedence or their virtue which, of course, depends upon the sex of the parent who is deemed inferior. When Lord Chesterfield wrote to his son that he would support as many illegitimate children as he cared to father but would never forgive him a mésalliance he was expressing a very Mediterranean point of view – as befitted an eighteenth-century nobleman – but he obviously would not have written the same thing to his daughter.

The ideal image of marriage in the pueblo where an honest and hard-working young man of honourable parents marries a girl of unstained reputation and sound stock after a courtship long enough to ensure the tenacity of the affections of both is far from adequate to cover all the marriages in an Andalusian township. The many-faceted nature of the conception of honour and the fact that its facets receive differing weighting by different social groups tempers the ideal, and since it attaches not only to virtue but to precedence – and precedence is ultimately a matter of power – one would expect the evaluation of marriage to vary according to social class, as indeed it does. Those with property are more concerned with maintaining their economic status – a statement so obvious that it would not be worth making if its implications were not so often ignored. The first implication is that a system of partible inheritance promotes endogamy among the propertied class, for if sisters take their share of the succession then wives of equal economic prospects must be found to replace them. Ultimately the perfect marriage is that between first cousins who reunite property that was divided in the parental generation, but perfect only from a financial point of view as we shall see.

Class itself is constituted of disparate criteria in which the past and the present combine so that wealth finds an honorific equivalent in descent. As much is true anywhere in western Europe where this principle provided the traditional means of integrating new fortunes into the aristocracy. In fact either established class or wealth can compensate for inadequacy of honour in the sense of virtue. At the furthest extreme the rich man's mistress, mother of an illegitimate family, feels no reason to hide her head in shame, save perhaps in relation to his legitimate family, for despite the ignominy of being an unmarried mother she enjoys the financial advantages and prestige which her man confers on her.

Honour is always connected with personal autonomy and here the notion of personal autonomy is expressed in a romantic attitude to marriage which makes it disreputable to marry for money rather than for love. Hence those who marry their cousins for the sake of property gain no esteem through doing so, if that is thought to be their motive. However much parents would like to marry their children to their sibling's children and thereby avoid the break-up of property and the dangers to their honour which, emanating from the same nuclear family, is shared, they cannot do so without the cooperation of their children who only too often have other ideas. The need for parental help financially to provide the means of setting up a home and in conducting the formalities of asking for the girl's hand in marriage is counter-balanced by the notion that arranged marriages are despised. Romanticism and prudence do not go together and parental advice is not welcome to those whose sentiment of honour is first of all centred on their emotions. Such considerations are basic to an understanding of the marriage customs of Andalusia and in particular of the conventions of courtship. The danger to a girl's honour is great while she is courted, for if she is unresponsive emotionally she will not get married, yet if she is suspected of granting the least favour she is vulnerable, since if she is then abandoned she loses her honourable status and hence her desirability as a wife for anybody else. In this quandary we find the explanation of the ideal image of courting through the *reja*, the iron bars which cover the windows, depicted on every romantic postcard, of the chaperoning of girls who must never go for a walk with a boy unaccompanied, of all the formalities of courtship, and its interminable length, and of the avoidance between the suitor and his future father-in-law who cannot recognise that his daughter is being courted until her hand in marriage has been asked for. This is not done until a few months before the marriage. However prior to this the suitor has normally been invited into the house by the girl's parents when the seriousness of his intentions has been recognised. Such an invitation is not issued lightly but only after years of assiduous courting. Before marriage the suitor is a threat to the honour of the girl's family. After marriage the responsibility for her honour passes from her father to her husband. The avoidance is then replaced by a relationship that tends to be close and even warm, for they are no longer potential enemies but committed allies whose common commitment brings them closer together than female in-laws.

The question of honour also explains the frequent elopements, for a daughter can attempt to extort the consent of unwilling parents to the marriage of her choice by compromising herself with her sweetheart as the various instances on page sixty-four showed. A suitor who is successful to the point where he has gained the girl's favours is virtually assured of her hand in marriage with all that goes with it in terms of property and social advantage. So the art of seduction ('knowing how to talk to girls') is often suspected to be used for material advantage. It is even employed on occasions for political rather than material reasons with the intention of damaging the honour of another family as in the instance of Don Juan, the destroyer of reputations – this is the basic sense of his title *burlador* – whose aspirations to self-aggrandisement were founded upon the notion that the honour you strip from others becomes yours.

In an agonistic society such as this, not only marriage but all romantic relations between the sexes have implications in the political realm even though these are seldom recognised. Thus the tenderest sentiments come together in the complex of honour with considerations of ethics, religion, prestige, economics and social preeminence to form a system of behaviour that determines the distribution and redistribution of respect among the families of which the community is composed. And this system, despite the disparate aspects that are combined in it and the contradictory assessments to which it gives rise, despite above all the apparent duality of the moral code that governs the actions of the individuals within it, can be understood only as a unitary system, for it corresponds to the dynamics of the social structure.

5 The law of hospitality

PROLOGUE

In an essay entitled *The Odyssean suitors and the host–guest relationship*[1] Professor Harry L. Levy discussed the final scene of the Odyssey and took issue with those authors who find it out of character with the spirit of the work as a whole. The apparent anomaly introduced by the unmerciful slaughter of the suitors whose faults went hardly beyond a certain absence of decorum he explained by the hypothesis of an earlier folk-tale in the peasant tradition which is evident elsewhere in the poem, he says. This is intertwined with the courtly tradition of the warrior princes which dominates the greater part. The ideal of courtly largesse is contrasted with the more material concerns of frugal farmers whose customs of hospitality contain a provision forbidding the guest to overstay his welcome and impoverish his host. Leaving to classical scholars the task of unravelling the origin of its elements, the anthropologist is entitled to take the story as it stands and attempt to relate it to what he can discover of the law of hospitality in general and of the code of hospitality of ancient Greece in particular. It appears to me that, regardless of any historical disparities in the sources from which it originated, the tale of the home-coming of Odysseus may take its place among those exemplary epics which provide us with a key to the principles of social conduct. Indeed the whole work may be viewed as a study in the law of hospitality, in other words, the problem of how to deal with strangers.

I

In one of the earliest professional monographs we have, Boas describes the custom whereby the Central Eskimo tribes receive a stranger and the curious combat to which he is then challenged:

> If a stranger unknown to the inhabitants of a settlement arrives
> on a visit he is welcomed by the celebration of a great feast.
> Among the south-eastern tribes the natives arrange themselves
> in a row, one man standing in front of it. The stranger
> approaches slowly, his arms folded and his head inclined toward
> the right side. Then the native strikes him with all his strength

on the right cheek [sic] and in his turn inclines his head awaiting the stranger's blow (*tigluiqdjung*). While this is going on the other men are playing at ball and singing (*igdlukitaqtung*). Thus they continue until one of the combatants is vanquished.

The ceremonies of greeting among the western tribes are similar to those of the eastern, but in addition 'boxing, wrestling and knife testing' are mentioned by travellers who have visited them. In Davis Strait and probably in all the other countries the game of 'hook and crook' is always played on the arrival of a stranger (*pakijumijartung*). Two men sit down on a large skin, after having stripped the upper part of their bodies, and each tries to stretch out the bent arm of the other. These games are sometimes dangerous, as the victor has the right to kill his adversary; but generally the feast ends peaceably. The ceremonies of the western tribes in greeting a stranger are much feared by their eastern neighbours and therefore intercourse is somewhat restricted. The meaning of the duel, according to the natives themselves, is 'that the two men in meeting wish to know which of them is the better man'.[2]

We can hardly suggest that such a desire to measure oneself against the stranger is peculiar to people of simple social organisation and dispersed settlements, as one might at first be tempted to imagine, for the custom in spirit if not in form, is reminiscent of the age of chivalry when knights on meeting found it necessary to test the 'valour' or 'value' of their new acquaintance, and we may therefore surmise that it springs from something fundamental in the nature of relations with strangers, such as a necessity to evaluate them in some way or other against the standards of the community.

Take the elements of the custom:

1. The feast offered to celebrate the stranger's arrival;
2. The challenge, issued to determine the stranger's worth;
3. The forms of the combat which estimate it in terms of the strength in his right arm;
4. His possible execution if he is proved inferior; and
5. The peaceful conclusion which is generally achieved, and which we may suspect to have been the intended outcome.

We are not told how often the right to execute the defeated stranger was, in fact, exerted. It is not essential that it should ever have been, for the belief that the right existed must surely have been enough to terrify the potential visitor from the East, particularly since duels inspired by vengeance also led to the execution of the loser. The existence of the right rather than the determination to exert it is all we require in order to understand the literal significance of the institution.

At the risk of appearing to throw my comparative net too wide, I would point out that the entry of an outsider into any group is commonly the occasion for an 'ordeal' of some sort, whether among British public schoolboys, freemasons or the initiates of the secret societies of Africa, but in these instances the character of the ordeal as a test of worthiness is less important than its character as an initiation rite. They might all be considered as 'rites of incorporation',[3] a variety of the rites of passage through which an old status is abandoned and a new one acquired. In this case it is the status of stranger which is lost and that of community member which is gained.

The social structure of Eskimo communities is notoriously flexible, yet it can hardly be supposed that a single occasion can admit a newcomer to full membership while he is still unacquainted with the other members of the settlement – the 'ordeal' of the British schoolboy lasts a whole year. The ordeal of the Eskimo would decide rather his right to remain, assuming he was either victorious or spared. Yet during the time he remained, what exactly would his status be? The combat enables the standing of the new member to be established within the hierarchy of prestige. From then on he is known to be a better man or not than his challenger. Unfortunately Boas tells us nothing more about the relationship which may have existed thereafter between the two men and it would be normal to assume, therefore, that it was in no way peculiar. Nevertheless, braving the bad name which speculation has rightly acquired in anthropology and on the basis of no evidence whatsoever, I should like to speculate on the relationship which subsisted between the stranger and his challenger, for such a guess would enable me to link up the Eskimo custom in this regard with that, so different in every way, of classical antiquity. The guess however does not claim to establish, but only at best to illustrate, the association between the two forms of custom which will be shown to derive from a common sociological root at a more abstract level.

Fustel de Coulanges explains that in the city of antiquity a stranger possessed no status in law nor in religion and that it was necessary for him to have a patron in order to gain the protection of the local laws and Gods. To offend the newcomer was to offend his patron since by the code of hospitality the two were allied in this way. 'L'étranger se rattachait par cet intermédiaire à la cité'.[4] The provisions of Arab hospitality are not dissimilar in this respect; indeed, in many countries similar customs are found.

In contrast to a member of the community whose status is identifiable by reference to its norms and is recognised by everyone, the stranger is incorporated only through a personal bond with an established member;

he has, as it were, no direct jural relationship with anyone else, no place within the system, no status save that of stranger (which is a kind of self-contradiction: the status of being statusless). On the other hand, in relation to his patron he possesses, however little may be known about him,[5] a clearly defined status, that of guest or client, which makes any further evaluation of him unnecessary. The status of guest therefore stands midway between that of hostile stranger and that of community member. He is incorporated practically rather than morally.

The essence of the stranger is, tautologically enough, that he is unknown. He remains potentially anything: valiant or worthless, well born, well connected, wealthy or the contrary, and since his assertions regarding himself cannot be checked, he is above all not to be trusted. For this reason the charlatan is always, must be, a stranger. In any case his social standing in his community of origin is not necessarily accepted by the people of another. For it is a matter of local pride that each community would set up its standards for itself rather than accept those which are dictated by foreigners. In this sense, every community aspires to autonomy. Therefore the status achieved in one is not directly transferable to another, nor is the status ascribed by one society necessarily recognised in another; indeed the possibility of finding an equivalent at all may very well be missing – you cannot be a Brahmin in the English countryside.[6]

The stranger therefore starts afresh as an individual insofar as he may be incorporated into the community. It must make its own evaluation of him in order to accept him. The simple logic of the Eskimo custom is apparent: lacking a wider society and a hierarchy of social status, the value of a man is no more than the literal strength in his right arm.

The problem of the treatment of the stranger includes another aspect. Does he possess the necessary knowledge of the culture of the people among whom he comes to behave correctly and make evaluations of conduct by their standards? Can he, in a word, subscribe to the rules of their culture? As a newcomer he will never know from the outset how to behave towards individual personalities, but if he knows the rules he will quickly distinguish who is who. No knowledge of persons is required of the guest who has a patron to protect him, but to fulfil the role of guest he must at least understand the conventions which relate to hospitality and which define the behaviour expected of him. Hence the distinction which the Greeks made between *Xenoi*, strangers who were nevertheless Greeks, and *Barbaroi*, outlandish foreigners who spoke another language. Franz Boas does not tell us, stranger as he was to the Eskimo, that he was obliged to wrestle with his right arm for his life and we may assume that the ceremony to which he referred was limited to other Eskimos who were practised in the art of such a combat and sensitive to the honour conveyed by a feast of walrus blubber, that is, to strangers capable of becoming incorporated, not 'barbarians'.

Let us suppose that the stranger's appearance in the community where he had neither kin nor friends constituted in itself a challenge to which the local challenger was doing in reality no more than respond in the name of his group, its self-appointed champion. He is likely therefore to be the chief or the strongest man within it, or at least one who claims to be so. It would follow that if the stranger defeats him, he is proved superior to all and this fact would entitle him to be honoured by the whole community. The precedence accorded to a guest may here be paid by everyone to recognised worth. Honour is gained by all through the visit of a superior person, since in accordance with its paradoxical nature it is gained by being paid (and lost by being denied) where it is due.[7] Moreover, it seems most improbable that the theoretical right to execute the defeated champion could be exerted where he was surrounded by his kin and the stranger was alone. On the other hand, in the instance where the stranger was defeated it seems unlikely that the right to execute him would be exerted unless he was suspected of coming with sinister covert intentions such as to avenge a blood-feud or commit a felony. Eskimos are known to change the affiliation of their community not infrequently, as Boas points out, and it hardly appears likely that this could be done only at grave mortal risk. Moreover they do not have the reputation of a bloodthirsty people who slaughter one another for glory. On the contrary their distaste for exhibitions of anger and violence has earned them the title of 'The Gentle People'. Is it not likely that this right to execute the defeated stranger existed *normally* only to be waived, establishing the fact that subsequent to his defeat, he 'owed his life' to his conqueror? The fact would surely find some social recognition in a kind of bond; when one has fought for one's life against someone, lost and been spared, one can hardly resume the relationship of mere acquaintances, especially in a society, like the Eskimo among so many others, where lives may be owed, avenged or commuted into payment. May I not infer that the defeated stranger became some kind of client to the man who had conquered him who became in this way responsible for him in the eyes of the community? Under such conditions his vanquisher would, in fact, have been literally responsible for his presence there, having preferred not to exert his theoretical right to kill him. The struggle, condemnation and pardon at the hands of his victor follow a well-known sequence of social death and rebirth into a changed status.

My guess – or is it mere phantasy? – amounts to this: the stranger who was recognised as the better man was accorded universal respect which posed no problem of his precedence within the community, whatever his subsequent relationship to his antagonist, while he who was defeated was thereafter 'attached to the community by the intermediary' of his victor. Those who know the Eskimo may have views about the the possible or probable existence of such a relationship which might conceivably, among a people so addicted to the notion of artificial kinship, have taken this form in the same way as war-captives are sometimes integrated into the lineage of their captors or as Dr Birket-Smith was adopted by his Eskimo host,[8] but my aim is not to make any contribution to their studies. The purpose of this imaginary ethnography, embroidering the solid work of Boas, is only to offer an exercise in the logic of social relations, the scales which one may practise before attempting to interpret the infinitely complex score of reality.[9]

II

We have dealt so far only with the social aspect of the problem posed by the stranger, unknown and perhaps unversed in the culture of the local community. The simplest solution of all – and one which was followed by many peoples while they were permitted to do so – was to refuse recognition to any person unable to claim an attachment of kinship with the tribe, that is, to treat the stranger simply as an outlaw who could be spoiled or destroyed with impunity. Such hostility towards him hardly requires an explanation since the threat which he represents to established norms and to the sanctioned order of society is patent, apart from any imagined dangers, natural or supernatural, which, in the absence of any knowledge of him, he may incarnate. Even when not suspect as a vampire or a child-stealer, the stranger is always potentially hostile. How then are we to explain that particular relationship, discussed by Professor Levy, between the stranger and Zeus? The idea that the chief of the Gods should choose to adopt such a disguise, that the most sacred of all should be allied to the outsider, must surely appear as something of an anomaly, especially to those who, following Malinowski, would expect to find in mythology a 'charter' for the social system. Taken at its face value the myth appears to contradict the first principle of social organisation: that every community must possess its own particular standards which are held sacred, ordained by the Gods and opposed to the customs of foreigners.

Let us examine the possible interpretations of this belief. To begin with, the stranger is also the beggar, since they both belong to the category of persons to whom hospitality is due. The fact that the God took the form of the stranger or beggar ensured the enforcement of the moral duty of hospitality upon which the free circulation of persons between Greek communities depended.[10] It may be viewed, then, as a sanction supporting a system of undifferentiated exchange: do as you would be done by; receive the stranger well so that when you travel you may be well received. Taken in this sense the myth furnishes a charter for the code of hospitality, but such a teleological explanation can hardly be held sufficient to explain the *existence* of the belief since, quite apart from any methodological strictures, a similar code of hospitality towards the stranger exists in the Arab world unsupported by any such charter and is regarded there as a *sacred* duty none the less. The notion of hospitality derives in this instance from the sacredness of the women-folk of the household.[11] Moreover, in both the Arab[12] and the Greek world, by dispensing hospitality honour was acquired within the community and allies outside it and considerations of personal advantage are thereby added to the general utility of the association between the stranger and the sacred. Yet they do not explain it. Granted the function of the association, the anomaly remains. For however convenient it may be in terms of the consequences to identify God with the stranger, whether as potentially the same person (Levy's little tradition) or as patron and client (Levy's great tradition), we can hardly suppose that a system of religious thought can be made to submit to anomalies uniquely for the sake of facilitating political and economic relations. Even the argument that the supreme God was the patron of all Greeks in opposition to local deities whose protection was geographically limited is insufficient, even were there no other objections to it, to account for the *priority* of the stranger in Zeus' favour and his connection with the sacred. In fact the stranger was not necessarily Zeus, but any God in disguise.

A more complete explanation can be deduced from a general consideration of the association between divinity and the unknown. Omniscience is a divine attribute and one which is jealously guarded. The moral lessons put forward in the Book of Genesis regarding the Tree of Knowledge or the myths of Icarus or Prometheus are quite unequivocal: the Gods possess knowledge which is forbidden to mankind and are prepared to punish any attempt to encroach upon their privilege. Their ineffability is the essence of their divinity. The esoteric character of communication with them and the mystery of their presence and their will (which follows none of the standards of human conduct) are the basis of the fear which they inspire. Once comprehended they would no longer be revered. Human knowledge desecrates by rendering known (and therefore secular) that which was mysterious (and therefore sacred), by reducing to the level of the known world that which is essentially unknowable. The character of the sacred as the inversion of the secular is implicit in all mythologies, those which define the status of the Gods or those which recount the origins of the world.[13] Both types of myth set the bounds of the mortal world and, doing so, establish the gradations of proximity to the Divine in space and in time. The mortal world is confined by an inversion of that which preceded it and that which lies beyond it. For this reason, we find Gods of foreign origin in so many parts of the world and for this reason also no prophet is accepted in his own country. In the light of this general principle the association between the God and the stranger appears generic, and the sacredness of hospitality and the honour which it confers *derive* not from any functional consequence of the belief but from the fact that the meeting with the stranger is a confrontation between the known world and the realms of mystery. The stranger belongs to the 'extra-ordinary' world, and the mystery surrounding him allies him to the sacred[14] and makes him a suitable vehicle for the apparition of the God,[15] the revelation of a mystery. Therefore, to put it in the phrasing of the popular epigram, it was not in the least odd of God to choose the Jews, but on the contrary exactly what the anthropologist should expect of Him. The ambiguity of their status, as at the same time belonging and not belonging, within the gates yet beyond the pale, and their reputation as the possessors of cryptic knowledge, the initiates of the mysteries of finance and of precious metals, made them strangers *par excellence*, perfectly endowed to be chosen both to provide the God in the beginning and to remain thereafter as his renegade kin. For this reason they were the 'sacred of the left hand' and the natural associates of the fallen angel. That these 'internalised strangers' should have served for centuries as the focus of the ambivalences of their Christian neighbours is in no way surprising; what is surprising is that psychological studies of anti-semitism should not all start with a profile of the mythological character of Jewry.

The stranger derives his danger, like his sacredness, from his membership of the 'extra-ordinary' world. If his danger is to be avoided he must either be denied admittance, chased or enticed away like evil spirits or vampires, or, if granted admittance, he must be socialised, that is to say secularised, a process which necessarily involves inversion. His transformation into the guest means therefore that, from being shunned and treated with hostility, he must be clasped to the bosom and honoured and given precedence; no longer to be suborned, he must be succoured; from being last, he must be first,[16] from being a person who can be freely insulted he becomes one who under no conditions can be disparaged. The inversion implies a transformation from hostile stranger, *hostis*, into guest, *hospes* (or *hostis*),[17] from one whose hostile intentions are assumed to one whose hostility is laid in abeyance. The word *hostis* claims therefore as its radical sense, not the obligation to reciprocal violence, but the notion of 'strangeness' which underlies this transition. The further extension to *host* is perfectly congruent, since strangeness is logically reciprocal, whether it enjoins distrust or hospitality. Both senses of the word, *l'hôte*, are conserved in French which must find other ways to distinguish between host and guest. While the behaviour enjoined by the relationship is essentially reciprocal, just as gifts are, there is a difference between reciprocal hostility and reciprocal hospitality: the first is simultaneous, the second can never be. Host and guest can at no point *within the context of a single occasion* be allowed to be equal, since equality invites rivalry. Therefore their reciprocity resides, not in an identity, but in an alteration of roles. Even the hostile hosts of the Kwakiutl observed this order. The hostility which underlies the relation of '*hôtes*' which they express so explicitly ('we fight with property')[18] can be vented, not in simultaneous combat, but (like the blows exchanged between the south eastern tribes of the Central Eskimo and their visitors) by turns. Reciprocity implies an alternation of roles, not an identity of roles. As Radcliffe-Brown saw in the case of avoidances and joking relationships, it is conflict which is prohibited; the laws of hospitality transpose the conflict to a level where hostilities are avoided.

This prohibition of the equality which leads to conflict applies to the beggar as well as to the guest, the one who cannot pay and the one who is not permitted to do so – is not a beggar simply one who aspires to be a guest? But if he aspires too assiduously, then his insistence implies a threat and at that point the host is liberated of all moral duty and instead of gaining honour by his charity he loses it through submitting to duress, for freedom of will is the first condition of honour.[19] Therefore the claim of the beggar is paradoxically one which is lost if it is asserted as a right and from the moment it loses its character as suppliance, it invites hostility. By pressing his claim too hard the would-be guest destroys its basis and falls back into the role of hostile stranger.[20] By asserting his rights he denies his status, for even though a diffuse obligation exists towards the beggar, he is not endowed with any corresponding right. He establishes his status by humiliating himself in the admission of indigence and the reciprocity which he concedes in return is on behalf of God. The customs regarding begging in Andalusia may be taken to illustrate the matter. The beggar establishes his status by the demand for assistance in the name of God (*por Dios*). Once gratified he replies: '*Dios se lo pague*' (May God repay you). 'May God repay you' means 'Because I cannot'. Here the association between the beggar and the Deity takes on a subsidiary meaning: the axis of exchange is no longer on the mortal plane. Repayment will only be made in Heaven; there will be none on Earth. The beggar is so to speak trading in the name of God, under His protection. The name by which he is known, *pordiosero*, rubs in the point. The refusal of alms is traditionally made in a formal phrase which carries the same import: '*Vd. perdone por Dios, hermano*' (Excuse me, in God's name, Brother). The refusal to lay up store in Heaven and assume on Earth the honorific role of patron to the beggar, includes the assertion of equality with him ('brother'), since inability to do so is the only excuse for refusal valid in the eyes of God. An alternative form, '*Dios le ampare, hermano*' (May God protect you, Brother) carries the same implication: 'Because I am not going to.'

To beg is always and everywhere shameful for it implies a loss of personal autonomy which is the negation of honour. Hence those who are reduced to this expedient are regarded as the lowest and treated with the least respect of all the members of a community.[21] This is not the case however, when they have sacerdotal status, for then they have not been 'reduced to begging'; their personal autonomy has been, not lost, but wilfully renounced. A vow of poverty derives from the will and commits it; it is not the same thing as the failed aspiration to affluence. We should recognise therefore that the action of begging does not suffice by itself to define the status of a beggar; the moral basis on which the begging is undertaken must be considered. Every town in Andalusia possesses a certain number of habitual beggars. These are known persons rather than strangers and they prey upon the local population. A certain number are gypsies whose reputation for shamelessness fits them for the role of beggar. Such beggars adopt a style which makes their loss of all claim to honour patent. They cringe and display their infirmity or their misery in such a way that no man can deny his good fortune in comparison with them and therefore his obligation to help them. But they are not the only persons who depend in fact upon charity. Andalusia is a land of large farms. Its rural proletariat live in their home town normally but go away to work either sporadically or regularly on a seasonal basis. Their lives are precarious and when necessity threatens they move forth in search of work. Frequently they find themselves away from home and without means of support, so that they are forced to depend on charity. Their style of begging is very different, however, from that of the professional beggar. They stop at the farm to ask for work and if none is offered, they expect and are prepared to ask for food to continue their journey in search for it. They are not seen begging on street-corners in the towns; they do not tug the sleeve of the passer-by; they do not cringe nor attempt to evoke pity and the techniques of moral blackmail practised by the beggars are denied them by their claim to shame. They tend on the contrary to adopt a gruff and manly style to differentiate themselves from the professional beggars, for they are strangers, not beggars, and they sacrifice their shame no further than the implied (but not stated) confession of indigence. They are not referred to as *pordioseros*, for they do not invoke charity in the name of God, but simply as *pobres*, persons who in better times at home would be prepared to reciprocate charity. The distinction is made clear in a telling passage in the memoirs of Juan Belmonte. When as a novice bullfighter he travelled round the countryside with a companion, they were accustomed to stop at the farms and contrive to be fed for nothing by asking to buy ten centimes' worth of oil.

> But one morning at a farm in Utrera which today is my own, the only answer I got was a dry *Dios le ampare, hermano*.
> The conventional refusal to a beggar! My face fell with shame. Had I sunk to that? I was seized with a great depression and a terrible indignation against the good-for-nothing vagabond who had degraded my lust for adventure to such a level. At least the San Jacinto gang never begged its bread from door to door. If we were hungry we robbed an orchard in gay defiance of watch-dogs and armed guards.[22]

The confusion between poorman and beggar is not commonly made, for the difference of status is usually clear from the style of begging. The distinction relates to the place of the supplicant within the social structure. 'Endomendicity' can promise no reciprocity other than through the Deity. 'Exomendicity' claims to be a system of undifferentiated exchange. The giver does not contemplate finding himself one day in the position of the endomendicant, for he has shame, but he may well expect to send his son off to seek work seasonally even if a change in his fortunes, the loss of his lease previously or of his post as bailiff, do not oblige him to take to the road himself. Therefore the response to the two types of supplicant are as different as their techniques. The honourable poor man may be received with honour (though this is not always the case); the professional beggar is treated with a disdain which the honourable man would not stomach. Moreover the former is a witness from the outside in whose eyes the reputation of the community is at stake, the latter is merely a nuisance and a threat. The former offers the opportunity of gaining honour through the role of patron, the latter is feared for her evil tongue and, as often as not, her evil eye. For there is a final difference between them: the former is more often a man, the latter more often a woman.

Convention demands that every stranger be made a guest in Andalu-

sia. The unincorporated stranger cannot be abided. The plebeian
etiquette with regard to eating illustrates this general sentiment. The act
of eating supposes a higher degree of intimacy than mere presence and to
eat in front of a stranger is to offend this sentiment. His status must be
changed therefore to that of guest and this is done by the formality of
offering food. The diner at a wayside tavern or modest restaurant invites
the new arrival with a standard phrase, the workman eating his lunch
uses the same phrase to the passer-by, the traveller in the third class
railway carriage presses his travelling companions to share his provisions
before he will begin eating.

A similar custom is found in North Africa where it has been explained
in terms of the magical danger of the envy of uninvited strangers who
might well be possessed of the evil eye.[23]

My own experiences with regard to hospitality in the town which I
have named Alcalá were not without significance. I was invited to a
drink by persons of various social classes and it was not long before I
was permitted to return such hospitality to members of the plebeian
community and even to play the role of patron to those with whom I had
formed an appropriate relationship, but I was never permitted to pay for
wine we had drunk together by men of the upper class of the town, the
señoritos, who insisted always on maintaining my status as a guest. (I
found it necessary to search for reciprocity in other ways.) They would
use various formulae to explain their refusal: 'We shall all one day come
to London and drink with you there. Then we shall ruin you' (laughter);
or they would simply remind me that I was a foreigner and that they
would be ashamed to let me pay in their town; or they would promise
that next time I should be allowed to pay – a 'next time' which never
came. The fact that I was never allowed to return hospitality within the
town was significant above all (since I was accepted as a social equal in
other ways), in regard to their conception of the stranger. For I was not
only a stranger to the local community but to the national community –
a foreigner, and an inquisitive one at that. The threat which I embodied
was represented in the belief that I was a spy, which was discarded only
after months of evident ineptness in that role. While my presence was in
itself honorific, my potential hostility was nevertheless very great.
Therefore I was never allowed to escape from my status as guest, where
I had no rights, into that of community member where I might assert
myself, make demands and criticisms and interfere in the social and
political system. This long-extended hospitality for which I remain ever
grateful carried the covert significance of a status barrier whereby the
leaders of local society protected themselves from the threat that my
strangeness represented. It was even suggested, after a minor govern-

mental authority with whom I had had a slight altercation happened to be transferred to another town, that I was really in the pay, not of the British government, but of the Spanish government. Zeus in disguise? An ingenuous young man hastened to take advantage of his connection with me to ask for a letter of recommendation which would get him into the secret police.

The extraneous example of my own experiences does not suffice to make clear the code of hospitality. The treatment of the stranger depends very much upon his social status. A person of high status honours the whole community by his presence and must be made a guest by a leading member, if he is not to be shunned as someone too suspicious to have any contact with. In fact, he can usually find someone with whom to establish at least a tie of common friendships. Persons of lower status frequently have similar contacts. There are also those who are glad to extend the range of their friendships as a source of prestige and with a view to an eventual reciprocity. The greatest overt distrust is that shown towards the groups of young men who come through the town on their way to the plains to seek work. The fact that they come in groups and that their destination is elsewhere makes them poor candidates for any form of hospitality.

There is however one class of stranger towards whom hostility is shown, the young men who come courting a local girl. An ancient custom relates how such a visitor was received. If he were not driven away by stoning he would be captured by the local lads and ducked in the fountain. It was not clear whether this might be done more than once, but if he survived this ordeal and persevered with his suit he was allowed to do so unmolested. He was then believed to have formed an unbreakable attachment to the place through the effect of the waters. It is not difficult to see the symbolism of this custom. The water of each *pueblo* is its pride and none is so brackish that it will not be proclaimed exceptional in taste and healthgiving qualities ('*una agua riquísima*', '*una agua muy sana*', etc.), superior to that of all neighbouring places. It is the source of the virtues of the inhabitants. The stranger who has been submitted to the ordeal of ducking survives no longer as a stranger but as a member of the community, one who has been reborn from its 'source'.[24] (The word used is either *pila* or *fuente*. *Pila* means both 'font' and 'fountain', *fuente* means both the town fountain and also 'source' or 'origin'. The town fountain is a white-washed edifice of great social importance as a meeting-place through which gossip is diffused and it is commonly surmounted by a cross). The hostile treatment is a prelude to acceptance at a level which is not attained by the guest. By presenting himself as a suitor the visitor denies his intention to depart; on the contrary he asserts his aspiration to enter the kinship system as an affine, that is, to acquire rights in the community.

III

The law of hospitality is founded upon ambivalence. It imposes order through an appeal to the sacred, makes the unknown knowable, and replaces conflict by reciprocal honour. It does not eliminate the conflict altogether but places it in abeyance and prohibits its expression. This is true also of the avoidance and the joking relationship. But whereas the joking relationship suppresses the conflict by the prohibition to take offence, hospitality achieves the same end by the prohibition to give offence; one by forbidding respect, the other by enforcing it, or it might be put: the avoidance of respect and the avoidance of disrespect. Both relationships are placed outside the struggle for supremacy by a tacit agreement enjoined by custom, but, while the custom of the joking relationship invokes the desecrable and employs the language of pollution in the exchange of obscenities, the custom of hospitality invokes the sacred and involves the exchange of honour. Host and guest must pay each other honour. The host requests the honour of the guest's company – (and this is not merely a self-effacing formula: he gains honour through the number and quality of his guests). The guest is honoured by the invitation. Their mutual obligations are in essence unspecific, like those between spiritual kinsmen or blood-brothers; each must accede to the desires of the other. To this extent the relationship is reciprocal. But this reciprocity does not obscure the distinction between the roles.

It is always the host who ordains, the guest who complies. The guest must be granted the place of precedence and he must eat first, but precedence is defined in relation to the host, on his right hand as a rule. (Only royalty takes the head of the table in the house of another, for the obvious reason that royalty always ordains, cannot comply.) The duty of ordering the precedence among guests is the host's responsibility and the guest who is dissatisfied with his treatment has no recourse but to retire from his role altogether by walking out. An intermediary solution was once furnished in diplomatic etiquette by the convention whereby a guest, dissatisfied with his position at table, could call attention to an error of protocol of which he was the victim by the gesture of turning his plate over and thereby making it impossible to serve him. In this way he retired from his role until the error was corrected, or at least until his protest had been registered, without showing any discourtesy to his host. To complain openly would infringe the host's prerogative in the placing of his guests, while to refuse the food would be impolite since refusal implies distaste and depreciation and amounts therefore to an insult. The Spanish peasantry, conscious of this implication, commonly uses the expression '*para no despreciarlo*' (in order not to despise it) when accepting food or drink. In this way the guest exonerates himself from the implication of being greedy or demanding and maintains that he accepts only out of respect for the host. Thus tipsy farmers down their umpteenth glass with the righteous air of obligation.

Whether it is mandatory to refuse or accept, or to refuse at first and then accept, is a particularity of custom. The logic of the law of hospitality provides a justification for either refusal or acceptance: whether honour is done best by declaring the offer of hospitality excessive (which might imply distaste) or by demonstrating it to be welcome (which risks the implication that it may be taken for granted) is something which can only be known by reference to local convention. To gobble the peasant's lunch in the railway carriage in order not to show contempt for it is incorrect because there is no reason why he, rather than another, should play the host in such circumstances. To refuse the food he offers in his home is another matter.

The roles of host and guest have territorial limitations. A host is host only on the territory over which on a particular occasion he claims authority. Outside it he cannot maintain the role. A guest cannot be guest on ground where he has rights and responsibilities. So it is that the courtesy of showing a guest to the door or the gate both underlines a concern in his welfare as long as he is a guest, but it also defines precisely the point at which he ceases to be so, when the host is quit of his responsibility. At this point the roles lapse. The custom of the desert Arabs made this abundantly clear. Such was the sanctity of hospitality that the host's protection was assured even towards those for whom he felt enmity. To take advantage of a guest or fugitive was unthinkable. Yet hospitality bequeathed no commitment beyond the precincts of the domestic sanctuary, so his guest might become his victim the moment he stepped outside them. Hence it was the custom for the guest to leave silently and unannounced during the darkest hours of the night for fear he should be followed and struck down. The custom of the Kalingas shows by a curious variation the true nature of this sociological space defined by hospitality. When the guest of a Kalinga is a local man his host is responsible for his protection only within the confines of his property. His hurt or murder on the premises must be avenged by his host. But if the guest is a foreigner his host remains responsible for his protection throughout the entire region.[25] The range within which their complementary relationship holds good coincides with the territory where their mutual status is unequal. Where neither has a greater claim to authority than the other their complementarity lapses. For, while a host has rights and obligations in regard to his guest, the guest has no right other than to respect and no obligation other than to honour his host. He incurs however the right and obligation to return hospitality on a future occasion on territory where he can claim authority. The reciprocity between host and guest is thus transposed to a temporal sequence and a spatial alternation in which the roles are reversed. Only then can the covert hostility be vented in customs such as the *potlatch* where rivalry takes the form of a hospitality which is more than lavish and where failure to reciprocate spells bankruptcy. The fable of the fox and the stork provides a model of the law of hospitality and an object lesson in its exploitation: an affront which masquerades as a generous and honorific gesture cannot be resented without violating the law of hospitality, since it is the host's privilege to ordain, but it can nevertheless be avenged by a similar ploy once the tables are turned.

For the same reason that the criminal is said to define the law the essentials of the law of hospitality can best be seen in the actions which constitute its infringement. How is the law of hospitality infringed? The detail varies of course from place to place. To inquire after the health of a spouse or child may be a requirement of good manners according to one code or a *faux pas* according to another. Yet a certain general sense informs them all, entitling us to talk about the *law* of hospitality in the abstract in contrast to the specific *codes* of hospitality exemplified by different cultures. There is, so to speak, a 'natural law' of hospitality deriving not from divine revelation like so many particular codes of law, but from sociological necessity.

A guest infringes the law of hospitality:

1. If he insults his host or by any show of hostility or rivalry; he must honour his host.

2. If he usurps the role of his host. He may do this by presuming upon what has not yet been offered, by 'making himself at home', taking precedence, helping himself, giving orders to the dependants of his host, and so forth. If he makes claims or demands, he usurps the host's right to ordain according to his free will, even where custom lays down what he should wish to ordain. To attempt to sleep with the host's wife[26] or to refuse to do so may either of them be infractions of a code of hospitality, but be it noted that the cession of the conjugal role always depends upon the host's will, like the precedence which he cedes. His wife's favours are always his to dispose of as he wishes. To demand or take what is not offered is always an usurpation of the role of host;

3. If, on the other hand, he refuses what *is* offered he infringes the role of guest. Food and drink always have ritual value, for the ingestion

together of a common substance creates a bond. Commensality is the basis of community in a whole number of contexts. Therefore the guest is bound above all to accept food. Any refusal reflects in fact upon the host's capacity to do honour; and this is what the guest must uphold. Therefore he may be expected to give thanks and pay compliments in order to stress that he is conscious of the honour done him. On the other hand it may be considered 'bad form' to do so since this implies that honour might not have been done and this in turn throws doubt on the host's capacity. The Victorian hostess who answered a florid compliment to her cook with the withering words: 'But did you expect to have bad food in my house?' made the point effectively. Failure to know what should be taken for granted can amount to insult. Therefore the details of codes of hospitality may be contraries, but, as in the treatment of twins or smiths in Africa, the contraries contain a common element of sociological meaning, which derives in this case from the law of hospitality.

A host infringes the law of hospitality:

1. If he insults his guest or by any show of hostility or rivalry; he must honour his guest.

2. If he fails to protect his guest or the honour of his guest. For this reason, though fellow-guests have no explicit relationship, they are bound to forego hostilities, since they offend their host in the act of attacking one another. The host must defend each against the other, since both are his guests.

3. If he fails to attend to his guests, to grant them the precedence which is their due, to show concern for their needs and wishes or in general to earn the gratitude which guests should show. Failure to offer the best is to denigrate the guest. Therefore it must always be maintained that, however far from perfect his hospitality may be, it is the best he can do.

It will be noted that, while the first clause is the same for both parties, the second and third are complementary between host and guest. This complementarity provides the systematic basis of the institution, which reaches its full symmetry in reciprocal hospitality when the roles of host and guest are exchanged. This is never the case with hospitality to a stranger whose chance of reciprocating necessarily remains in the blue. Lacking reciprocity between individuals, hospitality to the stranger can nevertheless be viewed as a reciprocal relationship between communities. The customs relating to the stranger therefore concern the degree to which he is permitted to be incorporated into a community which is not his own, and the techniques whereby this is effected. These may be divided into those which establish him as a permanent member of the local group and those which assume his departure in the future.

If he comes only to visit, the visit may be returned, but if he intends to remain and change his affiliation, the reciprocity between communities ceases to operate.

An 'ordeal' implies permanence since its significance is essentially that it marks an irreversible passage: the element of hostility in the character of the stranger is destroyed and he is able to emerge from it in a more acceptable status. He is no longer unknown, he has been tried. He forfeits his association with the sacred and his call upon hospitality which derived from it. The passage of an ordeal entitles the stranger to remain in a new role, more nearly incorporated even if he is not granted the full status of community membership; he may still be subject to a personal bond with one of its members through affinity, artificial kinship or clientship. Yet whatever his subsequent status it provides him with a mode of permanent incorporation. Where an elaborate code of hospitality applies to the stranger and he is made a guest by the mere fact of his appearance without any 'ordeal', an impermanent relationship is implied. His hostile character is not destroyed but inverted through the avoidance of disrespect. A limit is frequently set upon the time such a guest is expected to stay and, even when this is not so, it is always recognised that it is an abuse to outstay one's welcome. Thus while the mode of permanent incorporation solidifies in time, the status of guest evaporates. The one faces a potential assimilation, the other an eventual departure. While it lasts, the tenuous nature of the relationship of host and guest depends upon respecting the complementarity of their roles. Any infringement of the code of hospitality destroys the structure of roles, since it implies an incorporation which has not in fact taken place; failure to return honour or avoid disrespect entitles the person slighted in this way to relinquish his role and revert to the hostility which it suppressed. The sacred quality in the relationship is not removed, but polluted. Once they are no longer host and guest they are enemies, not strangers. Enemies *do* compete and it requires at least a tacit test of strength to determine which is the better man who will remain in possession of the field while the other takes his distance. The ordeal of the judicial combat may be appealed to so that Divine judgement may decide the matter or the struggle may be quite unformalised. The 'ordeal' which failed to take place on the way in takes place on the way out. Then the antagonists can part and become strangers again, in life or in death. This is why the process of reverting from guest to stranger in the Mediterranean follows a course reminiscent of that whereby the stranger was accepted in Eskimo society. Both represent variations on the theme of the ambivalence which underlies the law of hospitality. Both involve a combat which carries the host–guest relationship beyond that state of suspended hostility in which the exchange of honour overlays the contrast of allegiances, but beyond it in one of two directions: it may lead either to incorporation or rejection. Yet the logical foundation of the problem is the same and it is this which explains, perhaps, the similarity between Boas' ethnographical account and the last scene of the Odyssey.[27]

EPILOGUE

The feast[28] has been going on for years when the old beggar turns up. He is not, as one of the guests suspects, a god in disguise but the host. Only the old dog knows and the discovery is too much for him. The place is in disorder: the master's substance is wasting, the suitors plague his widow (who is not his widow), the guests play the host, abuse the maid-servants and plot the son's murder.

A challenge[29] is issued to a test of strength to see which guest can string the master's bow. The lady will espouse the winner, she says. Finally, when all have failed, the old beggar picks up the challenge amidst their scorn, and by the strength of his right arm[30] triumphantly reveals his true identity. After that, of course, the slaughter[31] begins. (How could one pardon guests who have so far usurped the role of host?) Anyway the gods see to it that no quarter be given, for it is justice which is at issue here, not sentiment. The world turns the right way up once more. Order and peace[32] are restored.

6 Women and sanctuary in the Mediterranean

> Woman is another being who lives apart and is therefore an
> enigmatic figure. It would be better to say she is the Enigma.
> She attracts and repels like men of an alien race or nationality.
>
> Octavio Paz
> (*The Labyrinth of Solitude*)

In the previous chapter I attempted to show, by reference to a proposed
universal 'law of hospitality', why the last scene of the Odyssey, the
slaughter of the suitors, is not, as certain authors have suggested, anomalous. I was concerned with the status of the guest as an intermediary
position between the hostile and mysterious outside and the interior
structure of the community. The relationship between host and guest is
subject to special provisions, I suggested, on account of the ambivalence
pervading it which derives from the fact that it represents a confrontation
between the internal and the external aspects of the host's social unit. My
explanation was complete in itself, I believe, but it raised at one point a
question that is worth examining: why is the notion of sanctuary in the
Arab world connected with the sanctity of women? Sanctuary is accorded in the first place at shrines where the fugitive becomes inviolate
through placing himself under the protection of the divine power to
whom the shrine is dedicated, but a right to domestic sanctuary also
exists for those who place themselves under the protection of the head of
a household who is thereby bound to protect them as his guests. In order
to claim this right the fugitive must make contact with the women of the
house. Is this connection fortuitous or does it derive from some fundamental association between the status of women and the status of guests
as, both of them, protected persons? The fact that in our own society we
tend to treat the two in a rather similar fashion might seem to suggest
that this is so, but it would be rash to jump to conclusions, since this is
not the case everywhere and notably in the Arab world. It is never, in
any case, on the basis of superficial resemblances in the modes of conduct
that the structural equivalence of institutions can be established. I shall

113

content myself with examining this connection in the Mediterranean and shall use once more as my point of departure that magnificent treatise on the law of hospitality which is the Odyssey.

I

Let us consider the scene in which Odysseus arrives upon the island of Phaeacia: he emerges from the sea and is soon befriended by the king's daughter, Nausicaa, who gives him clothing and counsels him how to obtain the royal protection. He then follows her to the palace and, hidden in a cloud by the watchful care of Athene, penetrates to the central hall where he finds Queen Arēte whom he clasps round the knees, taking up the traditional attitude of a supplicant.

The scene has given rise to speculations.[1] Why should he have to go to the queen rather than directly to the king beside her? Was clemency more likely to come from her? Was she more effective in authority than her husband? Though she is painted as a forceful character and is said to be much honoured by her husband, it is evident that the decision to grant sanctuary must come from him and we must remember that, according to many critics, Phaeacia is used by the poet as a model of the proper social order to be contrasted with the confusion Odysseus finds when he gets home. If this is so, there is something unlikely in the suggestion that here the queen wielded the power of decision over her husband, for this is not the proper distribution of authority in the society portrayed by Homer (and in any case she may be presumed to have been much younger than her husband, being his brother's daughter). The position of women was, in general, one of subjugation to male authority as it is in the Mediterranean down to the present and this is especially the case when the exterior relations of the household are in question. It appears then that here the distribution of authority is not the issue, nor is it a matter of female impressionability and that Odysseus was advised to go to the queen, not primarily on account of her individual character (though Athene makes much of her good qualities) but because this gesture was required of a supplicant according to Phaeacian custom. (Odysseus had already considered adopting such a posture when throwing himself upon Nausicaa's mercy.) It is to be noted that it is not the queen but the ancient counsellor who prompts the king to grant Odysseus hospitality. In fact we are dealing with a customary form of behaviour for supplicants as standard as that which follows the gesture in the scene in question: sitting in the ashes in the hearth. To explain it we must look not to evaluations of behaviour in our own society but to the moral division of labour between the sexes in the ancient Mediterranean, and in particular to that aspect of it which will explain the association between women and sanctuary.

This institution is not one which is often encountered in the modern world and where it is still to be found is in those areas where the authority of the state has yet to be exerted, for sanctuary supposes warring tribes whose strife is none the less subject to a code of rules accepted by both parties. It belongs to a world where the ethic of feud rather than written law provides the modes of offence and retaliation. Such societies have been called lawless or anarchic and they are certainly inclined to internal violence, yet their violence is subject to rules as strict as those of a sacred game. The persons to whom sanctuary is normally extended are therefore members of the same total society within which the rules are recognised, yet not members of the same social unit within it; they respect the sanctity of the same shrines within whose precincts violence is sacrilegious, yet they use violence freely in the struggle for power. The relationship between the social units which accept common norms of sanctuary is therefore similar to that between the exogamous sections of the same tribe or people who exchange their daughters. They stand in relation to each other upon the boundary of the known world.

Abou Zeid[2] has given us a description of the rules of sanctuary among the Bedouin of Cyrenaica who, in conformity with Arab custom, refer to it by the word *ḥaram*, from the same root as the words for womenfolk, sacred places and that which is prohibited.[3] His account of sanctuary is essentially the same as that given by Bishr Farès[4] in his study of the conception of honour in pre-islamic Arabia and it should be noted that when sanctuary is offered in the house or tent of an individual, the host gains honour through affording it, since it testifies to his power to protect. Like other authors who have written about the mores of the Arabs, Abou Zeid stresses the vulnerability of men's honour through their women, but he does not explain why the penetration of the women's quarters by a stranger should not constitute a violation of the honour of the owner ('outrage à la horma' in Bourdieu's phrase), why on the contrary his honour is enhanced not desecrated by the fugitive who reaches sanctuary there.

Varied as they are throughout the world, the customs that determine the reception of the stranger all provide a means of stripping him of some degree of his strangeness in order that he may be accepted into the community as a guest. His special status accorded by the code of hospitality derives from the necessity to establish norms of behaviour towards him in spite of the fact that he is as yet unknown and potentially hostile. In order that the rules of social intercourse may operate with regard to him the hostile stranger must be converted into a guest. This transformation is achieved through some ritual of incorporation which places the host and guest outside the bounds of the rivalry that governs relationships in a neutral setting. Between host and guest aggressive behaviour is forbidden and any act of discourtesy defiles the honour of both. Moreover the two are allied in the eyes of the rest of the community; the host is responsible for his guest, while the guest is dependent on his host and relates to others through him. In some societies the host may even receive blood-money in the event of the murder of a guest, but everywhere the same rule of hospitality is found: the guest submits to the authority of the host; the host extends his protection in exchange.

In the case of sanctuary the same rule may be said to apply though it is initiated by the visitor: instead of responding to an invitation to become a guest, the fugitive imposes himself as such by adopting an attitude of submission and by claiming protection in exchange for the honour which his submission conveys. By entering the women's quarters he tacitly renounces his power to affront. To enter them other than as a supplicant would be the gravest offence and a desecration of female purity, but a supplicant cannot affront for he throws himself upon the mercy of his host, and thereby forfeits all claim to the kind of honour by which he might impugn another man's. Having placed himself 'in balk', he cannot then challenge anybody until he resumes his liberty and with it his vulnerability.

Abou Zeid points out that the greatest honour falls to the man who extends sanctuary even to his own enemy whose entry into the women's quarters in the role of supplicant offers him the opportunity of accreting honour through a display of magnanimity; but it is not merely an opportunity, it is also a sacred duty, for to violate the right to sanctuary is sacrilege, as our own language implies. In the light of modern ideas about women, enmity and honour such provisions seem almost nonsensical. In order to find their sense we must attempt to transpose them to a higher level of abstraction.

Let us reduce to a simple schema the internal and external relations of a household such as is still commonly found in the Mediterranean prior to modern urban development:

(1) The house itself contains the inner quarters associated with the women and the intimate life of the family, and, for the purpose of receiving visits from neighbours, a hall or porch, its point of contact with the exterior. The latter part of the house, the guest-house, is commonly forbidden to women in Arab villages and the women's quarters are forbidden to any men but close kinsmen and servants or slaves, that is to say, persons attached to the household in an inferior status. The same

basic distinction is made between the interior and exterior aspects of the dwelling even when it is no more than a tent.[5]

(2) Outside the home are the common meeting-grounds of the whole community, composed of similar households with whom solidarity is shown in the face of external threats, who know each other's histories, marry each other's daughters and plot with and against each other in the struggle for wealth, prestige and authority within the community. Belonging to the same community, they stand in rivalry within it where they are conceptually similar: potentially equivalent and differentiated in fact by their relative preponderance. But their differences are forgotten when, facing the exterior, they are united on the basis of collective interests in opposition to those who are conceptually different.

Just as the household is divided internally and united in relation to the exterior, so the community is either divided or united according to whether its internal or external aspect is at stake.

(3) Beyond the community lies the outside world which is generally regarded as hostile, from which come strangers, that is, unknown persons who, unlike the fellow-members of the community with whom relations are habitual and clearly structured, remain mysterious, their nature and their power in doubt and who derive from their strangeness a preferential relationship with the Divine. The God of the Old Testament as well as Allah and Zeus protected strangers and the latter was also liable to appear himself in the disguise of a supplicant or beggar. Odysseus for this reason was mistaken for a god several times during his travels but by persons with whom he shared a common conception of humanity, fellow Greeks, as opposed to those with whom this natural affiliation was not shared, the sirens and the Cyclops.

Thus three main fields of social relations can be distinguished: those interior to the household, those exterior to it but interior to the community, and those that extend beyond the bounds of the community. On the axis of contact there is a progression from the private precincts where relations are intimate between members of the same household (and here is the only licit field of sexual relations), to the extraneous world with which contact is exceptional, sporadic and subject to special provisions, if not actually hostile. Between these two lies the community. Yet we can choose a different axis, that of similarity/dissimilarity, which makes opposition possible either on the basis of community or of sex: in the first case, own community is opposed to other communities – members of the known world versus non-members, habitual versus exceptional relations – in the second, own sex is opposed to other sex within a division of labour which endows the male with authority and the female with purity and correspondingly limits the activities of women in regard to public matters which are in the hands of men. Women are expected to stay at home, since they are the repositories of male honour to be shielded from contact with males of other households which would defile them. Therefore strangers are always masculine. Through the value attached to their purity women are endowed with sanctity of a certain kind, expressed by the notion of *haram* and associated not with any religious function but with the mysteries of sex and childbirth. Sacredness in this sense attaches in both cases to the dissimilar, whether they be of the same sex but a different community or of the same community but a different sex. The social structure enjoins the norms of behaviour which reign over the theoretical space between the two, that is to say, it classifies known male persons and dictates the rules by which they may triumph over or cooperate with one another. But females stand outside this structure in that they are allotted their place within the community by virtue of their relationship to males who are responsible for them as they are for their guests. Women are therefore not merely mysterious, opposed to males upon the moral plane, but on the social plane 'out of bounds', segregated and surrounded by taboos and literally, in the case of the Arabs, enclosed behind walls and veils like the tabernacle.

The essence of the notion of sanctuary is that it is a place where the 'normal' rules of aggression and retaliation are laid in abeyance. Its sanctity defines it as a context apart from the idiom of normal inter-course, 'out of bounds'. This suspension of the rules of normal inter-course applies not only to certain places such as shrines, but to certain persons, women as has been said and also guests who, from the moment that they are accepted, become subject to special treatment. Excluded from the councils of their host and denied authority, dependent upon his wishes just as women are, the guest receives respect nonetheless, for like women he possesses the power to act upon the honour of his host. One may distinguish therefore between relations which are 'in bounds' to the norms of interaction and those which are 'out of bounds' because concerned with persons mysterious and honorific who occupy a special status whether they derive it from their dissimilarity of sex or of com-munity.

The position of women in the tradition of the Mediterranean has, for all its variation, at least this constant: that they are viewed always in opposition to the world of men to which they are both essential for moral as well as practical reasons and yet contrary in terms of the values they symbolise; they embody, as it were, the counter-principle to the male-ruled society, antithetical to it and complementary, and this antithesis is illustrated in the conceptions which attach to the interior of the house or the life outside it: the wife is mistress within, the husband without. The moral division of labour of sexes relates, then, to their inverse roles within or without the house. The social order is founded upon this distinction. Hence the inversionary rites of the Mediterranean display to this day the theme of the reversal of sexual roles: men disguise themselves as women and women are granted the symbols of public male authority and the privileges of the male sex.

The masculine principle of power and authority determines the precedence and preeminence of the households of the community, but it recognises limits to the exploitation of advantage, as Bourdieu[6] has shown in his analysis of the dialectic of challenge and riposte in Kabyle society. Once preeminence has been established it requires to be confirmed by magnanimity, passing thereby from the realm of fact to that of right, for the gesture of magnanimity, to be accepted as such, must be endorsed by public recognition. You can demonstrate your power to win, but your right to pardon must be recognised by others, lest your magnanimity be mistaken for weakness. The granting of sanctuary is a public display of this right to magnanimity and for this reason a means of accreting honour. Complementarily, the demonstration of submission in suppliance invokes the claim to protection. The fugitive who seeks refuge among the women, violating the taboo which surrounds them, becomes thereby himself taboo and places himself 'out of bounds'. If therefore the union of the outsider and the women represents a conjunction of extremes on the axis of contact, on the axis of similarity/dissimilarity the two are associated as contraries of the bounded worldly order which stands between them but is eliminated by their union in favour of the other-worldly order represented by the sacred. Failing to escape *out* of the masculine order, the fugitive can therefore, if he is lucky, escape *in*. Hence Athene considerately covered Odysseus with a cloud while he ran the gauntlet of entrance into the palace, for the Phaeacians were notorious not only for their hospitality but for their hostility towards strangers.

This explanation attempts no more than to sketch the values symbolised in the notion of sanctuary and offer a logical connection between them, resolving the apparent anomaly of accepting the fugitive into the women's quarters, but it might seem fanciful and contrived if it did not accord with certain general principles long recognised in anthropology concerning the relation of women to outsiders.

II

Women are associated with outsiders first of all in the custom of exogamy which appears among primitive peoples from the moment that communities attempt to maintain structured relations with one another – as opposed to the hazardous contacts between jungle bands which are not exogamous. The exchange of women provides a form of sociation which establishes a permanent structure where political ties are too frail to do so. Yet this does not imply an end to all hostilities: the connection between the exchange of women and the hostility of outsiders is sanctified for all time in the well-known refrain 'We fight with those who give us wives' or 'We marry those we fight with.' Indeed, behind the theory of matrimonial alliance lies the premiss that those who are thus allied are defined as a group clearly enough to envisage fighting, even if they do not in fact possess sufficient autonomy to do so. This fact differentiates them again from those who live in a homogeneous society. Thus, too distant from each other, no alliance is possible; too close, it is superfluous, or putting it more exactly, the elementary structure upon which the exchange of women depends gives way to a complex structure where kinship is no longer the basis of social grouping; alliance can then only be between households or even individuals.

The custom of exogamy therefore serves to structure relations between social groups that recognise each other as different but capable of being associated. The point of my argument is not however the value of political and social ties established through the exchange of women – how frail these are is shown by the maxim – but that this exchange is also the exchange of knowledge,[7] the basis of sociation: unknown outsiders are reduced through marriage to a known element in the social universe, affines. The fact is clearly illustrated by those languages which derive the word for affine from that which means stranger, enemy or guest. Hostile these affines may remain and their hostility may be symbolised in a ritual of marriage by capture, but it is a mock-capture and asserts only that the hostility which persists is nevertheless subject to conventions recognised by both parties, like the rules of war. Once they exchange women they are sociated. There is however one area of the world which, though it is noted for being traditionally organised in corporate and even in kin groups, refuses to exchange women: the Mediterranean.

Now it is significant that Arēte was her husband's brother's daughter. Such a type of marriage is the basic model of patrilineal endogamy and is favoured still today by the Arabs. In fact it was perhaps in former times much more extensive than today.[8] Moreover we know that the classical Greeks recognised in the institution of the *epikleros*, the brotherless daughter of a line of descent, a preferential right to marry their patrilineal kinswoman whose estate was thereby kept within the lineage – if it were not more exact to put it the other way round and say that the woman went with the estate. It seems likely then that Arēte's kinship with her husband is a structurally significant detail; if not married strictly as an epikleros, she stood in relation to her husband in a similar situation, for her father, Rhexenor, had died leaving no other child. Nausicaa on the other hand, far from being married endogamously, is offered as a wife to a total stranger, Odysseus, on condition he remain upon the island. This offer is made on the night of his arrival and before he has revealed his identity (which he does only just before leaving).

One cannot help wondering about the Phaeacian marriage customs. Was patrilineal endogamy the rule for all or was it only the custom of the royalty? If in Homer's Mediterranean the king were no more than a chieftain, *primus inter pares*, rather than a sacred king, one would not expect the kingship to possess a special custom in this regard. On the other hand the royal house of Phaeacia was descended rather closely from the gods. Whether or not the norm of patrilineal marriage was general, there is an apparent contradiction in the fact that Arēte should have been married at one extreme of the axis of contact and Nausicaa offered in marriage at the other. Was there no classificatory father's brother's son available to claim her? The text implies there was not, since no collateral branch of the family is mentioned. At the time of Odysseus' arrival she was expecting to be married to a Phaeacian as soon as her father had made up his mind which one. Is one entitled to suggest that if all were turned down in favour of the stranger none was entirely satisfactory to his way of thinking? The higher the social status of a lineage the more likely it is to be endogamous. The royal house of Phaeacia faced a quandary in the case of Nausicaa if there was no available member of the royal patriline to whom she could be given and no neighbouring island with a suitable heir apparent. (Phaeacia's isolation is stressed in the text.) Odysseus furnished a possible solution to this quandary for the following reason.

To begin with marriage rules are always qualified by a rule of residence: to take *in* a son-in-law is not the same thing as giving a daughter *away*. In many patrilineal endogamous societies an in-marrying son-in-law can take place of a son. (The French or Japanese peasantries may be quoted as examples.) The status of son-in-law can merge into that of adopted son, if indeed some ritual of adoption does not precede the marriage as in Japan. In ancient Greece sons were sometimes adopted by the fathers of future epikleroi to avoid the inheritance being claimed by a more distant member of the patriline, and Lacey[9] has suggested that '... a great chieftain could obtain a following by bringing warriors into his house in order to secure their services ... often giving them wives ... Fathers of daughters gathered round them warrior sons-in-law like

Priam, who had twelve sons-in-law who lived with their wives in his palace' (p. 39). Odysseus was offered Nausicaa on account of the remarkable impression he made, according to Lacey (p. 40), though it must be retained that the impression was made purely from appearances; he had not yet excelled in the games. If Alkinoos was concerned only in acquiring a competent warrior-son-in-law she could have been married to a Phaeacian in the same way without the risk that the remarkable impression Odysseus had made should prove false. The question remains: why was the stranger chosen?

Marriage with the stranger appears on the axis of contact to be the antithesis of an endogamous marriage, but I have already suggested that this axis possesses by itself a limited explanatory power, since it marks only the points at which the inside and the outside can be opposed. The nature of the social relations changes according to their position on the axis. Nausicaa's marriage with Odysseus would have made an alliance, not with another patriline of the Phaeacians, i.e. outside the royal lineage, but with the totally unknown, i.e. outside 'outside the patriline', that is to say, outside the social structure altogether. One might say then that just as the fugitive who failed to escape *out* could escape *in*, so the Phaeacian royal family, unable to marry their daughter *inside* the field of normal competitive relations, could as the next best thing marry her outside it altogether and acquire thereby a surrogate father's brother's son for Nausicaa. For having no patriline upon the island himself he could without difficulty be accepted into that of his father-in-law. In this case outside the outside is equivalent to inside, just as in the case of *ḥaram* inside the inside was shown to be equivalent to outside.

This explanation rests on the possibility that the stranger could, with regard to the rule of marriage, be integrated into a system of patrilineal endogamy. Yet it leaves aside the generic nature of the connection between the stranger and the women, of which the case of Odysseus is merely a rather exceptional example which I have chosen to explain first of all in a more practical way. It should not blind us to the wider significance of offering Nausicaa in marriage to an unknown guest to whom sanctuary has been extended, a significance already suggested by the fact that she herself mistook him for a god at their first encounter.

The notion of sanctuary derives from the conjunction of the fugitive and the sacred (in either *ḥaram*, a sacred and prohibited place, i.e. a shrine, or *ḥarīm*, women's quarters, prohibited and therefore sacred also, if in a slightly different sense) and places the context 'out of bounds' to normal reciprocation under the aegis of a principle opposed to the logic of the profane community of everyday. Yet the principle on which exogamy rests is not in essence different, but only different in the use which is made of it, whether to establish ties of sociation with an 'outsider' group or to associate an individual outsider to one's own group. The principle may be stated that in either case the opposition between inside and outside is mediated through women. Exogamy denies access to the women of the community in favour of strangers who, through their conjunction with them, are established as guests, persons to whom a special code of conduct applies. Affines and guests, whether or not the conceptions are expressed in a single word, are *par excellence* the persons to whom extra-ordinary rules apply, either in the form of avoidances, joking relations or honorific behaviour, all of them ways of placing a person 'out of bounds'.

When it is said that 'we fight with those with whom we intermarry' or vice versa it is not asserted that individuals fight with their affines – the contrary is true, for in the combat between intermarrying groups a man must avoid striking his own affine – but that we, as individuals, give our daughters to members of the groups with whom we, as a collectivity, have relations of conflict. The two types of relationship, collective hostility and affinity through marriage, are the opposed aspects of an ambivalence and it is the second which qualifies the first and sets limits to it, bringing it under the control of the longer-term interests represented by the descendants who result from intermarriage.

The Arabs attempt to avoid intermarriage with those with whom they fight, conserving their women for the patriline, yet in according sanctuary in the *ḥarīm* they none the less accept, within rather than without the hearth, the principle that endows women with the power to proscribe hostility and invoke a relationship of respect. In either case, women provide the bridge with the outside, whether as wives given to outsiders or by providing a place of sanctuary for outsiders within the home. In either case the rules of profane conduct are placed in abeyance by the conjunction of the unknown with the unknowable, women.

One may note in passing that the same general area was noted in antiquity for the existence of a type of sacred prostitution whereby the girls of the community were offered before marriage and sometimes after also to strangers on the occasion of their visit to the shrine. This is no more than a variant, on the collective scale, of the syndrome of sanctuary. In either case the stranger's knowledge of women in sacred precincts operates an inversion of the normal rules of conduct. That this form of sacred prostitution should be found among endogamous peoples is surely to be expected: if women were destined to be given *away* in marriage there would seem to be little point in giving them to strangers outside marriage as well. Surely its significance is rather as a ritual inversion of a social order which ordained that women were to be kept, not given away – a gesture of recognition to that same principle which inspires exogamy by a people who have decided against foreign affines.

III

Exogamy and sanctuary are not the only forms of association with strangers established through women. There are peoples who include in their code of hospitality what has sometimes been called 'sexual hospitality'. Indeed, temple prostitution can be regarded as a collective form of this as Wake (*op. cit.*, p. 158) well realised. If the acceptable stranger is everywhere offered food, he is also in some parts of the world offered more than that. Commensality, the ritual ingestion of a common substance, establishes the common nature of host and guest and creates a bond between them. The symbolic equivalence of eating and copulation appears to be universal[10] and this fact leads us to recognise the significance of such a custom as the ingestion of the stranger's essence through copulation. Once more the opposition between the inside and the outside is mediated through the female sex.

In Mediterranean sanctuary the fugitive or stranger was not normally expected to have sexual relations with the women, yet the idea of sexual hospitality does not appear entirely foreign to the ancient Arab tradition, for Robertson Smith[11] who did not otherwise concern himself with the connection between women and sanctuary noted (p. 82): 'It appears from Arab sources that when a man sought protection within a tribe it was natural for him to ask to be furnished with a wife, as Cais ibn Zohair did when he joined the Namir ibn Câsit.' He summons evidence to show moreover (*op. cit.* pp. 139, 140) that some Arabs formerly practised sexual hospitality in the form of offering the guest access to the host's wife.

It can be seen then that if in one sense the stranger renounces his power to affront by taking sanctuary he does not renounce his masculinity in any literal sense. He removes himself from the sphere of agonistic social relations and becomes a client or dependant and therefore a person to whom the distaste for giving daughters away no longer applies and who becomes by virtue of that fact a preferential candidate for the role of son-in-law in a would-be endogamous society. The experience of Odysseus on Phaeacia runs parallel to the ancient Arab custom except that unlike Cais ibn Zohair he refused rather than demanded a wife, for the good reason that he did not wish to remain. Both stories hinge upon the same conception of hospitality which aspires to integrate the stranger not only temporarily through commensality but perhaps permanently through marriage. The connection between women and sanctuary in the

Arab world, expressed and in a sense validated by the complex of meaning attaching to the arabic root which gives us both words, can be seen
then to be merely a particular case of the more fundamental and wide-
spread principle concerning strangers and their integration into a
community, the condition of their entry being in the first place the
demonstration of their common nature through the consumption of food
and the condition of their remaining being adoption as an affine into the
kin group through the consummation of marriage. This principle, again,
derives from the universal logic of social structure which opposes the
interior and the exterior relations of a given social unit.

7 The fate of Shechem or the politics of sex

I was a pious child and around the age of ten I set out upon an enterprise that I considered necessary for my salvation: to read every word of the Bible. I started at the beginning and I intended to continue until I reached the end. I had not finished the Book of Genesis before I ran into difficulties. The stories I found myself reading seemed, apart from their basic improbability, anything but edifying. I possessed no vocabulary by which to identify the behaviour I encountered, but I sensed that practices such as incest, fratricide, filiocide, wife-lending, polygamy, homosexuality and prostitution were wrong. I did not know what a 'whore' was and my teachers seemed curiously incapable of explaining. Concubines, they said, were 'domestic slaves', so we adapted the word 'conk' for relationships of subordination in our games. I still remember the troubled amazement on the master's face when he heard me cry merrily 'Smith Minor is my conk this week, next week I shall sell him and have someone else.' Cheating, deceit and treachery were rampant and seldom apparently condemned – Cain was an exception though even he ended up 'protected', but Laban cheated Jacob and was robbed in revenge by his own daughters. The Pharaoh had Abram's wife, and Lot's daughters, spurned by the Sodomites to whom they were offered gratis, had Lot, having inebriated the old man first. It seemed positively unfair that Adam and Eve should have been cast out of Eden for such a trivial peccadillo as eating an apple off the wrong tree – in the cause of acquiring knowledge, which, as I understood it, was what I had been sent to school for. What should I conclude from such tales? They were not the moral lessons I had led myself to expect and if my faith failed to founder straight away it was only because I was convinced of the sacredness of Genesis. It was not moral truth that was being expounded, I realised, but historical truth and if God had allowed such events to occur it could only be that in His wisdom He had decided to accept the imperfection of human nature and hold in abeyance the divine message of the text. Caught upon the horns of theodicy I already faced unknowingly the problem of the relationship between events and the significance attached to them afterwards or, putting it the other way round, between

126

the lessons of the past and the events that inspired them – the relationship between myth and history, if you will – which underlies the more strictly anthropological problems confronted in this chapter. The reader eager to know the fate of Shechem may perhaps afford to skip the next three sections.

I

The reverence with which I once treated this text has long since been replaced by the respect which an anthropologist owes it, and if there remains much that I am unable to explain I think that anthropology has helped me to make sense of much more. If, as has been suggested, it is in the first place an origin myth of an ancient Middle Eastern tribe it falls clearly within the province of anthropology and if, on the contrary, it is to be treated as history then it is hardly less so, for it is the history not only of a people of an *other* culture but of a kind of society that is only studied elsewhere by anthropologists. Indeed it is hard to see how anybody would dare today to embark upon the study of Genesis without first equipping himself with a modicum of anthropological knowledge, for without it he has no comparative dimension in which to assess the meaning and functioning of the institutions described therein. This is not saying that I think I know more about the Bible than those who have devoted their whole life's work to its study – I know no Hebrew and my knowledge of the commentaries is scanty, to say the least – but there are problems in the elucidation of Genesis that can only be approached from an anthropological standpoint, so I would like to think that my experience of other cultures may in some degree compensate for my ignorance and inexperience in the realm of Bible studies, and that what I have to say may nevertheless not be without interest for those who know so much more than I do.

I am not by any means the first anthropologist to be attracted by the challenge that Genesis presents. First of all there was Frazer who found in it validation for his view of primitive mentality. His explanation of the story of the Fall of Man which opens the first volume of *Folklore in the Old Testament* remains one of the great passages in anthropological literature. He believed that symbolic values could be interpreted by reference to universal properties attaching to different objects and that these were to be discovered in myths from other parts of the world. Thus the significance of the serpent was provided by the fact that this reptile sheds its skin and thereby appears to escape mortality, for its old life is cast off at the end of its term yet the beast lives on. The association of serpents with immortality is identified in myths from many other parts of the world. The message whose sense is inverted is another theme which Frazer found in other mythologies relating the loss of eternal life and he wove this too into his explanation of the Garden of Eden: man was cheated of eternal life by the serpent who thus acquired it. Such a method, which was typical of his epoch, ignores the discreteness of cultures assuming that it is a question of how people think and that all primitive people think alike – a highly ethnocentric supposition – and it leads to arbitrariness in argument, since one can always find similarities somewhere to justify the significance attributed to any given symbol. It also led to the endless string of examples which enabled Frazer to fill so many volumes and thereby earn for himself a reputation for scholarship among his contemporaries and the distrust of future generations of anthropologists. But Frazer is silent about the problem which concerns me, the basis of the rule of endogamy, which has come to be accepted as the first principle of Mediterranean marriage, and this is all the more extraordinary since he paid attention to the marriage of cousins in the Old Testament. Frazer's view of kinship was anything but systematic and this is perhaps the explanation, but his successors have attempted to set this right. The most eminent of these, Sir Edmund Leach, who is also Frazer's most severe critic, has offered us a very different interpretation of the Old Testament, first of all in a demonstration of structural analysis entitled, 'Lévi-Strauss in the Garden of Eden'[1] which he followed with a second essay 'Genesis as Myth'.[2] In a third essay on the Old Testament the problem of kinship is attacked in relation to the 'Legitimacy of Solomon'.[3] Here he adopts again 'an explicitly Lévi-Straussian proce- dure'[4] though he expresses doubts about his grasp of certain aspects of Lévi-Strauss' thought. The procedure that he employs is to identify patterns of binary oppositions constituting a structure which recurs in different places in the text of the Old Testament, transformed or inverted into a mirror-image, and which is founded upon a theme on which his analysis focusses. The theme is a major contradiction between, on the one hand, a theological dogma, the promise of the land of Palestine to the descendants of Abraham, which he thinks implies the preference for endogamy (since in order to inherit this land the Israelites must be pure in blood and in religion) and on the other 'a less idealized form of tradition' constituted by the *fact* that the population of Palestine consists of a mixture of peoples intermarrying freely.[5] The early chapters of the Old Testament are concerned with the question 'how foreign is foreign?': from the point of view of endogamy how closely related must a spouse be for the offspring to be legitimate? The function of the text, whether myth or history, is to mediate this contradiction. 'The facts and the politico-religious theories are not mutually compatible'[6] and the Biblical account produces apparent 'solutions' to this fundamental contradiction (which is irresolvable in reality) by glossing it over, making Solomon appear at the same time pure in descent yet also descended from the original owners of the land of Canaan, from Esau the Edomite and from Heth the Canaanite.[7] This dual, if contradictory, attribution of descent also overcomes a second logical contradiction: that the Israelites' claim to the land is founded upon the right of conquest when they have conquered it, but remains valid subsequently despite conquest by others when the land is taken from them. The ambiguous status of the northern kingdom, Israelite in origin but opposed to Judah, makes the resolution of this conflict easier, for it can be considered, according to circumstances, either as belonging to the chosen people or opposed to them.

The demonstration includes discussions of the relationship of myth and history. The document must be treated as a unity, he says, regardless of the origins of different texts. Hence 'the historical portions of the Old Testament constitute a unitary myth-history which functioned as a justification for the state of Jewish society at a time when this part of the Biblical text achieved approximate canonical stability'[8] and 'To assess these structures we do not need to know how particular stories came to assume their present form nor the dates at which they were written'.[9] Thus he sets out[10] 'to demonstrate the existence of structural order . . . in specifically chronological sequences of events as recorded in Biblical history' and he does this by reducing the narrative from 1 Samuel (4) to 2 Kings (2) to a 'pattern' and arranging it as a three-act play developing, in parallel, two themes: sex relations and political relations.

While paying tribute to the richness of observation, and the sublety of the arguments, I have to admit firstly that I am not sure that I have followed them all correctly and secondly that this does not look to me very much like Lévi-Strauss' method, at least in its entirety, but rather more like certain aspects of it put to the service of quite different premises and aims.

To begin with, the treatment of the genealogies in the text is assumed to validate the geographical location of the tribes in accordance with the British tradition of studies, not of myth, but of social structures on the ground. (Evans-Pritchard and Peters are explicitly referred to.) This seems closer to Malinowski than to Lévi-Strauss as indeed does the notion of the function of Solomon's legitimacy which differs from Malinowski's notion of a charter only by being founded upon a paradox which it mediates, rather than upon a direct demonstration of what it validates. Even in this respect the difference is slight for Malinowski pointed to 'a special class of mythological stories which justify and account for the anomalous state of affairs' created by 'a conflict of principles' when the rule 'that land and authority belong to those who are literally born out of it' is endangered by the arrival of 'members of a sub-clan of high rank who choose to settle down in a new locality' and who 'cannot very well be resisted by the autochthons'.[11] Moreover the method of 'drastically reducing' the elements of the story in order to bring the pattern into evidence[12] and permit its representation as a three-act play does not look to me like a Lévi-Straussian procedure at all, for Lévi-Strauss has always insisted on the necessity to conserve all the details of a myth, that is to say *not* to reduce it.

But the chief difficulty concerns the validity of the enterprise in the first place which Lévi-Strauss has always denied, asserting that his method cannot be applied to a document that has passed through the processes of literary editing which places it in another class, no longer the unadulterated product of the structure of mind but deformed by the constraints of social life during the epochs of its reinterpretation. In reply to Ricoeur, who suggested that his method was applicable only to non-literate peoples but who maintained on theoretical grounds that there must be one and only one explanation of mythology, Lévi-Strauss remarked that his position was extremely prudent and *nuancée*[13] but his fundamental objection is that edited myths have been rehandled with a different aim in view in a different social context and therefore they have become a different intellectual operation.[14]

Leach does not appreciate the difference between pure and edited myth: 'Lévi-Strauss uses a narrow definition of myth which makes it appear that the myths of contemporary Amerindians are cultural products of an entirely different kind from the mythical-historical traditions of the Jewish people in the first century B.C. My own view is that this distinction is quite artificial and that the structural analysis of myth should be equally applicable to both the time of men and the time of Gods.'[15]

Leach has quite a lot to say about history in this essay, but he does not refer to Lévi-Strauss' views on this subject other than to point out that the latter views 'ethnology and history as complementary but quite distinct forms of enquiry'.[16] This is all the more surprising in view of the enormous importance of history in Lévi-Strauss' theory from the very beginning of his work up to and throughout the *Mythologiques*. Moreover the relation between myth and history must surely be primordial to a theory of myth since both are representations of the past. Leach lumps them together as 'myth-history'[17] Lévi-Strauss sees them as different mental operations belonging to different types of society.

To sum up then, Lévi-Strauss refuses to deal with Genesis as myth. Leach sees no reason not to; he uses what he believes to be Lévi-Strauss' method but refuses to restrict it to what he calls 'myth proper'[18] i.e. the myths of simple non-literate societies uncorrupted by editors. I accept Lévi-Strauss' limitation of his method to such societies and have attempted to elaborate a rather different method for the Book of Genesis, which I believe takes account of the problem of history that Leach appears to me to evade.

II

There are many theories of myth which I shall not go into but I would note like Percy Cohen[19] that they are not mutually exclusive; each can be valued for what it explains. Among British social anthropologists the influence of Malinowski's thinking on this subject was preponderant until a decade ago and, since one can distinguish several theories of myth in his work, it is worth examining what he thought were the functions of myth, for they are all related to its effects upon practical life. First of all, in *Argonauts of the Western Pacific*, he perceived that they give meaning to geographical features:[20] nature and the environment are represented and explained in the natives' minds by the stories about them which act as mnemonic devices in this way. In 'Baloma, the spirits of the Dead',[21] it had already been shown how myths lend authority to beliefs regarding such transcendental matters as the behaviour of ghosts and a connection is thus established with mortuary customs which take account of these beliefs. Beliefs in the supernatural world provide in the *Argonauts* the authority for practical functions in relation to the organisation of labour required for canoe-building or to the practices employed in fishing and gardening. He also perceived that they strengthen the morale of the natives and give them heart to face the rigours of work on land and the dangers of seafaring. By connecting myth with belief and belief with social organisation Malinowski came to elaborate his final theory of myth as a charter for customs and social institutions and this he expounded in 'Myth in Primitive Psychology',[22] together with the psychological theory already mentioned.

Malinowski distinguished between different kinds of mythical pronouncement, ranging from sacred myth, via historical tale to idle tale intended only to entertain and certainly we must recognise, not only that among the Trobrianders there are different kinds of oral literature, but that as Radin and Kroeber had already observed all cultures do not provide myths identical in character and in quantity; some are rich and some are poor in myth. But these distinctions gave rise to no further theoretical considerations and were subsequently ignored. Moreover, though Malinowski states that the way in which the natives regarded the sacred myths was very different from their attitude to the other two classes of stories[23] he was not always able to distinguish them himself, for the same story is told[24] as sacred myth that is cited in the *Argonauts*[25] as a fairy-tale.

Under Malinowski's influence it came to be accepted that myth serves the function of fixing certain values in the minds of people and acts thus as a charter which validates the social structure. This view has much in common with Durkheim's view of religion and like it, it is not so much wrong as inadequate to explain more than one aspect of the phenomenon. This it does moreover in a rather unmethodical way since it provides no clear rules of interpretation.[26] Whatever connection comes to mind will do by way of explanation. Nor is one ever difficult to find, since, given that cultures possess a certain intellectual unity, the same concepts and assumptions appear both in the myths and in other aspects of discourse connected with daily life. Myth reinforces custom in this sense if one is sufficiently selective in the choice of myths, but it throws no fresh light on social structure which is better investigated directly and for this reason such attention as the subject received for the next generation was limited to invoking myths in illustration where appropriate rather than as in itself a worthwhile subject for study.[27] In addition, this theory of myth, unlike Malinowski's first theory, takes little heed of what a whole myth means to the people who tell it. Though he frequently insists on the importance of 'the native ideas' he relates then only to particular institutions, pointing out that without an understanding of them one would misinterpret the myth. The phantasy employed in myth is left on one side unless it can be connected directly with the experience of the natives. In short it ignores all those features of myth that caused other scholars to liken it to dream whose essence is precisely as Freud showed that it should *not* be interpreted consciously by the dreamer but should convey a cryptic message that consciousness represses.

Lévi-Strauss (whose work often has Freudian undertones) produced a much more sophisticated theory of myth which brought in the factors Malinowski had ignored and provided a method for ordering the detail of myth and explaining the variation between differing versions of the same myth – a consideration which never crossed Malinowski's mind. Moreover he overcomes the difficulty that myths so often appear to be advocating the opposite of what society requires, by searching for its meaning in the structures that lie behind consciousness – 'myths get thought in the minds of men, unbeknown to them'.[28] But while he pays great attention to the general cultural setting and even more to the geographical setting and uses it in a far more significant way than Malinowski, he seems unconcerned with the social use of myths – how they are handled in daily life – and not much troubled by the fact that most of the myths he analyses were recorded not in the vernacular but in the language of the ethnographer. This is connected with his particular view of what the structure of myth is composed of – mythemes: simple literal elements of meaning – and his belief that myths are the product of mind unencumbered by practical restraints and, as such, closed systems of thought. What the people actually do when they're not telling myths is not *immediately* relevant, but only relevant insofar as it may oblige them to modify their thought in other ways: it affects the significance of the elements in the myth since this is never innate but 'de position' i.e. given by the relation of the symbol to other symbols. 'A myth can perfectly well contradict ethnographical reality . . . or preserve the memory of customs no longer practised or practised only elsewhere';[29] its relationship to ethnographical reality, though essential to its interpretation, is not one of direct representation but rather a connection between different levels related necessarily but as totalities.

At the same time he has restricted himself almost entirely to the myths of the American Indians which appear to be different not only from those written origin myths studied by Eliade, but from those of the Trobriand Islanders. The differences between the myths of the Amerindians and those of Melanesia or Africa[30] are yet to be discussed in detail, but Lévi-Strauss has produced throughout the length of his work reasons integral to the rest of his thought for not applying his method to the mythology of Western civilisation and complex societies. These reasons have not been well understood. In the discussions with Ricoeur and with Leach he explained only that once myths have been transformed into sacred texts such as the Bible, they have passed through many editorial hands and the pristine structures have been perverted beyond recognition. But he did not refer to the reasons he has given elsewhere for regarding what Leach calls 'the time of Gods and the time of men' as conceptually different and requiring different modes of interpretation. He had himself given a structural analysis of the myth of Oedipus and it might be asked: if Oedipus why not Adam and Eve? But the analysis of Oedipus was offered *then* only as a demonstration of method because it was a myth already known to his readers and Lévi-Strauss suggested at that time that 'its use is probably not legitimate in this particular instance'.[31] But the fact that it could be done at all implies that it could be done with other similar myths. The question remains however whether Genesis can be assimilated to the Greek myths.

Recently he has returned to the mythology of Europe and attacked the Legend of the Holy Grail.[32] It becomes evident from the account of his lectures that he is attempting an ethnological reconstruction of the original myth. That is, the structural analysis does not apply directly to the text of Chrétien de Troyes or any other of the literary accounts but is recomposed thanks to his understanding of the universal logic of myth, aided by some comparisons with certain Algonquin myths. But such far flung comparison is hardly likely to reassure his British colleagues, who already feel uncomfortable whenever Lévi-Strauss' faith in the psychic unity of mankind is pronounced for it reminds them of Tylor and Frazer. In fact he believes that, despite this unity, the modes of thought and the rules of conduct are assembled by primitive cultures in a different way and demand therefore a different framework of interpretation. In this way he marks a distinction which his British colleagues in the main refuse and not only in the realms of myth.

The distinction between primitive and complex culture was first marked by Lévi-Strauss in his thinking on kinship where he limits himself entirely to the elementary structures maintaining that complex structures operate in quite another way. He has little more to say about the latter than that certain kinship systems are in transition toward complex structure, because they are not really operating according to his rules for elementary structures. It is highly significant to me that the area of my particular concern, the Mediterranean, he has avoided even more studiously in kinship than in mythology: in the 600-odd pages of the *Elementary Structures* there is no mention of the kinship of any Mediterranean people, for he regards it as entirely complex in structure.

A similar distinction is made by Lévi-Strauss (which does not necessarily correspond to that between elementary and complex structures of kinship, but applies roughly to the same societies: simple primitive societies and complex societies such as our own) concerning the conceptualisation of time, and this relates to his theory of history to which anthropologists appear like Leach to have paid scant attention.

I do not refer here to his observations on the discipline of history to be found in *Structural Anthropology*, but to the way in which the past is related to the present in the thought of different cultures.

The distinction first appears in his essay 'Race and History' where he distinguishes between static and cumulative history and it is spelled out in *La Pensée sauvage* of which it forms as it were the theoretical backbone.

The conflict between diachrony and synchrony, between history and systems of classification, is fundamental and is resolved in two alternative ways by different cultures. He typifies societies as 'hot' or 'cold' according to whether they conceptualise their past as cumulative or static. Europe and Asia are a 'totemic vacuum' because 'these civilisations have chosen to explain themselves through history and this enterprise is incompatible with that which classes things and beings into closed groups',[33] which is the characteristic of totemic thought. He distinguishes also between strong and weak history according to the importance attached to diachrony.

Historical events play little part in Leach's work, either in the ethnographies of Burma or of Ceylon for in each he is concerned to find repetitive processes. In 'Cronus and Chronos'[34] he divides the many senses of Time into those that view it as cyclical and those that view it as irreversible, but though he has most interesting things to say about the former and the influence of religious dogmas in imposing it and of religious rites in establishing a means of measuring Time, the relationship between events in time which is irreversible – the main concern of historians – receives little attention. Classification is not opposed to history but encompasses it, whereas for Lévi-Strauss there is a fundamental antipathy between the two.[35] Congruently with this, when he came later to utilise Lévi-Strauss' method of establishing oppositions and mediators between them, he recognised none of the limitations by which Lévi-Strauss confined his method and ignored his basic distinctions between history and classification, between event and structure and between action and mind. Hence he found no reason to treat myth any more than history as a closed system.

In 'The Legitimacy of Solomon' the oppositions of which the structures are composed are not only between mythemes, minimal elements of meaning within the myth, but also and very often between the moral implications of the story or expressed rules of conduct taken from another book of the Old Testament. For example, the stories of Dinah (see below, p. 146–7) and Samson are said to be 'opposites', that is, to have the same structure, one being the inversion of the other.[36] But this view is conditional upon accepting the implications that Leach derives from the incidents. He regards the treachery of Samson's foreign wives as the counterpart of the 'dishonourableness' of the Shechemites in the story of Dinah. But why were the Shechemites dishonourable? Because their prince polluted Dinah by sleeping with her? This is to use a concept of honour which is anything but Mediterranean. Simeon and Levi take the humiliation or pollution of their sister as an affront and, unlike their father, they are prepared to respond to it. If treachery is the inferred moral value to be taken as an element of structure, then the counterpart is surely the treachery of Simeon and Levi which explains Jacob's attitude subsequently (Genesis 49.5) when they are displaced in the leadership of the Israelite tribe by their younger brother Judah. In any case neither treachery nor honourableness can be described as mythemes, for they are evaluations of conduct, not in themselves elements.

To take another example Leach states: 'Lot's virtue in Sodom turns to sin afterwards and the sin is that of ignoring endogamy altogether.' But Genesis does not say it was sinful of Lot to be seduced by his daughters. He did not know he had been anyway, because he was drunk at the time. He was the blameless victim of their plot to have children by him and it was entirely successful and rewarded by progeny. To claim that Lot was sinful one must have recourse to the prohibition expressed elsewhere in the Old Testament and this involves accepting that its various books have the same conceptual unity as a single myth.

This difference between the two authors with regard to structure rests upon another, the relationship between the myth and its ethnographical background: for Lévi-Strauss it is dialectical, for Leach it is direct, in the sense that the significance of the elements of a myth is given by reference to the customs and values of the people in everyday life. This has been illustrated by the example of Lot's 'sinfulness'. It is expressed clearly in a later publication,[37] where he explains:

> Any infringement of the standard conventions generates a sense of emotional shock which we experience *either* as embarrassment or as excitement.
>
> And even in a story, any reference to a transgression of taboo, however oblique, creates vicarious excitement. In this respect the myths of our own society have quite a different quality for *us* from the myths of other people. Myths everywhere make constant reference to moral offenses, but unless, as listener or reader, you share the same moral assumptions as the myth narrator, you will not be 'shocked' by what he says and you will then have difficulty in picking up the message. For it is the *shock* effect of references to breaches of moral taboo which gives myth its 'meaning'.

What is done in the myth derives its 'shock effect' from a direct comparison with what is thought to be proper in everyday life. In the same way the contradictions which run through 'The Legitimacy of Solomon' depend upon the rules of behaviour laid down in the prescriptive passages of the Pentateuch qualified by the anthropologists' estimation of their advantages and drawbacks. The moral rules of the society are necessary not merely in order to explain the myth as a whole but to interpret the incidents within it. The meaning of each element is given by its position in relation to the moral assumptions of the people, whereas, for Lévi-Strauss, by its position in relation to the other elements of the myth. The editors of Genesis do indeed appear to have edited the myths from which their text originated with their moral assumptions in mind, bringing their consciousness of diachrony to bear upon them in order to derive a 'kerygmatic' message,[38] but this is why Lévi-Strauss regards the final product as different in nature from the myths of societies which have no editors. Hence, while I agree with Leach that moral assumptions must be considered in interpreting Genesis, it is precisely this in my view that makes it necessary to distinguish myth from history and search for a different framework of interpretation for the latter; the framework of 'cold society' is no longer appropriate.

The contradictions on which Leach's interpretation is founded are not between aspects of the mortal or social condition that are irresolvable in reality, but between the rules of marriage and considerations of practical policy that are resolved in fact, within the Old Testament, by the political events that are the outcomes: the violation of Yahweh's proscription of marriage alliance with foreign women does not pay, it is always followed sooner or later by disaster. But quite apart from whether the contradiction is resolvable or not and whether the solution is provided by the myth itself or not, it appears to me that *rules* of marriage and considerations of policy do not have the same theoretical status: *belief* in the religious virtue of keeping the blood pure, which entails the recommendation to marry within the faith, is one thing – it is a rule frequently violated in practice – the political advantage of marriage alliances, including the possibility of laying claim to land through them, is quite another. It is never in any case formulated as a principle in the text, but only inferred by the observer, who if he is an anthropologist knows it to be real.

Moreover, the contradiction between claiming the right to land by conquest and claiming it by virtue of previous possession is a contradiction only in moral terms depending upon the assumptions of the observer. It involves what is called 'a double standard' which is a contradiction if equality is recognised as the basis of inter-tribal relations, but not if the system is defined as competitive; once there are winners and losers, and this is accepted, all standards are double in the view of those who do not accept this premise of inequality (as is argued in Chapter 4) and autochthony and conquest are merely alternative ways of validating the occupation of land to be used in pursuance of the same ethnocentric end which is the maintenance and expansion of the tribal territory. In such terms (in which reciprocity plays no part, for conquest can hardly be a reciprocal relationship) there is no contradiction involved in the ambition to keep what you have and get more at the expense of your neighbours. These are the terms which will, below, make it possible to explain the marriage customs of the Mediterranean.

Yahweh's injunctions to avoid entanglements with foreign women are plain: explicit in prescription and demonstrated by outcomes which are the result of divine anger. But the political advantages of taking foreign wives are never stated (not even in the case of Solomon's first marriage) and such marriages are represented, only when they are explicitly disapproved of by Yahweh, as lapses from fidelity. Concordantly, captured women who represent no threat to the faith are perfectly acceptable as concubines and even as wives. Deuteronomy 21.10 gives prescriptions as to the proper treatment of such women.

By constituting his structures from a mixture of what the narrative records and what the anthropologist infers from the injunctions of the laws and what his science tells him Leach appears to me to be fusing different levels of discourse and 'allowing on stage' considerations that are extraneous to the narrative which, if myth it is, is no longer a closed system. In the same spirit Beaumont and Fletcher wrote into their plays commentaries from members of the public who were given seats upon the stage. By allowing the latter to become part of the plot they bridged the gap between the actors and the audience. Such a theatrical device has been tried before and since: not only Pirandello but even classical Greek tragedy went some way towards breaking down the closure of the dramatic system, the former by pushing his characters into the audience, the latter by bringing the audience, vicariously through the chorus, on stage. Both manoeuvres aim to create the impression that the play is a spontaneous *event*. But this is an illusion for in fact Pirandello's actors still have their lines to learn and the Greek chorus' comments were written by Aeschylus, they were not really 'audience participation'. Like a conjuror's accomplice who volunteers to take a card, they guarantee the veracity of events on stage even if in so doing they betray the fact that it is after all only a performance. But the point is this: in breaking down the closure of the dramatic system they aim to take the play out of 'dream-time' and make it figure in historical time. If therefore Leach treats history as though it were myth he also in this sense treats myth as though it were history. The concept of 'myth-history' enables him to do both at the same time by simply denying any distinction between the two. But by offering as an explanation of his 'unitary myth-history' a function in relation to the state of Jewish society around three thousand years ago he appears to be covertly admitting a distinction between the two none the less. For once 'canonical stability' has been achieved the presence of the myth is no longer to be explained as a function of the present but as a bequest from the past.

I do not complain that Leach has not followed Lévi-Strauss' method *in toto* but has adapted it and grafted it on to different premises – surely he has every right to use it as he thinks best and in an endeavour of his own choice? I regret only that he has not pointed out where he has departed from it, for he can hardly be supposed to have done so unintentionally since he has devoted a number of articles and a short book to the analysis of Lévi-Strauss' theories. To offer as an 'explicitly Lévi-Straussian procedure' an analysis based upon theoretical assumptions that are the contrary of those from which Lévi-Strauss derived his procedures will hardly lead to a better understanding of this much misinterpreted author, to say the least.

While agreeing with 'The Legitimacy of Solomon' that the essential problem with which Genesis is concerned is that of endogamy and land rights, I find myself at odds with Leach at a number of points and believe that it may be helpful to summarise them briefly at the beginning so that the reader may keep an eye open for them as I progress:

(1) Leach assumes that there came a moment in time when the story was fixed in writing – the 'editorial present' he once called it – and this makes it possible to explain the genealogies of Genesis in terms of the relations between the tribes of Israel on the ground *at that time*. I do not believe that there was any 'editorial present' in fact but a process of sifting and collating of texts and sacred oral traditions spanning many centuries.[39] The hypothesis of the editorial present therefore appears to me methodologically inappropriate since it denies the accumulation of events over time. In Lévi-Strauss' terms he treats a 'hot' society as if it were 'cold'. I do not agree with him that myth and history can be assimilated. Moreover he treats all the narratives of the Old Testament as a single myth, while I believe that they constitute different versions of various myths and that these must be distinguished as to how 'mythical' they are. I see a progression in them which can be attributed to the ordering of the final text by the editors, and which gives them their meaning as sacred documents, a meaning quite different from that which derives from 'the comparative analysis (of different versions) which makes it possible to distinguish their common structure and their meaning'.[40]

(2) Leach fails to consider the Mediterranean nature of this document. There is no cultural setting; it might be from anywhere. It might be stated in counter-objection that Genesis is just as sacred for the Church of England as it is for anybody in the Mediterranean and therefore it is not a specifically Mediterranean document any longer. This would be taking an extreme functionalist and anti-historical point of view. It is worth considering only in order to raise the very interesting question of what changed significance is given to this story by the different cultural traditions which revere it. What Islam has done with it (including such thoroughgoing transformations as the replacement of Isaac by Ishmael in the story of the sacrifice) is something I am to my regret quite unable

to deal with.[41] What Western Europe has done with it is touched on in consideration of the story of Onan (see below, p. 169).

(3) Finally and in continuation of the previous point, Leach sees nothing worthy of comment in the particular form of endogamy practised by the Israelites; it is just endogamy as anywhere else, while I regard it as rather different from that found elsewhere and indeed I question whether we should speak of it as endogamy at all, save in the sense that the Israelites are constantly visited with the anger of Jahweh for contracting sexual liaisons with infidel women. But there is no equivalent anger reserved for Israelites who give their daughters to foreigners and in the rare instances where this appears to have occurred the matter is passed over without comment.

III

I would like to take the whole of traditional discourse whether recorded in writing by the people themselves or by the ethnographer – all that has been called myth, legend, epic, parable, exemplary tale, or even 'idle tale', all holy writ, all stories that are supposed or imagined to have happened – as a field within which to make distinctions and I would first of all distinguish them according to the degree to which they express a conscious fiat, that is to say, to which the listener or reader is aware that he is being told to do or not to do something. At one pole then one would put 'pure myth', the myths of non-literate societies such as Lévi-Strauss has analysed in the *Mythologiques*, and at the other those codes of divine injunction conveyed through the delivery of tables, the establishment of covenants or the emission of explicit moral judgements. No moral precepts are set forth in all the *Mythologiques* and the aetio-logical aspect of such myths, whatever custom they may appear to validate, entails no recommendation as regards behaviour; the loss of immortality, the acquisition of fire or the origin of a totem are not presented as guides to action in the sense that they can be imitated by living men who might wish to evade death, make fire or change their totem. Moreover, far from setting an example which reinforces custom they frequently contravene it: among peoples who respect the rights of primogeniture younger brothers get the best of elder brothers; Asdiwal's marriages were both matrilocal though the Tsimshians marry patri-locally.[42] In contrast the sacred texts of literate societies are full of moral precept expressed in a variety of ways. They are morally charged while pure myth is morally indifferent.

Corresponding to this distinction pure myth is expressed in terms that bear little relation to 'real' experience, while at the other pole a certain realism is obviously necessary if the injunction is to have any application. It is no good telling men to fly, to come to life again after being killed or to transform themselves into animals. The only sphere in which pure myth can be in any sense a guide is that of ritual, and the connection between the two has been rightly stressed ever since Robertson Smith, but ritual precisely allows no liberty of action to the participants, they do not have to decide what to do next, or what would be better. They have only to do it correctly or it is not considered to have been done at all.

The first pole might be said to relate to imagination, the latter to action. Both are placed in the past but in pure myth that past is unconnected diachronically with the present. 'Once upon a time' implies only 'not now'; it is not a point in time conceived as continuous down to the present, but simply a time opposed to the present, 'dream-time' as certain Australian aborigines have put it and as Leach has aptly cited.[43] We might then say that the past of pure myth is not the passed and gone, but only the 'not actually happening at this moment for all to witness'. It remains present in spirit in the rites which reactivate it on another plane. In millenarian prophecies it can even be projected into the future when the rites, so far from commemorating what happened, provoke what is expected to happen. But whether placed in the past or the future it has no perspective: it is not composed of periods *relatively* distant from the present, but of a single plane like a backdrop divorced by its very nature from the events that are represented in front of it. Experienced only in thought, its relation to temporality is different from that which is experienced in action which leaves its results behind able to be remembered but not altered. That which is done is done. But the happenings in myth can be undone or done again with the opposite result. In the absence of limitations of a practical nature pure myth resembles the dream, while mandatory myth must, if lessons regarding behaviour are to be drawn from it, be placed in the context of experienced reality. The significance of the notion of a miracle is precisely that, though it occurs in such a context, it interrupts the recognised regularity of cause and effect in favour of divine intervention which has licence to circumvent the rules of everyday experience and in doing so it harks back for an instant to the idiom of pure myth where there are no miracles since all is miraculous. It represents then the point of juncture between the two kinds of time and the two poles of discourse and brings to a realistic narrative of the diachronically conceived past the magical power of the free imagination, the instantaneousness of pure myth which incorporates the past into the present. Hence those nineteenth- and early twentieth-century scholars who strove, in the cause of reconciling their belief in Christianity with their belief in Science, to explain the miracles of the Bible in 'rational' terms, positing that the crossing of the Red Sea was able to be effected thanks to an exceptional hurricane or that Moses had a remarkable geological sense which enabled him to choose the right place to strike the rock at the critical moment, were simply de-sacralising a text that their successors no longer bother to read.[44]

The field of traditional discourse I have chosen does not of course include modern 'literature', but it is perhaps worth observing in parenthesis that our own secular writing varies greatly in the degree in which a fiat is explicit: from tales of phantasy to legal codes and from comic strips to political tracts. The writings of scientists and historians clearly belong, despite their apparent absence of moral injunctions, near the mandatory realistic pole, for they aim to explain what is or was with a view to enabling men to formulate principles of behaviour and those who do not themselves draw their conclusions regarding action are often accused by practically-minded persons (not without a certain irritation) of being in an 'ivory tower' as though it were evident that their duty was to 'provide the answers' not to day-dream. It is characteristic of the scientific outlook to believe that facts and conclusions must be separated, but why study the accounts of the Florentine bankers of the Renaissance if you do not believe that *ultimately* some profit may be drawn in terms of economic theory or of our understanding of the European past or even of human behaviour in general? The realism of science is inspired by the desire to find 'the answers' to the question of what to do. The place of 'science fiction' in such a scheme is not without interest, for it is a literature of phantasy masquerading as a kind of science and consequently it is always placed in the indeterminate future in a time discontinuous with the present from which it is separated by some new invention such as interplanetary communication. It is 'once-upon-a-time' that has yet to occur.

This scheme is not intended for the classification of myths but rather as an aid in understanding different aspects of myths that vary in the emphasis they place upon one or other end of the spectrum, that is, the degree to which their relationship to conduct is explicit. Pure myths do not concern themselves with recommendations as to behaviour, while at the other end of the scale we find the code of Hammurabi, the laws of Manu or the inscribed plates delivered by the angel of God to Joseph Smith in Ontario County, New York, in 1827. But the very fact that Smith's plates should have disappeared mysteriously, remaining ever since the object of a quest throughout the world (which includes some notable archaeological excavations by the New World Foundation) shows how the emphasis can change and incorporate elements from the other end of the spectrum. The Mormon plates, too sacred to remain tangible, have been whisked away to join the long line of sacred texts that have disappeared – a simulacrum among literate peoples of that hoard of divine injunctions whose message is lost or misconstrued that Frazer accumulated to support his interpretation of the Garden of Eden.

In any case, the relationship to conduct of even the most explicit extant code – surely this must be the Koran? – is always tenuous and dependent upon particular social situations which, in changing, pervert the meanings formerly attached to it. The mandatory pole is thus always, as it were, slipping into the obscurity of the past simply by remaining involved in a situation that is no longer operative. For each generation the explications must be renewed; the relevance pointed out afresh. The text itself recedes into a cryptic condition where it is no longer clear nor generally agreed what the injunction enjoins. It requires commentators to rescue it and no sooner have they done so than another century of change requires a change of commentators. Time like an ever-flowing stream bears all our past away and if it is not to be lost entirely, if its connection with the present is to be maintained, scholars must continually redraw the lessons of experience. The continuum therefore represents the degree of explicitness – which is never in any case total – with which the voices of the past are made to speak. In view of this Lévi-Strauss seems justified in contending that his method of structural analysis which, as it was elaborated in the *Mythologiques*, set diachrony on one side was applicable only to the mythology of those societies that have no editors. The myths he analyses have no connection with the lessons of experience and he views them as synchronic sets in which sequence has little significance. Their meaning is more akin to the meaning of dreams in Freudian theory than to that attributed to Pharaoh's dream by Joseph who by a scheme of equivalences derived his prophecy of the impending famine.

Now it may be objected that in fact, as Stephen Hugh-Jones' ethnography shows.[45] even the simple people of the Brazilian jungles use their myths to validate their conduct and in this sense they might be cited as charters for action. However the charter is not explicit in the myth but depends simply on the whim of the individual who, unaided by commentators and dogmas, invokes the precedent provided by myth as he sees fit and rather as literary authors once inserted references to the classics when they wished to support their views with the authority of the ancients. The use to which the myth is put in action is no guide to its structure – which might explain why Lévi-Strauss is unperturbed by the absence of such information. In fact in its *usage* myth might be likened to the body of proverbs that European peasantries like to quote. The proverb does indeed pretend, unlike the myth, to lay down principles of conduct, advise regarding expectations, point to regularities, and can be cited to provide authority for a given course of action, but taken as a whole it is not clear what course, for the notable characteristic of a *body* of proverbs is that it recommends *all* courses of action; its lessons all contradict one another. 'Out of sight, out of mind' but 'absence makes the heart grow fonder'. 'A stitch in time saves nine' but 'sufficient unto the day is the evil thereof' and 'don't count your chickens before they're hatched'. In a study I made of those repeated in an Andalusian village I discovered that a proverb could always be found to justify any course of action and therefore it was used only as a validation of that chosen for quite other reasons. Moreover the body of proverbs included many that were not applicable at all but were repeated for their alliterative charm; these appeared to have entered the popular treasury via the radio's folklore programmes among other ways and came presumably from other parts of Spain where they had once been applicable. In this class were proverbs advising the month in which vines should be tilled or fruit-trees pruned which were never followed and weather proverbs quite inappropriate to the Sierra de Cadiz where I collected them. They cannot then be said to be mandatory but only at the most validatory and very often not even that. They furnish an armoury of weapons not a strategy.

That proverbs should be able to be used in this way is surely due to the fact that they involve no dogma and are commented on by no professional scholars who feel it necessary to elucidate their message and draw a moral from them. Those such as Rodriguez Marín who have turned their attention to proverbs have been content to collect them as things in themselves, 'gems of peasant wisdom', without ever attempting to elaborate a theory of the popular wisdom contained in them. The quality and above all the quantity was what counted for Rodriguez Marín, as the titles of his compendia showed,[46] but his gems remained unset, in a pile as it were, in which the relation between one and another was of no significance. The whole spirit of the endeavour, thoroughly in accordance with the notion of folklore, was to collect them for the aesthetic pleasure they could give to the unknown reader without any regard for what in terms of action they might imply. In the same spirit a British publisher produced in 1937 *The Bible designed to be read as literature* which presumably meant: without regard for the edification that might be derived from it, for it was 'intended for all readers, of whatever belief, opinion or bringing-up'. One senses that it was meant for unbelievers, and in the same way folklorists are 'unbelievers' in peasant culture, viewing it from outside and with aims quite different from those who use it but do not collect it.

I trust I have convinced the reader that despite their mandatory form proverbs provide anything but a blue-print and a guide to conduct. Their purpose is rather to provide a means to ratify any event which may occur and thus strip it of its novelty and preserve society from innovation. They classify events immediately in terms of tradition and thereby place them in the timeless past of peasant wisdom 'out of harm's way'. They bolster in a quite illusory way by reference to a supposedly unchanging past the notion of stability to which they cling in the face of the many threats to their way of life and thereby they provide the urban commentator who believes in progress with an excuse for complaining of peasant traditionalism and backwardness.

If the usage of myth in everyday life is not dissimilar from that of proverbs in that it provides a frame of reference within which individuals can comment on events and justify their actions, its structure and its inspiration are quite different, for it has no pretension to furnish recommendations or account for how things really work. For this reason its imagination is quite unfettered by conscious understanding of experience. Hence all the inversions of commonsense and of moral precept: animals talk, humans are transformed, fly or disappear suddenly, the gods commit incest, contend with each other, punish out of spite. That which is forbidden is not merely allowed but pays off handsomely as in those apparently immoral events I read about in Genesis forty-odd years ago. But the Book of Genesis also contains clearly enunciated rules of conduct – (even if the Ten Commandments do not appear until the next book) whose infringement is punished – especially it seems when the guilty are not Israelites. There is a general if irregular movement throughout the Old Testament from the first pole to the second, and the Israelites of later books get it in the neck for infringing the rules laid down by Yahweh.

IV

We might place the Book of Genesis at the point of transition where the age of myth begins to give way to the age of philosophy:[47] Its messages are hidden only too often yet sometimes they are set forth clearly in the form of commands. The stories are not simply a structure of 'mythemes' mediating an insoluble contradiction, as in Lévi-Strauss' theory, an unfocussed recognition of the mortal and social condition, but they lead towards plain injunction. Not simply a wandering fantasy through the kingdom of the *id* but an attempt to enunciate a mandatory message in a language which, despite its intermittent explicitness, still owes much to the myths from which the different sources, especially the Yahwist and Elohist derived. Hence even within Genesis we find a broad spectrum of styles of thought (quite apart from the literary differences in style which enabled the scholars of the last few centuries to establish the different versions), I mean a coming-and-going between the style of 'fantastic' myths of origin, the practical style of empirical reality and clear imperatives which take pride of place later in Leviticus. There is a general movement from the former to the latter – the ages to which the patriarchs lived decrease gradually – and not without reversals such as Methuselah – but Jacob still gets to one hundred and thirty, despite the limit of one hundred and twenty set in Genesis 6.3 and Joseph reaches one hundred and ten at the end of the book. Elements of the legendary past preceding literature and law remain embedded in the narration and provide the ambiguity which is the hallmark of the sacred and the means for its professional interpreters to justify themselves. These professionals hold the power, like the priests of Delphi, to say what the Divinity ordains by his enigmatic utterances. Thus they translate from the fantastic to the realistic pole and thereby assure the continuity of their society through time by making a contemporary sense out of messages that were intended for other ears. Hence they might be called 'anachronisers' in that they provide a modern gloss on legends recorded in very different times whose original sense is lost or obscured. And when they cannot find a satisfactory interpretation they can always decide that a given portion of the text is to be set on one side for technical reasons ('too manifestly apocryphal to merit serious consideration') or ignored by ordinary people as in the case of Shechem whose sad fate provides the focus of this essay. It is one of the least illustrated chapters of Genesis[48] and I have never heard it given in an Anglican lesson nor mentioned in any sermon and the commentators themselves who cannot evade their duty show by the startling variety of their comments the uncertainty that weighs upon this incident's interpretation. Indeed Gerhard von Rad confesses that to him it seems that 'ultimate scientific clarification is no longer possible'.[49] After such a pronouncement from a great scholar I fear only a fool would rush in, but the gentle reader will perhaps make allowances for the innocence of the anthropologist and may even wonder, like him, whether in any case *ultimate scientific* clarification can be provided by a hermeneutic analysis.

In view of the confusion the story has caused I would do well to give a brief summary of it as it is told in Genesis 34. Jacob has just arrived with his sons in the neighbourhood of Shechem, the modern Nablus, where he has bought a field and erected an altar. It was here that Abraham (Genesis 12.6) on his way to the Negueb received from Yahweh the promise that his descendants will inherit the land. Dinah, Jacob's only mentioned daughter, goes out to meet the local girls and gets seduced or raped[50] by Shechem, prince of the town of Shechem and son of Hamor. Hopelessly enamoured of the girl, he wishes to have her for his wife and offers to pay any bride-price that is proposed if only he may marry her. He gets his father, Hamor, to go to Jacob to ask for her hand in marriage. Jacob says nothing since his sons are away with the flocks. When they return they hear about it and are very angry. Hamor proposes a contract of matrimonial exchange starting with Dinah and offering to Jacob's people, in addition to wives, the right to remain and acquire property. Jacob's sons answer cunningly that they cannot give their women to people who are not circumcised since this would be shameful for them.[51] They would only agree if all the Shechemites get circumcised. Hamor and Shechem agree and convince their people and they all get circumcised. On the third day, 'when they were sore' in the King James Version, Simeon and Levi, the second and third of Dinah's six full brothers, fall upon them and slaughter all the men and the other sons of Jacob join in to capture all the women and pillage their houses. Jacob explains to Simeon and Levi that their behaviour has spoiled the Israelites' public relations and they all risk now seeing the Canaanites and Perizzites uniting to outnumber and defeat them. But Simeon and Levi answer proudly: 'Is our sister to be treated as a whore?' At the beginning of the next chapter Yahweh tells them to clear out quick in order to escape vengeance.

My object is to find sense in this story which perplexed me so deeply forty years ago.

How can we treat it? The obvious way, and one favoured by not a few commentators, is to assume that it is 'history': a regrettable event in the past of the Israelites which honesty has conserved in the sacred text, but which need not be dwelt on since it shows the patriarchs in a somewhat discreditable light as Jacob recognises in his blessing.

But it is not the only incident of the kind and to assume that all such incidents have been preserved only out of respect for the facts is to credit the sacred text with intentions and methods that would become a modern historian but hardly concord with the work as a whole if indeed it can be maintained that it is a whole despite the varied origins that scholars have attributed to different sections.

Such an approach appears to me to consist in hiding from reality behind the facts, for the reality that requires explaining is the presence of this story in the founding legend of three world-wide religions. Can it seriously be maintained that the story of Shechem has been retained in preference to all the other events, creditable or discreditable, that might have been, simply because it is supposed to have happened?[52] It forms no link in a narrative that would be incomprehensible without it: Dinah is never again mentioned in the Bible, save in Genesis, 46.15, where she is numbered among those who go to Egypt (the Haggadah suggests that Asenath, wife of Joseph, was Dinah's daughter). But that is all.

This treatment reduces the book of Genesis to the level of a column of news items, which have been selected by the editor from the mists of antiquity but are only there in fact to fill the page; in other words, the historicist explanation by itself is simply a denial of any innate significance in the text. It follows then that if there is any message to be found it resides in the events themselves and this gives free range to kerygmatists of every hue who can always find in events anything they choose: the Hand of God, the national destiny or the dialectical process of history – or it leaves the reader free to reject all hermeneutic explanations and content himself with a theory of history that treats events as in themselves fortuitous or at least explicable only in terms of unpredictable conjunctions of circumstances, unknowable in themselves, which a later age puts to its uses.

If, as Edgar Morin has suggested, 'history is a harlot who gives herself to the victorious soldier of fortune'[53] the event of his victory remains devoid of explanation or significance and we are forced back to interpret the text simply in terms of the social consciousness of the editors, i.e. to the position of Leach. This anti-historical mode of explanation seems plausible to an anthropologist since he assumes that culture is not an arbitrary matter and the *record* of events (as opposed to the events themselves) is part of culture, that is to say, he is committed on *à priori* grounds to search for significance in the *story*, regardless of the historical facts that may lie behind it in time. This significance is to be found in its relation to other stories and its place within the work as a whole, whereas the historicist looks for significance in the relations between events themselves regardless of how they may be related in different texts or archives. To me both positions appear unacceptable for the simple reason that each ignores the reasoning of the other whereas the problem of diachronic interpretation is precisely that it must respond both to the accumulations of culture and to its synchronic coherence. Nor is this problem new in anthropology for it was the basis half a century ago of the difference between the diffusionists and the functionalists who each failed to come to terms with the valid observations of the others. If history, as events, is essentially incoherent, like the fortuity of the soldier of fortune's triumph, it is because it is a random accumulation and if it is coherent it is because it has to be for the historian to be able to write it. Not even the chroniclers, they least of all in fact, manage to record events without any attempt at coherence.[54]

Let me start then by an overview of the Book of Genesis, bearing in mind that it is the first book of the Old Testament. The past is represented as either a recorded succession of events or as a validation of the present by reference to origins or, by the kerygmatists, both. The further we go back in time the fewer and less certain are the records and the more difficult to interpret; therefore the more the latter view predominates, until we reach a mode of thought from which consciousness of diachrony – the past as a succession of events – is missing altogether; we are in the realm of pure myth, timeless because placed at the beginning of time, *in illo tempore*, according to Eliade, when all is back to front and upside-down to prove that you can go back no further.

In the case of Genesis the element of myth is strong as one would expect in a text explicitly concerned with origins. Especially in the early chapters the events recounted do not correspond to our experience of reality. On the contrary they resemble the origin myths of primitive peoples. In its movement from pure myth to history Genesis resembles, rather than those myths of the Middle East with which it might be thought to have an historical connection, the *Popol-Vuh*. In that great corpus of ancient Maya mythology we find the first men created from clay, the Flood, idols and various other features reminiscent of Genesis which might be attributed to the influence of the missionaries at the time that it was first thought to have been written down but that such details are also to be found in the myths of so many other parts of the world. What distinguishes the *Popol-Vuh* from them and likens it to Genesis is that first of all it is a *single* story rather than a class of stories arranged in no order and awaiting the ethnographer in order to become a 'collection'. Secondly a concern with sin which was characteristic quite as much of the pre-Columbian high civilisations of central America as of Christianity. Thirdly its concern with genealogy and finally the fact that it *progresses*, changing its style as it approaches modern times until it reaches the moment when it was written down; the royal genealogy ends, fourteen generations after the Creation, with Don Juan de Rojas and Don Juan Cortès, the contemporary hispanicised kings of the Quiché. The editorial present is dated with fair precision as 1554–8[55] (though the original manuscript has disappeared). It is clear that editorial policy is not the same throughout. How could it be when the materials were so different in nature? The editors were no doubt personally acquainted with Rojas and Cortès and knew by experience what they were recording while in the earlier chapters they depended upon oral tradition of which vestiges are found in the syncretised myths which still survive to this day.

The editors who bring together such materials into a single narrative have the task above all of ordering them; they are responsible for sequence, and for concording them in some degree only, for since such materials are already sanctified by tradition, the editors cannot tamper with them freely.[56] The logic and coherence of the text – since the sacred is not required to be logical and coherent – matter less to such editors than the duty to preserve the elements in their entirety. Hence different versions of the same story are included, repeating and often contradicting each other, but necessarily placed in sequence. In the *Popol-Vuh*, as in Genesis, the creation and early development of man is not a steady flow of narrative but a series of efforts to find the solution to a problem which can be taken as resolved after that, rather as a child's exercise book shows repeated attempts to reach the right answer by the method of trial and error. Hence the diachronic ordering of the presentation, the product not only of the editorial process but of the materials themselves, betrays a hermeneutic intention.

Lévi-Strauss speaks of 'diachronic structures' as conceivable but better left aside for the moment.[57] I am proposing that when the theologians 'historicised' the myths of the ancestors of Israel[58] they in a sense stood them on their end, reordering the myth's different versions that were formerly distinguished spatially into a temporal order and assembling the incidents within the original myths which once formed synchronic sets into a progressive sequence. To give an example, it is not vital to Lévi-Strauss' analysis of the story of Asdiwal whether his first marriage precedes or follows his second marriage as long as both are there;[59] the message is in the structure. But in a 'historicised' myth the message is in the progression (as in cumulative history) and it is revealed by the final solution – which is authoritative because final and has therefore the power to prescribe action. If when myths die they become charters,[60] it would be equally true to say that when they become historicised they die, slain by the hermeneutic zeal of the commentators.

In Genesis we are offered two accounts of the creation, attributed to different sources but which the compilers thought both worthy of retention despite their discrepancy, or perhaps one would say, on account of their discrepancy for they represent quite different aspects of the Creation. The first is concerned with the physical world and the creation of men and women together as a biological species. The second starts with the creation of *man* and named places. It is homocentric and moral and recounts the origin of the sexual division of labour and its logical correlate, death. Eros implies Thanatos. Once out of Eden we are a clear stage nearer to experience. *Social* relations begin with the slaying of Abel, the pastoralist, by his agricultural brother who is punished by the loss of his sedentary way of life. Thence we proceed to the appearance of tribes and within them a certain economic division of labour: five generations after Cain we find Adam's descendants divided into those of the tent and the flocks, those of the lyre and the pipe, those of bronze and iron: shepherds, musicians, and smiths – and the rest. Then comes the Flood and humanity is off to a fresh start. This time we proceed to the division into nations at the level of the sons of Noah and relations of hegemony among them. Cultural variation is introduced with the Tower of Babel, perhaps the first glimpse of an historical event. (At any rate the Oriental Institute of Chicago displays a model of it.)

Social structure among pastoral nomads is first and foremost a matter of kinship – and kinship as a system depends upon the rules of marriage. A series of incidents presents the possible solutions to the questions: whom shall we marry? whom shall our sisters marry? Abram takes a wife, Saraï, noted for her beauty. He goes to Egypt and presents her as his sister, telling her to say so too, for he fears that if he admits her to be his wife he will be killed to get him out of the way, as Uriah the Hittite was later to be dealt with by David. Pharaoh takes her on. The adultery brings copious material advantages for Abram and Divine punishment for the Egyptian in the form of sores (a most un-Mediterranean distribution of deserts!). The deception is discovered and Abram and his wife are asked to leave unrelieved of their acquisitions. The narrative is judged by von Rad[61] 'offensive and difficult to interpret'. There is hitherto no serious mention of a kin relationship between Abram and Saraï. A problem is posed by the fact that Saraï is barren and getting on in years. Conscious of her failure in this respect she sends her Egyptian slave, Hagar, into Abram's bed as a proxy and Hagar gives birth to Ishmael. Pleased as Abram is by the birth of his son, the foreign and servile origins of his mother are clearly a disadvantage and her insubordination to her mistress angers Saraï. When Isaac is born to her, around the age of ninety, it is clear that *he* is the legitimate heir. Ishmael and his mother are sent off into the desert.

Despite her years Sarah (formerly Saraï) appears to have lost none of her charms and the incident with Pharaoh is repeated, this time with Abimelech, King of Guerar, who is warned by God in time to avoid the same misfortune as the Egyptian. This time Abraham (as he is now, having established the covenant with Yahweh and been circumcised) says again that Sarah *is* his sister and later he explains she is his half-sister. It is thought by learned commentators that she was his father's, Terah's, daughter by another mother and that this was an acceptable form of marriage among the Israelites of early times. Von Rad[62] maintains that marriage with a half-sister was still possible at the time of David on the grounds that Tamar (2 Samuel 13) suggests to her half-brother Amnon who is attempting to rape her that he should ask their father David to give her to him instead. Ezekiel later complains that among other sins committed by the Israelites brothers violate their half-sisters (Ezek. 22). Others have suggested[63] that she was Terah's *adoptive* daughter. But the incident is repeated once more a few chapters later when Isaac presents his wife Rebekah to the unfortunate Abimelech as *his* sister. Now we know that Rebekah was not Isaac's sister but his father's brother's son's daughter, his patrilateral parallel cousin, the preferred marriage of many Middle-Eastern peoples to this day. Abraham's assertion that Sarah was his sister would seem to be insufficient to maintain that this was literally the case. One would be tempted first of all to suspect that 'sister' is being used in a classificatory sense to include patrilateral cousin in the same way as in some kinship terminologies male patrilateral cousin is called 'brother'. Unfortunately there is no other evidence that this was so and the modern Middle East makes no such assimilation. However it does not follow that 'sister' cannot be used figuratively. In Genesis 24.59 Rebekah is referred to as 'sister' of Bethuel's people and it was used as an honorific title for wife in ancient Egypt and indeed it appears in this sense in the Bible (Songs 4.9; 5.1–2; 10.12; Tobias 7.15; 8.4, 7.21, 10.6; and in the latter not only in address but in reference). This usage moreover is congruent with a patrilineal system in which wives become members of their husband's patriline, as Ruth's behaviour illustrated so strikingly.

Whether in fact Sarah was Abraham's half-sister, adoptive sister or merely patrilineal kinswoman is vital only for the historian. I am concerned in historical events insofar as significance can be given to them and it is the essence of sacred texts that they should contain enigmas, mysteries and contradictions. It is somewhat incongruent that Sarah's place in the patriline should not be given, if indeed she was Abraham's sister, when Milcah and Iscah are recorded as Lot's sisters, though they are otherwise mentioned only in reference to the fact that Milcah marries Nahor and becomes the mother of Bethuel. If I knew for certain that the Israelites practised brother–sister marriage at that time it would enable me to place Abraham nearer to the pole of experience, whereas if I knew the contrary I would conclude that his incestuous marriage assimilated him to the divine ancestors who so frequently indulge in incest. But the text is unclear, and the commentaries unconvincing. Placed within the context of Genesis as a whole, the significance of these stories is precisely this uncertainty as to whether sisters should be kept and married within the patriline or given away to foreigners for the sake of political advantage. Yahweh's attitude is unequivocal: they should *not* be given away at all. But the quandary is fairly represented. It

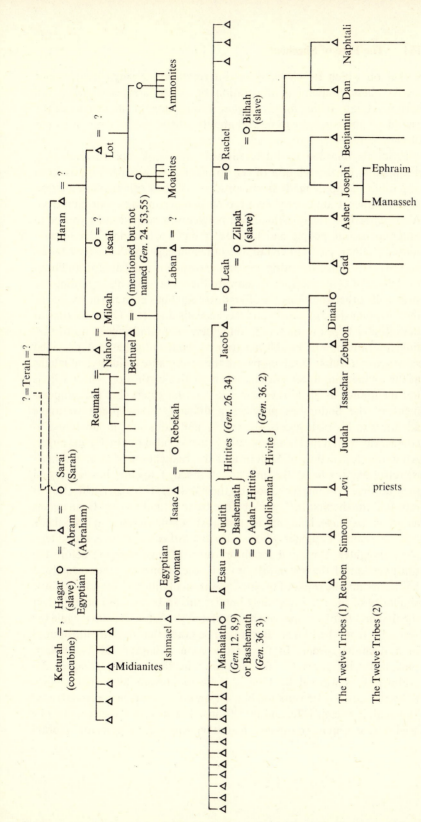

Fig. 2. Genealogy of the Patriarchs.

is that on which Leach bases his interpretation, though he does not invoke these chapters in illustration but only later ones which are perhaps equally telling for his purposes. Accepting the importance of the quandary, there is more to be said about its presentation from my point of view, however.

From the Garden of Eden onwards the book can be read as a disquisition on the relation of self to other. Eve was part of Adam in origin but the apple made them conscious of their otherness in relation to each other. Cain clearly went too far in asserting his separation from Abel. After that the questions are: how closely related must you be in order to be one people and how other must you be in order to be a spouse? Other sex? Other family? Other lineage? Other tribe? Other nation? The limits of endogamy and exogamy are debated throughout the length of Genesis. Interwoven with the three incidents regarding the sister-wife other solutions are offered. Ishmael has been borne by Hagar the Egyptian slave of Saraï – and has been disinherited. Lot has settled at Sodom and hopes to marry his daughters there and indeed up to that time the attempt to establish a rule of endogamy has not provided satisfactory results; Saraï has passed the menopause childless and laughs at the divine announcement that she is to give birth. Lot, whose wife is not mentioned as his kinswoman, has two daughters, but the temperament of the Sodomites provides a difficulty; they prefer to make advances to his male guests, the angels, and Lot's sons-in-law refuse to come away with him. Homosexuality is firmly ruled out by Divine anger. After the destruction of Sodom and the castigation of their mother's regretful glances back, the girls are stranded. Exogamy has failed and they fall back on impregnation by their father. The sister-wife story is repeated for the first time then, before Isaac is finally born. Isaac makes a correct marriage, in accordance with Abraham's wishes, to his father's brother's son's daughter who is also his father's brother's daughter's son's daughter. Esau and Jacob are born of this marriage before the third version of the sister-wife story is told. Repetitions are usually, it has been said, the result of the incorporation of different versions and the similarity of the detail certainly implies this to be the case here. In fact the first and third versions are attributed to the Yahwist source while the second is from the Elohist. But it is to be noted that they are introduced in a declining order. In the first version (Chapter 12) Pharaoh is punished with sores for the adultery; in the second (Chapter 20) Abimelech is warned by God in time to prevent him. In the third (Chapter 26) he discovers for himself on purely empirical grounds that Rebekah is Isaac's wife, and he refrains. The three versions can also be seen to represent a progression in another sense: in the first story Abram says Saraï is his sister; there is no suggestion in Genesis 12 that she is his half-sister. In Genesis 20 Abraham claims that Sarah is *really* his paternal half-sister. In Genesis 26 Isaac says simply 'my sister', but we know from Genesis 24 that Rebekah was his father's brother's son's daughter. The versions thus take us from incest to the preferred marriage of later times.

The marriages of Esau and Jacob which occupy the next few chapters form an exemplary tale: Esau marries two Hittite girls and this so annoys his mother that she organises his replacement by Jacob as their heir. Isaac sends him off to marry his father's father's brother's son's son's daughter (who is also his mother's brother's daughter) with the injunction to avoid these Canaanite women. Esau then marries his father's brother's daughter, Ishmael's daughter, but this makes no difference to his position, because of the second-rate status of Ishmael's mother and the fact that Ishmael was disinherited. It appears to be established that the Israelites *should* marry within the Covenant, though in fact four of the founders of the twelve tribes are born to slave mothers who were not perhaps foreigners like Hagar but were acting like her as proxies for their mistress, and two tribes are descended from Joseph's Egyptian wife Asenath, daughter of Potipherah, priest of On. At this point the story of Shechem is told.

This time it is not a question of where shall the descendants of Abraham find their wives but – and this is the first instance mentioned – where shall a daughter find a husband. However it is also a question of whom shall one's sister marry or be given to and in that sense it is the continuation and conclusion to the sister-wife stories, though curiously none of the commentators I have read considers it in this light. Abram, Abraham and Isaac offered their sister (or patrilineal cousin) to whom they were already married to the local ruler as concubine for the sake of political safety and material advantage. Jacob hesitates to complain about the seduction (or violation) of his unmarried daughter and his sons settle the matter negatively by political means to material advantage (pillage) but at subsequent political risk. The rules of marriage are spelled out in detail in subsequent books, but it is never again implied that it might be honourable to give daughters away to foreigners – though heroic harlots serve the national interest on occasions by giving themselves away.

Old Testament commentators always face a choice, the same that I faced myself at an early age, between interpretations based upon moral precept and those based upon historical fact. Those tales that are both edifying and plausible present no difficulty: history has demonstrated Divine purpose and with luck moral truth is supported by archaeological digging. But where edification and historical plausibility do not coincide the commentators tend to accept as moral parables those stories that are implausible from a practical viewpoint granting the text the licence to be allegorical and figurative, and accept as historical truth those that provide no moral lesson. As Professor A. S. Herbert says:[64]

> This book of Genesis gives tantalizing glimpses of this period: but we have to remember that it is not primarily a history but a teaching book. Nevertheless it gives occasional glimpses of a historical situation such as we see more fully documented in extra-Biblical material.

Those stories that are both implausible and frankly unedifying, if not simply ignored or attributed to Divine arbitrariness, the privilege and proof of Divinity, can be relegated to the category of traditional folk-tales incorporated by editors too careless of their hermeneutical duty to perceive the uninspired origin. Whenever the phrase 'traditional folk-tale' is used one can sense that the commentator is in difficulties, for to tell the reader that it is a folktale is a means of reassuring him that however implausible historically the incident may nonetheless be discounted from the moral viewpoint, placed in parenthesis, and no lesson need be drawn from it. Such an interpretation is frequently invoked in discussions of the 'sister-wife' stories where there is full justification for avoiding a moral interpretation based upon modern values: Abraham (or Isaac) takes a cowardly and deceitful line and does extremely well in material terms as a result; all three versions stress in similar words how wealthy he becomes. Sarah (or Rebekah) lend themselves to his ploy without complaint and Yahweh punishes the victim of his deceit.

The story of Dinah is hardly easier to draw an appropriate lesson from. It is a tale of the treacherous slaughter of ingenuous hospitable neighbours whose only fault was that their prince expected the same deal as Pharaoh and Abimelech. If her sexual honour was so important what was Dinah doing when she went unchaperoned into the foreign town? Even stressing the justification of avenging rape and the need to liberate their sister, which the text taken as a whole hardly confirms, Simeon and Levi come out of it very badly, as Jacob recognises in his will (Genesis 49.5–7), and their brothers not much better. Hence many modern commentators have recourse to a theory that one might call 'tribal history expressed allegorically'. Despite the fact that of the whole of Genesis this is perhaps the most graphically human story, they explain that the characters are merely personifications of tribes.[65] A tribe of Israelites, descended from Dinah and called Dinah, is immured within

Shechem and eventually rescued by the tribes of Simeon and Levi who succeed in entering the town by the deceit of a forsworn pact of alliance and liberate the men of Dinah putting the Shechemites to the sword. The tribe of Dinah replaces the girl and Shechem's sentiments go by the board. Marriage exchange, bride-price, circumcision and the punch-line of the story ('shall our sister be treated as a whore?') become pointless and redundant embroidery and what is really being said concerns only a successful military coup. It takes a commentator as ingenious as Professor Herbert to draw a moral from the story[66] as demonstrating 'the impropriety of subordinating Israelite to Canaanite culture'. Such semantic impoverishment can hardly provide an adequate explanation quite apart from the anomalies that are thus introduced: if this thirteenth tribe of Israel was *rescued* why is there no further mention of it in the Bible? It disappears leaving no trace, having served its purpose which was only to enable the commentators to evade the moral implications of the story. Moreover it is hard to imagine how the anomalous accretions have been introduced. If it is not a story about people but about tribes and not about sex but about military operations how has it been transformed in this way? 'This is a mode of presentation which is unfamiliar to the modern Western mind, but normal to the mind of ancient Israel' says Herbert[67] who cites in illustration Hosea 11.1–4 in which the people of Israel are momentarily referred to as if a single person. In fact the mode is no more unfamiliar to us than referring to France as Marianne or England as John Bull; it is simply a rhetorical figure in the case of Hosea. But the notion of a rhetorical figure can hardly be blown up to explain away an entire chapter of Genesis, save for those who like the anthropologists of the late nineteenth century believe that primitive mentality is incapable of abstraction and unable to understand anything except in terms of individual personalities.

The connection between the two stories, sister-wife and Dinah, depends upon recognising in marriage rules a moral issue, which indeed they are in most societies. The first implies that if Sarah were really sister and not wife she might legitimately have been given away to a powerful stranger. The second implies, since Dinah is really sister and only sister, that women cannot be given away at all. There is a progression therefore from the first to the second in the direction of restricting the access of foreigners to Israelite women. Moreover there is a further progression in that this access is denied not by God or by the fear of Divine retribution on the part of the would-be adulterous monarch but by the action of Simeon and Levi, who settle the matter with their swords. The solution to the problem of exogamy, the refusal of the notion of exchange of women, comes at the point where political events are represented realistically for the first time. Such a progression from the mode of myth to that of realism is present in the repeated version of many stories, often in much later books. A telling example is to be found in Judges 19.22–30 which reproduces the incident of Lot and the angels. But this time the visitor is human not supernatural, a Levite travelling home in fact. No miracle saves the situation and his concubine is abused and left dead on the doorstep. The outcome is a terrible war of vengeance against the Benjaminites who perpetrated this crime. Structural similarity there certainly is in such repetitions, but they are not simple transformations of the structure of the original version, they progress and always in the same direction.

The Mediterranean endogamy of historical times was reached, as I have suggested in Chapter 6, via a more ancient tradition that included sexual hospitality in various forms. In ancient Arabia the stranger was given a temporary wife while he remained with his hosts, a form of marriage that is still recognised in certain parts of modern Islam (though it is regarded, I am told, as no more than a form of transient concubinage if not simply prostitution). Temple prostitution was also practised in many parts of the Middle East. Herodotus' account of it in Babylon, however suspect, indicates at least that prior to marriage girls were made available to visitors in a dedicated role in the shrines. The temple of Aphrodite at Corinth was a famous centre among seafaring men. Herodotus also records the manner in which the girls of Crete received visitors from Egypt. Early anthropologists, aware of this tradition, regarded it as evidence of an anterior state, a survival of communal marriage. Frazer explained it in terms of fertility cults.[68] Biblical commentators are on the whole agreed that some such form of temple prostitution was practised by the Canaanites in Old Testament times; when the Israelites went 'whoring after strange gods' as, to the fury of Yahweh, they frequently did, they appear to have done so more than figuratively (2 Kings 23.7; Jeremiah 5.43; Hosea 4.14; etc.). Solomon in his old age tolerated the religions of his various foreign wives and his son Roboam whose mother was an Ammonite is explicitly stated to have introduced temple prostitution into Judah during his reign (1 Kings 14.24; 15.12; 22.47). During the hellenisation of Antiochus the temples were dedicated to Zeus and in that of Garizim temple prostitutes were installed in accordance with the wishes of the inhabitants who appropriately enough happened to be the people of Shechem (2 Maccabees 6.4). In the main however temple prostitution in the Old Testament was a matter of Israelites frequenting the shrines of foreign gods and it implied religious infidelity. In view of the emphasis from the story of

Dinah onwards on female sexual purity and virginity at marriage it is understandable that it should less frequently be found practised by Israelite women. The prostitutes of Israel have a shameful and profane status.

This observation is relevant to the stories we are considering, for are not Abram, Abraham and Isaac operating a form of sexual hospitality in offering their 'sister' to the local ruler when they enter his territory? Sexual hospitality usually means receiving the stranger who comes alone, but if he comes with his women he can hardly be received in the same fashion. He cannot become, as it were, a temporary or momentary affine since he already has a family, but he *can* establish alliance in the other direction by offering his sister or daughter. In the light of this logic 'the sister-wife problem' takes on a new significance for, if such a temporary alliance is to be practised through the wife, she must be presented as sister, i.e. available for the exchange of hospitality by which the women of the visitors are taken in return for receiving them in the vicinity and granting them pasture. The mores of later times in the Mediterranean would condemn almost equally and in the same terms the offer of sexual access to either, but prior to Genesis 34, there is no sign of such attitudes and Genesis 20.13 implies that Abraham's behaviour was customary rather than exceptional: 'this is the kindness you must do me, *at every place* [my italics] to which we come, say of me, he is my brother'.

This form of sexual hospitality has received little anthropological comment, yet its existence is amply testified from ethnographies of many nomadic peoples, who use their women as a means of establishing relations with the sedentary population. The gypsies are a good example or the Zapotecs of the Isthmus of Tehuantepec who make their living in the fairground business and curiously resemble gypsies in a number of ways. The women of both practise the art of seduction and at the same time endeavour to avoid literally giving their favours, for this is resented by their menfolk. Strictly endogamous in theory and placing high value on female purity, the gypsies are nonetheless ready to exploit the sexual charm of their women for the sake of political advantage. Hence they have provoked the most inexact opinions regarding their mores in the populations among whom they dwell.[69] Being by reputation shameless in that they do not react with visible signs of shame nor respect the rules of behaviour that govern the neighbourly relations of the community – they steal and cheat and lie – it is assumed that they are sexually shameless and their women's brazen behaviour is taken as testimony of this. In fact this behaviour, which includes inveigling attempts to inspire pity, supernatural threats and sexual provocation, is limited to the context of their relations with *gajé* (non-gypsies) and due to the contempt that all gypsies entertain for those who are not of their own race. It is due also to the fact that contact with the hostile locals is conducted by the women rather than the men. But within the gypsy community the women are subjected to a strict code of morals by their menfolk and are expected to show a high sense of shame. The supposed sexual shamelessness of gypsy women in the view of the *gajé* is due, first, to the different connotations and contexts of gypsy shame but above all to the fact that it is required only in relation to other gypsies. The *gajé* do not count as moral persons.[70] Gypsy women rarely go in for prostitution and never while they remain integrated with their people and in the countries where on occasions a sexual relationship with a *Gajo* is accepted it is not a stray liaison with peasants but a lasting one with the powerful whose patronage is extended to their kin. The nobleman's gypsy mistress was a feature of Spanish and Hungarian society where they enjoyed fame as musicians with a style of their own. Their role as entertainers brought them into contact with the upper class, but regardless of this they have always maintained better relations with the upper than with the lower classes who are the chief victims of their predations. They succeeded so well in gaining the protection of the nobility in seventeenth-century France that Colbert complained that this was the reason they could not be got rid of.[71] Those who live close to the knuckle dependent upon their more powerful sedentary neighbours cannot afford to ignore the overbearing value of political protection.

The gypsies are in many ways unique but the principles by which their customs are to be explained are not, for they derive from a social structure of a certain type, one in which nomads live in habitual contact with sedentary peoples of a different culture upon whom they depend, whom they despise, yet whom they fear to confront. The nomadic Somalis and Fulani in Africa, and the Guajira and Guajibo in South America are similar to the gypsies in that their women are encouraged to make contact with the sedentary townsmen, are frequently preyed upon sexually by them, and this is resented by their menfolk, unless it is advantageous to them. I conclude that the sister-wife stories depict a situation that is typical of nomadic people living in political and economic dependence upon townsmen who extort a sometimes grudgingly given sexual hospitality from their visitors in exchange for tolerating their presence.

Bearing this in mind let us return to the story of Dinah. It is an amalgam of two versions, the Elohist and the Yahwist which according to Osty are distinguishable by the text and which combine two rather different interpretations giving rise to internal inconsistencies. In the

Elohist verses (1, 2a, 3b, 4, 6, 8–10, 13, 15–18, 20–5a, 25c, 27–9a) Dinah is seduced rather than raped and she returns to her people. In the Yahwist she is possessed by violence and held captive. In the first Shechem's father Hamor negotiates the pact of marriage alliance, in the second Shechem offers the bride-price himself. The verses telling of the action of Simeon and Levi and their final comment come from the Yahwist. The hesitation of Jacob whose 'part in this story seems curiously ineffective'[72] is part of the Elohist.

The difference in orientation which Osty finds between the two sources reflects the difference between a less intransigent and a more intransigent attitude towards the seduction of Dinah. Simeon and Levi do not come into the Elohist text but they set the tone for the rest of the Old Testament in regard to sexual honour: 'Is our sister to be treated as a whore?', a question that might well have been asked of Abraham or Isaac.

This is the first appearance of the notion of sexual honour and it corresponds not only to the assumption of military dominance by the Israelites but also to their first attempt to abandon the nomadic way of life. For this reason the texts referring to this period are called the 'sedentarisation chapters'. Once they are masters of the land they no longer need to use their womenfolk for their external relations. The fate of Shechem was determined by his failure to appreciate that such nomads are liable to change their minds about the necessity to offer their women once they are strong enough to refuse them. Hamor's offer of direct marital exchange implements a conception of marriage that is no longer acceptable to the Israelites, who have learned through the hard experience of political subordination to keep their women to themselves, once they can.[73]

V

There is much to be said of the connection between political power and sexual honour – it is a favourite theme in the literature of 'anti-honour' – and some of it is said in Chapter 2 and in Chapter 4 of this book. Here I am concerned only with the effects of this connection in the realm of kinship. By making men's honour vulnerable through the sexual behaviour of their women Mediterranean culture gives to sex a kind of political significance it lacks in primitive societies. The marital exchange, direct or indirect, of women between groups reflects a consciousness of social equivalence that western civilisation, whether tribal or urban, has long since lost. Ever since the foundation of cities there have been differentiations of class which hinge upon the nuclear family and those who retain a pastoral way of life and a corporate organisation in tribes live nonetheless in relation to the cities and under their political sway.

Marriage is here an affair first and foremost of the nuclear family whatever the depth of the patriline and the future of a family in terms of power, wealth and prestige depends upon its marriages. Marriage choices thus become a function of its strategy and consequently marriage rules can no longer be phrased in general terms as the rules of a system but depend upon a given *ego* whose strategy is particular to himself. The system no longer assures equilibrium through reciprocity but dominance through accumulation for those whose strategy is successful.

However, before this point can be developed it must be asked whether what has been called Mediterranean endogamy is rightly so called, for in the strict sense a rule of endogamy would, precisely, preclude marriage as a means of political alliance between groups and therefore diminish rather than increase its political significance – or so it might be thought. But Mediterranean endogamy is, rather than a rule forbidding marriage outside a given social range, a preference for keeping daughters as close to the nuclear family as the prohibition of incest permits. Though there is a general preference for marriage within the patriline, the preferential right to the hand of the father's brother's daughter in the Arab world applies strictly only to the literal father's brother's daughter not to any member of the patriline.[74]

In correct usage the terms exogamy and endogamy refer to rules of marriage concerning a given social group which is either forbidden to intermarry (exogamous group) or forbidden *not* to intermarry (endogamous group), that is to say, marriage within the group is forbidden in the first case and in the second marriage is forbidden outside it. Thus they are logical contraries and as such they set either an interior or an exterior limit to valid marriage. But in application to concrete examples this does not entail that if a group is not exogamous it is endogamous nor vice versa for such reasoning would exclude the intermediary sphere between the two limits where valid marriage takes place. Even less does it justify the usage of the terms to mean the *fact* of marriage outside or inside a given group rather than the *prohibition* of the opposite. This is, alas, a frequent error in anthropological writings and it leads straight to confusion, for not only it confuses a fact of behaviour and a rule of conduct, it obscures what the rules are by calling exogamous a marriage that is merely not a violation of the rule of endogamy and vice versa so that the sphere of valid marriage can be called either one thing or its contrary according to whether it is considered in relation to its interior or exterior limit.[75] From this it is evident that a preference *for* a given marriage is not at all the same thing as a prohibition *against* its opposite, for the first takes place within a range of acceptable choices – and the notion of preference presupposes the existence of choice; the second allows no choice and therefore no possibility of preference. As long as marriages that do not respect the preference are valid there is no question of endogamy for it may be due not to the kinship system at all but to factors quite contingent to it such as economic or political advantage and the preference operates upon it only at the statistical level in the sense that more than a random number of such marriages are made because they are favoured for extraneous reasons. For example it brings luck to the bride to marry in May in England, since May brides are under the special protection of the Virgin in the month of Mary, but October brides are no less married. The old belief may even have been materially beneficial for dietetic reasons quite apart from the grace bestowed by the Virgin's patronage, for May brides were likely to produce their first born in the spring and, on a higher than normal protein diet, to produce more milk and therefore nourish their child better. Such considerations have obviously nothing to do with the kinship system even before it is recalled that the custom is the reverse on the Continent where May marriages are considered improper. Yet the example poses the question of how to distinguish the elements of a kinship system from extraneous pressures upon it deriving from beliefs such as those that recommend a particular month for the marriage or the preferential choice of a husband. A Spanish music-hall ditty provides the limiting case of the latter by invoking Santa Rita, the patroness of fiancées, to provide, in defiance of statistical possibility, for every girl a millionnaire husband.[76] The fact that a saint is invoked in order to achieve this ideal already implies that it is not within the range of everyday choices. But the notion of preference covers a whole spectrum, from the norm to which conformity is expected by the community when practically possible or at least convenient, to the ideal attainable by an individual only in the most exceptional cases with the miraculous aid of Santa Rita. Both are preferences but the first is normal in the sense of habitual, the second is not.

The example is obviously frivolous. But when a preference is expressed for marriage between the children of two brothers and endorsed as the obligation to give your daughter in marriage, if claimed, to your brother's son it is easy to slip into the unexamined assumption that this is part of the kinship system. In fact it may well be a matter of political or economic advantage, like the marriages of monarchs made to cement an alliance or assure the fidelity of a powerful vassal.

What has been called 'Mediterranean endogamy' appears to belong to this class. In ancient Greece the right to marry the *epikleros*, the heiress of a family holding, was explicitly an economically motivated preferential marriage since, as the word implies, the bride went with the estate and such a marriage thereby guarded against the alienation of the inheritance to another patriline. But the term applied only to women who inherited property in default of a male sibling, that is to say, they could not be allowed to marry out, since having acquired the male status of property owner they were condemned to remain part of the patriline. Numbers 36 lays down an exactly similar prescription. The cousin marriage of southern Europe and parts of the Arab world can also be seen to be similarly motivated: where women have rights to a share in the inheritance of land it is advantageous to marry them rather than allow the estate to be divided. Peters has shown in the case of a Lebanese village how the land-owning class especially control their marriages in order to control their property.[77] Recently he has submitted the notion of *bint ʻamm* marriage to scrutiny, pointing out that this preference is much less general in the Arab world than is commonly assumed[78] and that in such instances where it is the custom it accounts for only a small number of marriages, despite the fact that *ʻamm* may mean father-in-law as well as father's brother. The right to claim the *bint ʻamm*'s hand is in no sense an obligation for the groom, but merely an option which he can waive at will. At most it may require that the girl's father must obtain his brother's son's acquiescence before giving her in marriage to someone else, and this he can probably contrive to do if he wishes.[79]

Now it would be a gross error to assume that modern Arab marriage can be taken as a model for ancient Israelite marriage even though both peoples disapproved of taking unbelievers as wives, but it is at least more reasonable to compare them rather than to accept a general notion of endogamy as covering both the Mediterranean and also the castes of India and elsewhere. For a *tendency* to marry within the patriline has quite different implications to a *prohibition* to marry outside the caste. The Israelites of the Old Testament are continually in fact taking foreign wives, especially, it appears, the kings, and captured foreign women were acceptable as wives as has been pointed out. One can hardly therefore refer to the customs of the Israelites, either their distrust of foreign women or the preference for marriage within the patriline as endogamy in the proper sense of the term.

The reason for divine disapproval of foreign wives appears to me, most unoriginally, to be the danger to the faith resulting from the introduction of women who do not belong to it by birth. Indeed this is explicitly stated in 1 Kings 11.1–3. On the other hand Ruth's fidelity to Yahweh and to her husband's patriline (Ruth 1.16, 3.10) entitled her to become assimilated and to be counted among the ancestors of Solomon, while Samson's wife more typically showed no such fidelity (Judges 14) and demonstrated the wisdom of the divine injunction. The preference for marriage within the tribe, clan or patriline is a separate issue to be explained by quite different considerations relating not to the unity of the faith among the descendants of Abraham, the people of the Covenant, but to marriage strategy, that is to say marriage is an economic and political matter, whether or not it bears upon the problem of the faith. And this indeed it is among the ancient Israelites, the modern Muslims or even the peoples of the whole Mediterranean.

We have so far considered only the question of where to find wives; where daughters are to be given in marriage is another matter and one on which the Old Testament is curiously silent save for a very few examples. One learns of the existence of women who have married foreigners for the most part only by the mention of persons with Israelite mothers and foreign fathers. They are few in any case and their fathers are mostly men in the service of the Israelite monarch, that is to say are in-marrying sons-in-law.[80] In brief, there is no mention of daughters being given *away* to foreigners, with the single exception of Ibzan (Judges 12.9) whose thorough-going reversion to the principle of exogamy – he brought in foreign wives for his thirty sons and married his thirty daughters out – receives neither praise nor blame and provokes no recorded consequences.

The connection between masculine honour and the purity of women which makes a man vulnerable not only through his wife but through his mother, sister, or daughter, is common to all the traditional peoples of the Mediterranean and it poses a problem to the men of the nuclear family. Since they cannot impregnate their women themselves, to whom shall they give them? The fusion of honour that takes place in marriage alliance clearly inclines them to choose those who are closest and best known and who already share the collective honour of the common patriline.[81] But such a consideration applies only to the marriage of daughters not of sons. Anthropologists are accustomed to regard these as the same thing, since if daughters are not given away then sons do not receive them. But this argument only holds within a closed system of kinship in which there is not only a preference for marriage in, particularly with regard to daughters, but a prohibition on marriage out for both sexes, that is to say, within a system that is truly endogamous. It does not hold at all however if marriage is a political affair in which there are winners and losers of women, more powerful and less powerful, patrons and clients and social classes between which a certain mobility of families takes place, as in the Mediterranean where the agonistic quality of social relations has so forcibly struck the anthropologists who have worked there. In fact those who have attempted to treat Mediterranean kinship as a closed system have committed the mistake of supposing that marriage necessarily involves *exchange* of women. It might be given the name 'Shechem's fallacy' in honour of its first perpetrator who paid more dearly than any anthropologist for his mistake. Expressed in anthropological terms it is his error of attempting to interpret a complex structure of kinship on the basis of an assumption that is valid only within elementary structures.

From the moment that the notion of honour is attached to female purity kinship loses its basis of reciprocity and becomes political and ego-centred, a competition in which the winners are those who keep their daughters and take the women of other groups in addition, giving only their patronage in exchange. Hence from being the means of establishing sociation on a conceptually equal basis, women become the means of establishing dominance, a conception against which the egalitarian peasant community has led an unsuccessful struggle down to modern times. Their concept of honour, so different in its sexual connotations, illustrates this struggle (see Chapter 2).

Accepting the political significance of marriage within such a framework it follows that marriage strategy can be either conciliatory, defensive or aggressive. To give women in exchange for political protection and/or economic advantage involves accepting domination and profiting from its counterpart. This was Abraham's strategy. A more defensive strategy attempts to reserve its women within the group and avoid outside involvement. But the aggressive strategy aims both to deny its women to outsiders and take in their women. Simeon's and Levi's was the extreme of aggressive strategy: they took the women and children and they wiped out the men – and they did so in the name of their sexual honour. Moreover the effect of such a strategy is of course to increase their numbers in the future and thus their political power – 'sons are guns' – which in turn enables them to acquire more foreign women in exchange for their value as allies, while avoiding the risks to their honour involved in giving daughters away. Competition for women, however it may be conceptualised by the people themselves, is competition for power. On the sole condition that the sons thus produced can be maintained in patrilineal fidelity – a condition which was not always met in the Old Testament – those who receive most women expand fastest and attain a position of domination.

Such a political usage of marriage depends of course upon polygyny of one form or another, and in the age of the patriarchs Israel practised both polygamy and concubinage. But there are dangers in an aggressive strategy and an expansive policy which are illustrated in the subsequent books of the Old Testament for, not only foreign women cannot be trusted nor can their sons – Abimelech of Judges 9 is a fair example – foreign wives lead to segmentation and the possibility of fission.[82] Yahweh whose overriding concern is religious fidelity appears to favour a defensive strategy which consists in keeping women born within the Covenant and avoiding entanglements with foreign women, a strategy which eventually led the Israelites, unlike the Muslims, to monogamy. Foreign wives are a constant source of trouble but sexual relations with foreign women also lead to infidelity and are usually punished ferociously. In Numbers 25, the Israelites appear to be offered sexual hospitality by the Moabites – so it appears to Osty[83] – and to be tempted into alliance with them. The lesson is clear. Sexual hospitality is not only not to be given, it may not be received either, not even (the text finally adds, vv. 6–8, 14–18) in the form of the Midianite Cozbi, daughter of Zur, who is brought into the Israelite camp by the Simeonite prince she has seduced.

The incident is an exact counterpart of the story of Shechem and Dinah save in the distribution of the blame and the moral lesson drawn. This time it is not the prince of the sedentary people who seduces the daughter of the visitors, but the local girl who has seduced the prince of the visiting tribe. They are both speared by Phinehas when they approach the Ark of the Covenant. Phinehas later (Chapter 31) leads an expedition against the Midianites who are all, if male, put to the sword and Moses subsequently (Chapters 31, 35) decrees that all the adult women be massacred as well. The Israelites are allowed to keep only the thirty-two thousand virgins and the children. Simeon and Levi were blamed for their intemperate action but Phinehas (25.13) went further than them and was rewarded with an hereditary high-priesthood. On account of its similarity it can be added to the story of Shechem and Dinah as an extension of the series on which it marks an ultimate progression. The defensive strategy of Yahweh is now complete. The story comes appropriately as a prelude to the final settlement of Canaan.

Interspersed with the account of the fate of the Midianites the problem is posed (Chapter 27) of the inheritance of the daughters of Zelophehad who died with those who were punished for their incredulity in the desert and left five daughters and no son. The rule is laid down clearly by God to Moses that the order of inheritance is to be: sons, daughters, brothers, father's brothers, patri-clan. Chapter 30, deriving the lesson from their example, ordains that heiresses must marry within their tribe to prevent land from being alienated to another tribe (v. 9) and verse 11 specifies that they all married a father's brother's son. A clearer description of the *epikleros* could hardly be given. By the end of the Book of Numbers, the last narrative book of the Pentateuch (for Deuteronomy is almost entirely composed of laws), the rules of marriage appear to be established, and though they are frequently violated it is clear – save in the curious case of Ibzan cited above – that Yahweh disapproves when this occurs. It is within this framework that the story proceeds after the Pentateuch and it does so on a realistic basis: the style of myth has given way almost entirely to history. The events recorded in subsequent chapters show that the defensive strategy is the wisest in the long term. Solomon's departure from it leads to expansion and empire, but eventually to the break-up of Israel. The *interpretation* of the past validates the religion of the present at any point in time but this is not to say that the events that are thus reinterpreted had no reality in the first place.

VI

The question remains: to what extent does the Old Testament reflect history? To what extent is it myth? Biblical scholars have long recognised that it is not all equally historical throughout – compare the Garden of Eden with the reign of Solomon! – and even within the Book of Genesis, which is my concern, there is a change of tone which implies an increase in historical pretensions. Were there any events at all behind it or are the historical pretensions an illusion? Leach is prepared to treat all history as structure and thereby eliminate events altogether. (By assimilating history and myth he surely invites the question: does he believe that history also gets thought in the minds of men unbeknown to them?) But by refusing the opposition between structure and event he reduces structuralism to a method of detecting mnemonic devices, a way to see how 'memorable events' were rendered memorable.

I believe that in the Old Testament, even in Genesis, events have left traces however difficult or even impossible it may be to use them to reconstruct an account of them comprehensible to modern minds. Very often the bones have been picked clean and we are left with nothing but names, as in the interminable genealogies scattered through the Pentateuch which list the forebears in the patriline but add no further information about each than that he begat somebody else about whom nothing more is known either. One could get more edification out of a telephone directory! For this reason the attention paid to them by biblical scholars has been limited to strictly historical considerations based on the reckoning that their names have conserved clues as to the tribal movements and alliances of the past. But then of a sudden a story is told which relates an event in detail. Its original sense, that is the sense it had for those who witnessed it, is lost to the eyes of later generations and what is left of the record remains as a riddle incorporated into the comprehension of the day by generations of anachronisers who weave a thread of meaning into it for the sake of their contemporary public which is expected to be edified by it and to be able to use it to guide their conduct in the present. Take the example of Onan (Genesis 38.8–10) who refused to give children to his elder brother's widow because he wished to keep the inheritance for himself. He was punished by death, but his sin was not 'onanism' but *coitus interruptus* practised by deceit for selfish ends and contrary to custom and paternal instructions. While the institution of the levirate was understood there was no difficulty in understanding this passage, but once impregnation of a deceased brother's widow was not a duty but sexual access to her was forbidden, the possibility of misinterpreting it was greatly increased.[84] Given the obsession of the nineteenth century with masturbation, biblical authority for its prohibition was required and Onan was the best that could be found in the Bible. The belief that masturbation leads to debilitation and death found its authority in a misunderstanding of Genesis 38.

To understand the past is like understanding another culture. Bartlett's[85] experiments of half a century ago already demonstrated how time and translation into an alien idiom deform the original sense of a text. To understand one cannot but employ the criteria of one's own life, however refined they may have been by the study of history or anthropology, but the essence of the sacred is mystery and it is not necessary to understand in order to revere sacred texts, for their words not their meaning are what links them to the sanctity of origins and it is always permissible therefore to place a passage in hermeneutic brackets labelling it a mystery or to maintain that it is 'clearly apocryphal'. Hence the book of Genesis appears to me to be the product of quite a different process from those pure myths that are found in illiterate unstratified societies who have no sense of the historical past and even from those which can be sensed rather than perceived *behind* the text of the early chapters of Genesis. Rather than stories each of a piece, complete in itself and related to other such stories by no established order, those of the Old Testament are diachronically ranged, even if the order differs slightly in the different versions (Torah, Vulgate, etc.), and rather than the unreasoned product of the collective consciousness, they are the consciously reasoned constructs of individual men attempting to find in the debris of events a pervasive sense, and looking to the past for an authority to be exercised in the present. They are like coral reefs built by a process of accumulation and bearing at any given moment a relation both to the past on which they are founded and to the ecology of the ocean around them which hides their foundations from view.

What went on at Nablus some time about three and a half thousand years ago we shall never know, but the story of Dinah and Shechem records how, when the Israelites first attempted to become sedentary, they ceased to allow their women to be preyed upon by their more powerful neighbours and abandoned the custom of offering sexual hospitality in the way that went with their nomadic condition. As a result the conception of marriage they subsequently adhered to was opposed to the notion of exchange; they accepted the predatory premises regarding women of which they had themselves been the victims. This 'sexual revolution' inevitably covers the whole realm of sexual relations and bequeaths to subsequent generations an evaluation of 'women's favours' in terms of honour, shame, purity, etc. that this book has largely been concerned to analyse.

If it may be posited that the peoples of the Middle East once practised a system of marriage involving the exchange of women, an elementary structure of kinship like those of the great majority of the primitive peoples of the world, some such transition must have taken place and the growth of cities and the conditions of political instability such as the Old Testament describes provide circumstances favourable to the development of the kind of situation described in the story of Dinah. But there is no possibility of bringing any exterior evidence, historical or archaeological, to confirm the story, other than conceivably that the town of Shechem, such as it could have been, was sacked – and all the towns of Palestine appear from the Old Testament record to have been sacked at one time or another. Such evidence would tell us nothing about the events which led to its destruction. The story of Dinah depicts this change in terms that correspond, not to the free phantasy of the unconscious mind, but to a real experience of events which were unlikely to have been unique – that is to say that the historical inspiration of the legend was in social history rather than in political history. The social theory implicit in Genesis' account – for there is an implicit theory in any account, ethnographical or historiographical is, briefly, for it has been elaborated throughout this essay, that sex is a political matter, a function of a system of status and power manifest in the idiom of honour. This it has been in the Mediterranean ever since and the notion of honour as fundamentally a matter of sexual behaviour is a correlate of this. This is not the case, necessarily, elsewhere. The fate of Shechem then marks the transition from an elementary to a complex structure of kinship, from a closed kinship system to a system of marriage strategy dominated by political values, and the adoption by the Israelites of the concepts of honour and shame which go with that system.

EPILOGUE

It is understandable that Lévi-Strauss, now that he has come to tackle the mythology of Europe, should choose the Holy Grail rather than the Book of Genesis. The former is not holy writ and therefore it has escaped the attentions of the anachronisers: no edifying message was to be extracted from it and it has been used only in the fabrication of literary conceits – and opera. If I appear bolder, not to say foolhardy, in accepting the task the author of the *Mythologiques* refused, it is because my aspirations are in fact different and more modest. Lévi-Strauss' grasp of the logic of myth enables him to unearth the structure of the original version of the Holy Grail behind the literary accounts that have preserved it and even ultimately to give a demonstration of how it evolved down to the operas of Wagner, an exercise in diachronic structure he had judged intrepid earlier. In approaching the Book of Genesis I make no attempt to discover either the structure of the myths of origin behind it, nor like Leach the structure of the finished product, for him the King James version. I have tried only to show that the story of Shechem contains, for those who accept my premises regarding the relationship of history to myth, a meaning which is both less contrived than those given it by commentators who have sought edification in it and less arbitrary than the interpretation that treats it simply as factual, political, history. It records in the cryptic fashion of such legends a truth about the origin of Mediterranean civilisation.[86]

Notes

Preface

1 Cf. my article 'Honour' in the *Encyclopedia of Social Sciences*.
2 Cf. Pierre Birot and Jean Dresch, *La Méditerranée et le Moyen Orient*, Paris, 1953, for a consideration of the contrasts and similarities. It is significant too that this great work is divided into two volumes not by latitude into the north and the south shore, but into the western and eastern Mediterranean.
3 Fernand Braudel, *La Méditerranée et le Monde Méditerranéen à l'époque de Philippe II*, Paris, 1949.
4 Cf. Julian Pitt-Rivers, 'Contextual Analysis and the Locus of the Model' in *Archives Européennes de Sociologie*, 1969.

Chapter 1: The anthropology of honour

1 E.g. Erving Goffman, *The presentation of self in everyday life* (Edinburgh, 1956). Also: 'Deference and demeanour', *American Anthropologist* (1956).
2 An excellent example is T. Hooker, *An essay on honour* (London, 1741) but this was equally true of the Italian Renaissance literature on the subject.
3 Montesquieu ['Esprit des Lois', *Oeuvres* (Paris, 1951), Vol. 2, p. 354] viewed this opposition as indicative of a corruption of the principle of monarchy: 'Il se corrompt encore plus lorsque l'honneur a été mis en contradiction avec les honneurs et que l'on peut être à la fois couvert d'infamie et de dignités.' ('It is further corrupted when honour has been put in contradiction with honours and it is possible to be covered at the same time with infamy and with titles.')
4 'Para Tirso, como para muchos ostros autores, habia venido a ser lugar común literario que "el honor se fué a la aldea."' Américo Castro, *Cinco ensayos sobre Don Juan*, Santiago de Chilé, n.d., p. 22 ('For Tirso, as for many other authors, it had become a literary commonplace that "honour has gone to the village."')
5 *Questions sur l'Encyclopédie: Honneur* (Geneva, 1774), Tome 3, p. 438. He quotes the Regent, the Duke of Orleans, saying of a certain gentleman: 'C'était un parfait courtisan; il n'avait ni humeur ni honneur.' ('He was a perfect courtier; he had no moods and no honour.') 'Le misérable caractère des courtisans' had been discussed, in fact, in *L'Esprit des Lois*, *op. cit.* p. 255.
6 Thomas Hobbes, *Leviathan*, Ch. 10.

7 Cf. F. R. Bryson, *The point of honour in Sixteenth Century Italy: an aspect of the life of a gentleman* (Chicago, 1935), p. 84.

8 The rituals of dishonour also centre upon the head, of course, as the prevalence of the custom of scalping testifies. Some psychological theories regarding the significance of such customs are discussed from the anthropological point of view by E. R. Leach, 'Magical hair', *Journal of the Royal Anthropological Institute* (1959).

9 Montesquieu suggests, following Beaumanoir, that since knights disputed honour with their faces covered, in contrast to plebeians, the offence to the face carried the connotation of treating a knight as if he were plebeian, that is, of denying his status.

10 'The laundry of honour is only bleached with blood.' Théophile Gautier (in *Le Capitanie Fracasse*) quotes it as a Spanish saying.

11 G. Simmel, *Sociology of Simmel*, translated by Kurt Wolf (Glencoe, 1950), p. 321.

12 Montesquieu, *op. cit.* p. 826.

13 'Honour and Shame', in J. Peristiany (ed.), *Honour and Shame: the Values of Mediterranean Society* (Chicago, 1965), p. 95.

14 It is true that there have been cases of duels between women, particularly – and this seems to me highly significant – in the later nineteenth century, but, like lady-bullfighters, these clearly involve a travesty.

15 *Op. cit.* p. 820.

16 Cf. Montesquieu, *op. cit.* p. 262.

17 Tirso de Molina, *El Burlador de Sevilla y Convidado de Piedra*, Jornado Tercera, lines 641–5

D. JUAN: Honor	Honour
Tengo, y las palabras cumplo	I have and I keep my word
Porque caballero soy.	Because I am a gentleman.
D. GONZALO: Dame esa mano: no temas.	Give me that hand. Don't be afraid.
D. JUAN: Eso dices? Yo temor?	What's that you say? Me afraid?
Si fueras el mismo infierno,	If you were hell itself
La mano te diera hoy.	I would give you my hand today.

18 *The approach to the Spanish drama of the Golden Age* (London, 1957), p. 13.

19 Ernestine Friedl, *Vasilika: a village in modern Greece* (New York, 1962), pp. 80, 86.

20 The ambiguity which surrounds this problem is reflected in the discussions of the jurisprudence of duelling; an insult may be answered not by a challenge but by an indictment of lying (the Mentita) which throws on to the insulter the obligation to challenge. Since the challenger loses the choice of weapons there was every advantage in provoking rather than issuing a challenge. The function of the Mentita was to entitle the affronted party to gain the choice of weapons, but it also tended to enable the professional duellist 'to place a chip on his shoulder', provoke whom he pleased and stick to his preferred arms.

21 Marcel Mauss did in fact suggest such a translation. *The Gift* (London, 1954), p. 36.
22 *Mana: an Inaugural Lecture* (London School of Economics, 1974).
23 Cf. *Eclaircissements sur L'Esprit des Lois, op. cit.* pp. 1169, 1180–3. Also, Emile Faguet, *La Politique comparée de Montesquieu, Rousseau et Voltaire* (Paris, 1902), p. 3.
24 The motto of the Order of the Garter, 'Fie on him who thinks ill of it.'
25 *Op. cit.* p. 36.
26 Cf. Meyer Fortes, *Oedipus and Job in West African Religion* (Cambridge, 1959).
27 Rather more attention is paid to this point in my article 'Honour' in *Encyclopedia of Social Sciences* (New York, 1968).
28 Hans Speier, 'Honour and social structure' in *Social Order and the Risks of War* (New York, 1952), pp. 36–52.

Chapter 2: Honour and social status in Andalusia

1 J. A. Pitt-Rivers, *The People of the Sierra* (London, 1954).
2 Cf. *Fuero de los Españoles* (1945), Article 4. Cf. also *El Código Penal*, Articles 467–75, 'Delicts against honour'. It is also implicit in the articles against duelling (439–47) and in the concept of adultery (448–52).
3 Pitt-Rivers, *op. cit.* p. 168.
4 Cf. E. Friedl, *op. cit.* p. 86.
5 There are two words for honour in Spanish, *honor* and *honra*, which are not clearly distinguished in meaning. *La honra* is more common in speech perhaps, but Manuel el Conde uses the word *honor*. For further discussion cf. Caro Baroja, *op. cit.* and *Diccionario Espasa-Calpe* which attempts to distinguish *honor*, as the internal aspect of honour, from the public recognition of honour, but admits that the two are generally confused.
6 Pitt-Rivers, *op. cit.* p. 113.
7 It was commonplace of the theatre of honour, yet its aristocratic cuckolds appear not to be much concerned with questions of responsibility. Their unfortunate women get killed, not as punishment, but because they represent a living testimony to male dishonour.
8 *Op. cit.* p. 116.
9 Cf. the definition of *cabrón* in the *Diccionario de la Academia:* 'One who consents to his wife's adultery'.
10 For the Nuer of East Africa, adultery creates a state of pollution but 'it is not the adulterer but the injured husband who is likely to be sick' (E. E. Evans-Pritchard, *Nuer Religion* (Oxford, 1956), p. 189). A parallel can be found in South Africa in the first-fruit ceremonies before which it is prohibited to touch the crops. 'In most South African tribes a breach of this taboo threatened ritual danger not to the transgressor, but to the leader whose right of precedence "was stolen".' Those who broke the taboo were nevertheless punished by the chief. (Max Gluckman, *Rituals of Rebellion in South-East Africa* (Manchester, 1954), p. 12.)
11 G. Brenan, *South from Granada* (London, 1957), p. 48.

12 Pitt-Rivers, *op. cit.* Ch. 10.

13 Approximately 2 per cent of the children born in the period of 1940–50 have no paternity.

14 *Op. cit.;* cf. also: 'El honor   'The honour

que de mi padre heredé	which I inherited from my father
El patrimonio mejor	The best of patrimonies
Que en Valencia espejo fué	Which in Valencia was a mirror
De la nobleza y valor'	Of nobility and valour.'

Tirso de Molina, 'La Villana de Vallecas', *Obras Dramaticas* (Madrid, 1952), Vol. 2, p. 792.

15 Thus, in place of the symbolism of the head 'standing for' the genitalia as in the Freudian interpretation, we have here a word for the genitalia being used to 'stand for' the quality which is commonly expressed by an analogy with the head.

16 *The Spaniards in their History*, trs. Walter Starkie (New York, 1950), p. 121.

17 Cf. Michael Kenny, *A Spanish Tapestry* (Bloomington, Ind., 1962).

18 In the cases of ostracism on account of sexual conduct of which I have heard, the victim was always a woman whose status was insecure from the point of view of birth.

19 This sense of the word cuckold is not, of course, unique to modern Spain. Anouilh, in *Ardèle ou la Marguerite* (Paris, 1949, p. 81), ridicules the notion of honour contained in this conception of cuckoldry by making the lover challenge the husband to a duel on the suspicion that he has seduced his own wife.

20 Another figurative form produces the word *cabronada* which according to the *Diccionario de la Academia* means: 'an infamous action which is permitted against one's honour' and applies in fact to any shameful action. We might also point out that in Mexico the word *cabrón* has lost, in popular usage, all association with cuckoldry and, with this, the symbolism of the horns which is not understood outside the circle of the educated. A comparison of the values and symbolism of honour in Spain and in the New World is badly needed. A tentative beginning is made in J. A. Pitt-Rivers' 'Contextual Analysis and the Locus of the Model', *European Journal of Sociology* VIII, pp. 15–34.

21 Carl A. Thimm, *Fencing and Duelling* (London, 1896) gives statistics, only unfortunately for Italy, in the period of 1879–89. It is interesting however that he finds the causes distributed among politics, card-games, religious discussion and only 8 per cent of 'serious insults' which may be taken to include sexual honour. I do not have the impression from the many duels cited by Thimm that Italy was exceptional in this regard.

22 Robert Redfield, *The Folk Culture of Yucatán* (Chicago, 1941).

23 *Don Juan* (Buenos Aires, 1942). Marañon is another writer who fails to perceive that Don Juan is a man of honour = precedence and that the theme of the play is, precisely, a critique of this theory of honour – a fact which is surely congruent with the circumstance that the author was a priest.

24 *El Chichisveo impugnado por el R.P. Fr. Joseph Haro* (Seville, 1729).

25 *El mayor imposible.* Lope makes clear in the last line of the play that he thought his thesis was unlikely to be put to the test.

26 Cf. Stendhal: 'L'amour s'empara bien vite de l'usage des sigisbées.' *Promenades dans Rome* (Paris, 1940), vol. 3, p. 88. Stendhal, incidentally, followed certain Italian authors in attributing the introduction of the *cicisbeo* in Italy to the Spaniards, thus paying back Father Haro in his own coin.

27 Pitt-Rivers, *op. cit.* p. 175.

28 Haro *op. cit.* p. 12: 'que las mugeres naturalmente son ambiciosas del mando y de la libertad y que quieren invertir el orden de la naturaleza, solicitando (aunque sea con la execución de las mayores crueldades) dominar a los hombres'. Father Haro's appeal to the order of nature cannot be dismissed as the ranting of a baroque Sevillian priest. It bears some relation to those universal values which were examined, for example, by Robert Hertz in his great essay 'The Pre-eminence of the Right Hand' in *Death and the Right Hand* (London, 1960). The association between the male sex and the right side and the female and the left with all the figurative meanings of the left which different languages give it testifies to the generality of the fear and envy that men feel towards women and express in their domination over them.

29 Andrés Pérez de León, *La Pícara Justina* (Madrid, 1912).

30 'Quelques fois la jeune fille dupée se charge elle-même de la réparation de son honneur en poursuivant – souvent travestie en homme – l'usurpateur', P. W. Bomli, *La femme dans l'Espagne* (The Hague, 1950).

31 The difference in social status between the two was not in fact great. Voltaire's father held a 'charge' and he was entitled to consider himself 'noblesse non achevée' while Montesquieu's family was but recently promoted to the 'noblesse de robe'. But Voltaire was not accepted as noble, as the incident of his quarrel with Rohan shows, while Montesquieu was. It is near the frontiers of a social barrier that the distinction which it marks is stressed.

32 Cf. Luc de Heusch, 'Pour une dialectique de la sacralité du pouvoir' in Heusch (ed.), *Le Pouvoir et le Sacré* (Brussels, 1962).

33 E. Durkheim, *The Elementary Forms of the Religious Life*, trs. J. W. Swain (London, 1915), p. 204.

Chapter 3: Spiritual kinship in Andalusia

1 George M. Foster, *Empire's Children, The People of Tzintzuntzan*, Smith-sonian Institution Publication No. 6 (Washington, 1948). It has also been called 'fictive kinship' though there is in fact nothing fictive about it and this regrettable appraisal confused it with adoption (which *may* legitimately be called 'fictive kinship') and for a long time obscured its nature which is to be opposed rather than assimilated to kinship.

2 Sydney W. Mintz and Eric H. Wolf, 'An Analysis of Ritual Co-parenthood (Compadrazgo)', *Southwestern Journal of Anthropology*, Vol. 6, No. 4, 1950.

3 George M. Foster, 'Cofradia and Compadrazgo in Spain and Spanish America', *Southwestern Journal of Anthropology*, Vol. 9, No. 1, 1953.

4 J. A. Pitt-Rivers, *The People of the Sierra*.

5 A notable and unique exception is Stephen Gudeman's admirable article 'The *compadrazgo* as a reflection of the natural and spiritual person', *Proceedings of the Royal Anthropological Institute*, 1971.

6 Frédéric LePlay, *Les ouvriers européens* (Paris, 1866).

7 Mintz and Wolf, *op. cit.* p. 364.

8 Ibid., p. 348.

9 E.g. 'En Andalucía y en algunas otras partes, se suele llamar así a los amigos y conocidos, y aun a losque por casualidad se juntan en posadas o caminos.' *Diccionario de la Lengua Española de la Real Academia Española* (Madrid, 1956).

10 L'Abbé Jules Corblet, *Histoire dogmatique, Liturgique et Archéologique du Sacrement de Baptême*, 2 Vols (Paris, 1881), is the authorative work on the subject.

11 *Colección de Canones de la Iglesia Española* (Traduccion de D. Juan Tejeda y Ramiro, Madrid, 1849).

12 Jean-Baptiste Thiers, *Traité des Superstitions qui regardent les Sacremens* (Avignon, 1777).

13 The distinction between natural and ritual kinship is spelt out in my article 'Pseudo-kinship' in the *Encyclopedia of Social Sciences* and in 'The Kith and the Kin' in Jack Goody (ed.) *The Character of Kinship* (Cambridge, 1974).

14 Foster, *op. cit.* pp. 7–9.

15 Cf. Ch. 4 (pp. 84–90) and *People of the Sierra*, Ch. xi for a fuller description of the nickname.

16 In the folklore of Andalusia the window, protected usually by an iron grille, is the place where courting is conducted and where romantic postcards picture the courting couple.

17 Corblet, *op. cit.* vol. 2, p. 209.

18 Paul, quoted by Mintz and Wolf, *op. cit.* p. 355.

19 Foster, *op. cit.* p. 7.

20 Mintz and Wolf, *op. cit.* p. 342.

21 Covarrubias' dictionary of 1611 gives the following definition: 'Quasi compater, aunque nuevo y barbaro. Llamanse compadres a los que nos sacaron de pila . . .' But he also gives in his definition of *comadre*, together with the sense of midwife and as a familiar form of address for neighbours and acquaintants, the following: 'Llamanse comadres las que acompañan la criatura y la reciben de mano del padrino quando la sacan de la pila. Y comadre la que asiste con la novia el dia de su casamiento, aunque a esta la llamamos no comadre, sino madrina.'

22 J. Pitt-Rivers, 'Ritual Kinship in the Mediterranean: Spain and the Balkans' in J G. Peristiany (ed.), *Mediterranean Family Structures* (Cambridge, 1976).

Chapter 4: The moral foundations of the family

1 Cf. J. Pitt-Rivers, 'A critique of Mediterranean Endogamy' (in press).
2 Cf. Chapter 6. The statement is somewhat qualified in chapter 7.
3 Cf. Jack Goody, *Succession to High Office*, Cambridge Papers in Social Anthropology, No. 4 (Cambridge, 1966), p. 4.
4 Such an accusation was even formulated as a concept within the social sciences by Edward Banfield who invented the phrase 'amoral familism' to express it and who found in it a justification for regarding an Italian rural township as 'backward'. *The Moral Basis of a Backward Society* (New York, 1958).
5 J. G. Peristiany (ed.) *Honour and Shame*, p. 179, cf. also p. 14.
6 The double standard is defined by Cornelia Butler Flora in Ann Pescatello (ed.) *Female and Male in Latin America* (Pittsburgh, 1973) as 'when extra-marital sex was presented as permissible for men, but not for women'. Ann Pescatello, *ibid.*, p. 35, speaks of 'a society rife with a double standard of morality'. A much more perceptive use of the notion is made by A. L. Maraspini, *The Study of an Italian Village* (Paris (Mouton), 1968) p. 177, who speaks of a 'dual code' to distinguish between the standards of conduct expected of each sex. Maraspini's sensitive account of the mores of a village in the Salento bears innumerable similarities with the Andalusian materials on which this essay is based.
7 e.g. Anouilh, *Cécile ou l'école des pères*.
8 In Mary Douglas (ed.) *Witchcraft Confessions and Accusations* (London, 1970).
9 *ibid.*, Introduction.
10 Douglas, *ibid.*, p. xxix.
11 For comparison, see Juliet du Boulay, *A Greek Mountain Village* (Oxford, 1975).
12 Cf. Pierre Bourdieu, 'La Maison Kabyle ou le monde renversé' in J. Pouillou and P. Maranda (eds.) *Echanges et Communications: Mélanges offerts à Claude Lévi-Strauss à l'occasion de son 60ème anniversaire*, 2 vols. (Paris, 1968), pp. 739–58.
13 Cf. du Boulay, *op. cit.*, see also p. 115 below.
14 Alan MacFarlane in Douglas, *op. cit.* and Keith Thomas, *Religion and the Decline of Magic* (London, 1971), p. 671.
15 A description and analysis of these institutions is given in my *People of the Sierra*. They were mentioned in another connection on page 60.
16 For example the nicknames of Wales are not transmitted to the children nor are those of the Chatillonnais as Françoise Zonabend (in press) has' shown. Many reasons can be found for this: the place of the nickname within the total naming system, its usage in relation to the Christian name and the degree to which surnames are known and used, that is to say, to which the official system of appellation is accepted by the community. Such *prima facie* explanations do not exhaust the materials, however, for in the Quercy nicknames can still be found that have been inherited from forebears – though they are used without the Christian name and surnames are all known.
17 *La Pensée Sauvage*, p. 283.

Chapter 5: The law of hospitality

1 Transactions and Proceedings of the American Philological Society, 1963.
2 F. Boas, *The Central Eskimo* (Washington, 1887), p. 609. Strangers are greeted with a feast in many parts of the world and are also frequently subject to a contest of skill or strength.
3 'Rite d'intégration', in the words of A. van Gennep, *Les rites de passage* (Paris, 1909).
4 Fustel de Coulanges, *La Cité antique* (Paris, 15e éd., 1895), p. 232.
5 According to Farès, ancient Arab custom forbade asking the guest who he was, where he came from or where he was going (B. Farès, *L'honneur chez les Arabes avant l'Islam*, Paris, 1932, p. 95). Similarly Odysseus was asked such questions only as he was leaving Phaeacia.
6 Even within a single society whose communities are roughly similar in structure, an individual easily forfeits his status when away from home. The point was made tellingly by a plebeian member of the town of Alcalá; to a drunken summer visitor who attempted to patronise him he answered: 'You may be Don Fulano de Tal in your own home, but here you're just sh . . t' (the story is probably apocryphal; I have only the testimony of the speaker that he actually said the words). In accordance with the same notions the system of nicknames in the townships of Andalusia seldom recognises an outsider by any identity other than the place of his origin. Only exceptionally and after many years of residence will he acquire a nickname which defines him as an individual, that is, as a member of the community. Since place of birth is what defines the essential nature of the individual, an outsider can never become totally incorporated. Cf. J. Pitt-Rivers, *The People of the Sierra* (London, 1954).
7 See above, Ch. 2.
8 K. Birket-Smith, *The Eskimos* (London, 1959), p. 173. It is significant that the officiants at rites of passage frequently establish through them relationships of ritual kinships, as for example in the instance of godparenthood.
9 I admit none the less to a certain satisfaction when it was confirmed to me by Mr Keith Basso who was then immersed in Eskimo ethnography that there is indeed one tribe among whom the stranger, defeated in the ordeal of entry, is made the ritual kinsman of his victor. Here however the contest took the form of a wrestling match of which the object was to kick the opponents' legs away from under him. Strength in the right leg, not arm, was the measure of superiority as indeed it is among the football fans of modern society.
10 'L'humeur voyageuse et sociale des Grecs, les fêtes, les besoins du commerce et très souvent aussi les exils politiques rendent toujours l'hospitalité nécessaire dans toutes les parties du monde grec' (Ch. Daremberg and E. Saglio, *Dictionnaire des antiquités grecques et romaines*, vol. III, Paris, 1900, p. 294).
11 Cf. A. H. Abou-Seid, 'Honour and Shame among the Bedouins of Egypt', J. G. Peristiany, ed., *Honour and Shame: the values of Mediterranean Society* (London, 1965). So powerful is this idea that every home becomes

a sanctuary guarded by the honour of the owner who is in duty bound to receive any fugitive who ask for refuge. Even his own enemy can demand sanctuary of him, and rest assured of protection against himself, since his obligation to respect the sanctity of his own home takes precedence over his right and desire for vengeance. It should be noted however that the sacredness of the home makes it a sanctuary only to the stranger, not to the fellow-member of the community. Further instances of the association between the sacred and the stranger are given by A. M. Hocart, in 'The Divinity and the Guest', *The Life-giving Myth* (London, 1935).

12 Bishr Farès, *L'honneur chez les Arabes avant l'Islam* (Paris, 1932).

13 'The first possible definition of the *sacred* is that it is the opposite of the profane' (M. Eliade, *The Sacred and the Profane*, New York, 1959, p. 10).

14 'The sacredness of the stranger in many societies was recognised long before Van Gennep who refers to earlier discussions of this topic' (Eliade, *op. cit.*, p. 36).

15 'Le sacré n'est pas une valeur absolue, mais une valeur qui indique des situations respectives. Un homme qui vit chez lui . . . dans le profane . . . vit dans le sacré dès qu'il part en voyage et se trouve, en qualité d'étranger, à proximité d'un camp d'inconnus' (Van Gennep, *op. cit.*, p. 16; cf. also p. 36 et sq.).

16 The guest who is received in a house for the first time is given precedence over its habitual guests with whom a greater familiarity exists. In the same way diplomatic etiquette forbids placing a countryman of the host in the place of honour if foreigners are present.

17 See Daremberg and Saglio, *op. cit.*, p. 303: 'D'après Servius, certains auteurs anciens employaient le mot *hostis* pour *hospes*.' The Greek word ξένος possesses the same two senses.

18 R. Benedict, *Patterns of Culture* (London, 1952) p. 136.

19 See above, Chapter 2.

20 The problem of the 'sturdy beggars' in sixteenth-century England revolved around this distinction of roles. The nursery rhyme preserves the terms of the choice which they imposed on the villagers: 'some gave them black bread and some gave them brown, and some gave them a big stick and beat them out of town'.

21 Cf. M. Mauss, 'Le don', in *Sociologie et Anthropologie*, p. 258: 'Le don non rendu rend encore inférieur celui qui l'a accepté . . .'; cf. also p. 169.

22 J. Belmonte, *Juan Belmonte, killer of bulls. The autobiography of a matador* (New York, 1937), p. 109.

23 Havelock Ellis, *The soul of Spain* (London, 1908), p. 17. It might be noted that whereas the evil eye is a female attribute in Andalusia, it is also exerted by *men* across the straits.

24 A recent article by Susan Tax Freeman, 'The Municipios of Northern Spain: a view from the fountain' in *Essays presented to Sol Tax* (in press) examines in detail the symbolic value of the fountain and marks the analogy between *pila*, the baptismal font, and *pila*, the fountain.

25 R. F. Barton, *The Kalingas* (Chicago, 1949), p. 83. Regarding the status of stranger in Africa, see Meyer Fortes, 'Strangers' in *Studies in African*

Social Anthropology: essays presented to I. Schapera, (eds.) M. Fortes and Sheila Patterson (London, 1975).

26 Cf. Van Gennep, *op. cit.*, p. 47 et sq.

27 In order to demonstrate the universal validity of the logic of the law of hospitality, I have deliberately taken evidence from different spheres: ritual custom, the conventions of manners, habitual practice and the inventions of the poet. It is not intended to imply that there is no difference between them and that they must not be distinguished for other purposes.

28 See numbers on page 95.

29 See numbers on page 95.

30 See numbers on page 95.

31 See numbers on page 95.

32 See numbers on page 95.

Chapter 6: Women and sanctuary in the Mediterranean

1 It was also used to buttress conjectures regarding primitive matriarchy. On this point see M. I. Finley, *The World of Odysseus* (London, 1967), pp. 103–14.

2 A. H. Abou Zeid, 'Honour and Shame among the Bedouins of Egypt' in J. G. Peristiany (ed.) *Honour and Shame: the Values of Mediterranean Society* (London, 1965), pp. 7–23.

3 See Bourdieu's discussion of this term 'La maison kabyle ou le monde renversé', J. Pouillon and P. Maranda (eds.) *Echanges et Communications: Mélanges offerts à Claude Lévi-Strauss à l'occasion de son 60ème anniversaire*, 2 vols. (Paris, 1968). Excerpts from this essay are published in English in Mary Douglas (ed.), *Rules and Meanings*, Penguin Modern Sociology Readings (Harmondsworth, 1973). C. Staniland Wake, *Serpent Worship and Other Essays* (London, 1888), p. 227, tells us of the Bedouins that 'The respect paid to [women] is so great that, if a homicide can succeed in concealing his head under the sleeve of a woman and cry "fyardh'ek", "under thy protection", his safety is insured.'

4 Farès, *op. cit.*

5 Cf. E. Laoust, *L'Habitation chez les transhumants de Maroc Central* (Paris, 1935), p. 19 et sq.

6 P. Bourdieu, 'The Sentiment of Honour in Kabyle Society' in J. G. Peristiany (ed.) *Honour and Shame*.

7 The expression 'carnal knowledge' retains the association between knowledge and copulation. Romantic love is said to be blind, but the marriage rules of the primitive know what they are up to. Westermarck, when he attributed the prohibition of incest to the absence of sexual desire produced by familiarity, confused the two (as well as confusing much else besides), but it is an error based upon a profound truth that many other writers have touched on in different ways: that the sexual division of labour offers a road to escape from self. It will not become clear in anthropological terms until some brave man undertakes the structural study of love.

8 'Lorsque nous examinons la diffusion de ce type de mariage endogame,

nous constatons qu'elle correspond à une région vaste et homogène: tout l'Ancien Monde.' G. Tillion, *Le Harem et les Cousins* (Paris, 1966), p. 36.

9 W. K. Lacey, *The Family in Classical Greece* (London, 1968), p. 39.

10 Cf. Lévi-Strauss, *The Savage Mind* (London, 1966), p. 105. The interpretation is reinforced by the observation that semen is in certain instances used in the place of food or blood, in the rites which effectuate the tie of blood-brotherhood.

11 W. Robertson Smith, *Kinship and Marriage in Early Arabia* (Cambridge, 1903).

Chapter 7: The fate of Shechem

1 *Transactions of the New York Academy of Sciences*, February 1961, pp. 386–96.

2 *Genesis as Myth and Other Essays* (London, 1969).

3 *Ibid.*, pp. 25–85.

4 *Ibid.*, p. 25.

5 *Ibid.*, p. 31.

6 *Ibid.*, p. 54.

7 *Ibid.*, p. 64.

8 *Ibid.*, p. 81.

9 *Ibid.*, p. 33.

10 *Ibid.*, p. 65.

11 *Myth in Primitive Psychology*, Chapter 2 (reprinted in *Magic, Science and Religion and Other Essays* (New York, 1954)).

12 Leach, *op. cit.*, p. 74.

13 *Esprit*, n.s., 11, November 1963, p. 631. The whole passage, pp. 629–35, is a clear exposition of Lévi-Strauss' argument in this regard.

14 There is nonetheless a mythological residue in the Old Testament, *ibid.* p. 632.

15 Leach, *op. cit.*, p. 114, n. 8.

16 An unfortunate editorial slip gives the wrong reference for this view which clearly comes, not as attributed, but from the Introduction to *Anthropologie Structurale*.

17 *Ibid.*, p. 81.

18 *Ibid.*, p. 38.

19 'Theories of Myth', *Man*, Vol. iv, 1969.

20 It is not without interest that Lévi-Strauss in his discussion with Ricoeur (*Esprit*, p. 634) at one point invokes precisely this function of myth in order to deny that the myths of the Australian Aborigines are lacking in 'kerygmatic' sense (see below, n. 38). He would appear then to look more kindly upon Malinowski's theory expressed in *Argonauts* than upon his subsequent elaborations.

21 *Magic, Science and Religion*, pp. 149–274.

22 *Ibid.*, pp. 93–148.

23 *Ibid.*, p. 107.

24 *Ibid.*, p. 103.

25 *Argonauts*, p. 307.
26 See above, Chapter 5, where Malinowski's interpretation of myth as a social charter is considered in relation to Zeus' appearance as a beggar.
27 There is no contemporary equivalent among the British anthropologists to the study of myth in France by the school of M. Griaule and indeed the first is Jack Goody's *Myth of the Bagre* (Oxford, 1972).
28 'Nous ne prétendons donc pas montrer comment les hommes pensent dans les mythes, mais comment les mythes se pensent dans les hommes, et à leur insu', *Le Cru et le Cuit* (Paris, 1964), p. 20.
29 *Ibid.*, p. 53.
30 Cf. Luc de Heusch, *Le roi ivre ou l'origine de l'état* (Paris, 1972), which causes one to wonder whether the difference has not been exaggerated by the interests and methods of the ethnographers who worked in the different continents.
31 *Structural Anthropology* (London, 1963), p. 213.
32 *Annuaire du Collège de France* 1974 and 'Perceval or Parsifal', lecture delivered at the French Institute, London, 23 October 1975, in which he took up again his interpretation of the myth of Oedipus.
33 *La Pensée Sauvage* (Paris, 1962), p. 308.
34 In *Rethinking Anthropology* (London, 1961), pp. 124–32.
35 *La Pensée Sauvage*, p. 307.
36 Leach, *Genesis as Myth*, pp. 39, 40.
37 'Structuralism in Social Anthropology' in David Robey (ed.) *Structuralism: an Introduction* (Wolfson College Lectures, Oxford, 1972), p. 51.
38 That is to say, an announcement or promise of what is to follow. The word 'kérigmatique' was introduced into the discussion by Ricoeur (*Esprit*, pp. 611, 612, 616, 621, 634, 652).
39 Emile Osty and Joseph Trinquet, *La Bible* (Paris, 1973), pp. 23, 'a slow process' covering several centuries and, pp. 284–5: 'the composition of the Yahwist and Elohist texts dates from the 9th and 8th centuries respectively but incorporated much earlier traditions known in oral or written form. It even brought together the remains of the most ancient literature of Israel which celebrated the epoch of the conquering march towards the Promised Land.' As a theoretical construction the 'editorial present' creates problems from the moment that it is recognised that things may be repeated over a period of time and written down only much later. Thus the 'earliest genealogies were in a source no older than the Davidic period' but 'late sources might nevertheless contain early material'. Robert R. Wilson, 'Genealogy and History in the Old Testament', unpublished Ph.D. thesis, Yale University, 1975, p. 2. The fact that editors incorporate materials, not simply because they make sense to them, but because they are *there*, introduces contradictions – for example the contradictions in the genealogy of Esau noted by Wilson (p. 200) – that remain for subsequent editors to face if they wish to draw historical conclusions.
40 Jean Pouillon, *Fétiches sans fetichisme* (Paris, 1975), p. 65.
41 The extent of the transformation can be seen most simply by consulting the entry 'Ishmael' in the *Encyclopedia of Islam*.
42 Cf. 'The Story of Asdiwal' translated into English in E. R. Leach (ed.)

The Structural Study of Myth and Totemism, A.S.A. Monographs No. 5 (London, 1967).

43 M. Eliade, *Myth and Reality* (London, 1964), pp. 8, 18. Leach, op. cit. p. 29.

44 In the same spirit the myth of the origin of Rome was explained by the suggestion that Romulus and Remus were raised by a wet-nurse of the name of Lupa. Tylor poured deserved scorn on the method in *Primitive Culture*, Vol. 1, *The Origins of Culture* (Gloucester, Mass., 1970), p. 281.

45 Stephen Hugh-Jones, *Male Initiation and Cosmology among the Barasana Indians of the Vaupés Area of Columbia* (Cambridge, forthcoming).

46 *Mas de 21,000 Refránes Castellanos* (1926); *12,600 Refránes mas* (1930); *6,666 Refránes de mi Ultima Rebusca* (1934); *Todavía 10,700 Refránes mas no registrados por el maestro Correas* (Madrid, 1941).

47 Lévi-Strauss, *Du miel aux Cendres* (Paris, 1966), p. 407.

48 Apart from Bugiardini on the jacket of this book I have been able to trace only two other pictures and a few illustrated manuscripts. The British Museum Library contains, composed around the story, an epic poem in German of the eighteenth century and a play about Dinah by A. G. Oehlenschläger (Copenhagen, 1842), but that is all.

49 Gerhard von Rad, *Genesis* (London, 1972), p. 330.

50 'Seduced' according to King James, Hasting's *Encyclopedia* and de Vaux, 'raped' according to Speiser and von Rad (and Bugiardini). The difference depends largely upon whether preference is given to the Elohist or Yahwist passages – see below.

51 According to Osty and others the Canaanites already practised circumcision and there are many intermarriages with them both before and after this passage, though always through Israelites taking Canaanite wives.

52 Cf. Leach, *Genesis as Myth*, p. 42.

53 *Autocritique*, Paris, 1959. 'L'histoire est une catin qui se donne au soudard vainqueur.'

54 Cf. Bernard Lewis, *History remembered, recovered, invented* (Princeton, 1975), pp. 55, 61–2, 69.

55 Adrian Recinos, *Popol Vuh, the sacred book of the Ancient Quiché Maya* (Norman, Oklahoma, 1950).

56 'It must be stressed that late Bible editors as a rule did not tamper too much with their sources, often transmitting them in "fossilized" form. Thus as regards *Genesis*, E. A. Speiser, in particular, has shown that many of the narratives have been conveyed, untouched for generations, and included by the editors basically without change, the original meaning of the tales eluding them.' Abraham Malamat, 'Comments on E. Leach "The Legitimacy of Solomon – some structural aspects of Old Testament History"', *Archives Européennes de Sociologie*, Vol. VIII, No. 1, 1967.

57 *Esprit*, p. 649.

58 Cf. *ibid.*, p. 636.

59 Some critics have reproached Lévi-Strauss with paying so little attention to sequence – unlike Propp (V. Propp, *Morphology of the Folk-tale* (Austin, Texas, 1969)). But Propp was concerned with analysing the folktales of a hot society: Eastern Europe.

60 Cf. Lévi-Strauss, 'Comment meurent les mythes' in Jean-Claude Casanova

(ed.) *Science et conscience de la société* (*mélanges en l'honneur de Raymond Aron*) (Paris, 1971).

61 von Rad, *op. cit.*, p. 167.
62 von Rad, *op. cit.*, p. 222.
63 Cf. Speiser, *Genesis* (New York, 1964); de Vaux, *Histoire Ancienne d'Israel* (Paris, 1971).
64 *Genesis, 12–50: Abraham and his Heirs* (London, 1962), p. 110.
65 Herbert, *op. cit.*, p. 111. Von Rad, *op. cit.*, p. 335. R. de Vaux, *op. cit.*, hesitantly, p. 227.
66 Herbert, *op. cit.*, p. 112.
67 *Ibid.*, p. 111.
68 *The Golden Bough* (abridged edition), Chapter 31.
69 Cf. Judith Okely: 'Gypsy women: models in conflict' in Shirley Ardener, *Perceiving Women* (London, 1975), p. 55: 'the extraordinary contrast between the outsider's stereotype of the Gypsy woman and the ideal behaviour expected of her by the gypsies themselves' is the subject of this essay and the author illustrates it amply. Okeley's study relates to English gypsies whose women exploit their sexual charm much less than their cousins in Spain and elsewhere, cf. Luc de Heusch, *A la découverte des Tsiganes, une expédition de reconnaissance* (1961) (Brussels, 1966), p. 39.
70 Anne Sutherland, *Gypsies: the hidden Americans* (London, 1975).
71 'Il a été impossible de chasser entièrement du Royaume ces voleurs par la protection qu'ils ont de tout temps trouvée et qu'ils trouve encore journellement auprès des Gentils hommes et Seigneurs justiciers qui leur donnent retraite dans leurs châteaux et Maisons . . .' (Quoted by de Heusch, *op. cit.*, p. 24).
72 Herbert, *op. cit.*, p. 114.
73 I am grateful to Mr Ibrahim Tahir for an account of a similar incident from West Africa in which a tribe of pastoral Fulani, angered with the sexual abuse of their women by their sedentary neighbours, rose and sacked the town. The source is a Ph.D. thesis of the University of Zaria, 1970: Saad Abubakar, 'The Emirate of Fombina, 1809–1903'.
74 E. L. Peters, *infra*, note 78.
75 Cf. Pitt-Rivers, 'A critique of Mediterranean endogamy', in press.

76   'Santa Rita, Santa Rita
                            Cada una necesita
                            Un marido milionario
                            Para el uso de diario.'

77 E. L. Peters, 'Aspects of Rank and Status among Muslims in a Lebanese Village' in J. Pitt-Rivers (ed.) *Mediterranean Countryman* (The Hague, 1963), pp. 176–94.
78 'Among all Muslim Arabs, first paternal parallel cousin marriage is permitted, among some it is a preferred form (as far as expressed sentiments go, at least), and in a few communities, exceptionally so I am sure, a man has a right to his father's brother's daughter.' 'Aspects of affinity in a Lebanese Maronite village' in J. G. Peristiany (ed.) *Mediterranean Family Structures* (Cambridge, 1976), p. 61.

79 Cf. Abner Cohen, *Arab Border Villages in Israel* (Manchester, 1965), p. 74. Cf. Malamat, *op. cit.*

80 'Israelitish women also married aliens (1 Kings 7.14) but usually as it would seem, under the condition that their husbands settled in Israel (2 Samuel 11.3, 1 Chronicles 2.17)', Hastings *Encyclopedia.*

81 Only among the Slavs is the patriline exogamous, while the prohibited range extends to second cousins on both sides among the modern Greeks.

82 Jean Cuisenier, 'Family Units and Kinship Ties in the Structure of Maghreb Societies'. Paper for Conference *Modernization and Family Life in Mediterranean Society*, Rome 1973. This paper is published in J. G. Peristiany (ed.) *Kinship and Modernization in Mediterranean Society* (American Universities Field Staff, Rome, 1976). See also *Economie et Parenté, leurs affinités de structure dans le domaine arabe* (Paris, 1975). Pierre Bourdieu, *Esquisse d'une théorie de la Pratique* (Geneva, 1972) chapter 3, gives an admirable analysis of marriage strategy among the Kabyles.

83 *Op. cit.*, p. 334.

84 Webster gives the original meaning as well, but the *Diccionario de la Real Academia de la Lengua Española* does not, nor does the *Oxford English Dictionary*.

85 F. C. Bartlett, *Remembering, a study in experimental and social psychology* (Cambridge, 1932).

86 In an otherwise unpublished comment ('Systèmes de parenté' in *Entretiens interdisciplinaires sur les sociétés musulmanes* (Ecole Pratique des Hautes Etudes, Paris, 1959), Lévi-Strauss concludes a comparison of the theories of Barth and of Murphy and Kasdan regarding Islamic endogamy with the observation that in the preference it accords to marriage with the father's brother's daughter Muslim society introduces the historical dimension, that is to say, where women are exchanged not for other women but for political advantage, the maintenance of the lineage to which they belong depends upon marriages that either reinforce or isolate it. In this way, he says, a dialectical relation is created between marriage system and political history. He sees a connection between on the one hand the creation of diachronic consciousness with its correlative passage from 'cold' to 'hot' society and from myth to history and on the other the refusal to give daughters away in exchange. The fate of Shechem represents in that case not only the sexual revolution that initiated the Mediterranean concept of honour, but the starting point of the history of Mediterranean civilisation itself.

Index